History and Conscience:
Studies in honour of Father Sean O'Riordan, CSsR

HISTORY
and
CONSCIENCE

Studies in honour of
Father Sean O'Riordan, CSsR

Edited by
Raphael Gallagher, CSsR and
Brendan McConvery, CSsR

GILL AND MACMILLAN

Published in Ireland by
Gill and Macmillan Ltd
Goldenbridge
Dublin 8
with associated companies in
Auckland, Delhi, Gaborone, Hamburg, Harare,
Hong Kong, Johannesburg, Kuala Lumpur, Lagos, London,
Manzini, Melbourne, Mexico City, Nairobi,
New York, Singapore, Tokyo

0 7171 1613 1

Print origination by
Irish Typesetting & Publishing Co. Ltd, Galway

Printed by the Camelot Press, Southampton

Contents

Contributors

Michael Baily, CSsR is an historian and scripture scholar. He has written *Small Net in a Big Sea: the Redemptorists in the Philippines, 1905-1927* (1978). Currently residing in Rome, he is doing archival research on the history of the Irish Province of the Redemptorists.

Brendan Callanan, CSsR is Superior of the Vice-Province of Fortaleza, Brazil and teaches moral theology at the Institute of Theology and Philosophy in Fortaleza.

Gerald Crotty, CSsR teaches at the Redemptorist Pastoral Centre, Marianella, Dublin and is a well-known lecturer and retreat giver.

Charles E. Curran was Professor of Moral Theology at the Catholic University of Washington until 1987. Among his many writings on moral theology are *Catholic Moral Theology in Dialogue* (1982) and *Directions in Fundamental Moral Theology* (1986).

Josef Fuchs, SJ is Professor Emeritus of the Gregorian University, Rome. Significant among his many contributions to the development of moral theology are *Natural Law: a Theological Approach* (1965), *Personal Responsibility and Christian Morality* (1983), *Christian Ethics in a Secular Arena* (1984) and *Christian Morality: The Word Becomes Flesh* (1987).

Raphael Gallagher, CSsR is Provincial Superior of the Irish Redemptorists and has taught moral theology at St Patrick's College, Maynooth, Trinity College, Dublin and the Holy Ghost Missionary College, Dublin.

Bernard Häring, CSsR is Professor Emeritus of the Alphonsian Academy, Rome. He is best known for his seminal work on moral theology, *The Law of Christ* (1959) and more recently *Free and Faithful in Christ* (1979).

James Healy, SJ teaches moral theology at the Milltown Institute, Dublin, and has written and lectured widely on the moral aspects of alcoholism. He is author of *The Just Wage: A Study of Moralists from St Alphonsus to Leo XIII* (1966).

Brian V Johnstone, CSsR has taught moral theology at the Catholic University of America, Washington, and is currently teaching at the Alphonsian Academy, Rome.

Kevin T Kelly is both pastor in a Liverpool parish and lecturer in moral theology at Heythrop College, London. He has published *Conscience: Dictator or Guide?* (1967), *Divorce and Second Marriage* (1982) and *Life and Love: Towards a Christian Dialogue on Bioethical Questions* (1987).

Terence Kennedy, CSsR teaches at the Alphonsian Academy in Rome where he specialises in the relationship between modern philosophical questions and moral theology.

Richard McCormick, SJ teaches moral theology at the University of Notre Dame, Indiana, where he is currently the John A O'Brien Professor of Christian Ethics. He is well known for his 'Notes on Moral Theology' in *Theological Studies.* On bioethical and health ethics, he has written *How Brave A New World?* (1981) and *Health and Medicine in the Catholic Tradition* (1982).

Enda McDonagh is Professor of Moral Theology at St Patrick's College, Maynooth. He has written extensively on moral theology, including *Invitation and Response* (1972), *Gift and Call* (1975) and *The Making of Disciples* (1982).

John O'Donnell, CSsR is Rector of Clonard Monastery, Belfast and chairman of the General Commission on Redemptorist Spirituality.

Kevin O'Shea, CSsR is Provincial of the Australian Province of the Redemptorists. Prior to taking up this position, he lectured in theology at Fordham University, New York.

Marciano Vidal, CSsR is Director of the Instituto Superior de Ciencas Morales, Madrid. He has published *Moral de Actitudes* in three volumes (1977–85).

Foreword

THIS volume contains the papers delivered at a conference held at the Redemptorist Pastoral Centre, Dublin
from 14–18 December 1987. It was the tribute of the Irish
Redemptorist Province to two men, the one who founded
and the other who, in more recent times, powerfully
shaped its tradition of response to pastoral need. The year
1987 marked the second centenary of the death of Alphonsus Maria de Liguori at the age of almost ninety-two. As
founder of the Redemptorist family, pastoral and moral
theologian, and less than one hundred years after his
death, Doctor of the Church, Alphonsus' legacy formed
not merely his own spiritual family for more than two
hundred and fifty years, but has also been a source of
richness for the whole of Catholic life in that time. The
second cause for celebration was the seventieth birthday
of a lively exponent of that tradition, Father Sean
O'Riordan.

Alphonsus' life is too long to summarise adequately
here. Born in 1696, the eldest son of a patrician family in
Naples, he graduated as a doctor of law at the age of
sixteen, left a promising career at the Bar to be ordained
priest at twenty-six, and at thirty-two, founded a group of
missionaries to work in the obscure hinterland of the
Amalfi coast. No doubt, Alphonsus' project would have
flourished and died within the span of his own life-time
like many similar groups of its time and place had he not
tapped deeply into a finely-wrought pastoral sensitivity
and an insightful clarity of mind. The history of his literary
activity alone gives some hint of the scope of that sensitivity and insight.

Alphonsus did not come to the writer's craft until 1744.
Before that, his literary output consisted of a few hymns of
mediocre but melodious quality, and a handful of short
devotional leaflets. His first work, published anonymously,

was a short compendium of christian doctrine, intended for the priest or missioner. It was followed within the next seven years by a number of works destined to become best-sellers in 20,000 editions in over seventy languages—the *Visits to the Blessed Sacrament* (1745), the first edition of the *Moral Theology* (1748), the *Glories of Mary* (1750), *Reflections on the Passion* (1751). Alphonsus was not a writer by choice: pastoral necessity thrust the task upon him. It has been suggested that his writing career might be divided into three parts, and if, in this first phase from 1744–51, the sources on which he draws seem second-hand and derivative, that should not blind us to their instinctive response to pastoral need which is the essential characteristic of Alphonsus. Nor are the devotional works mere pot-boilers: they are at once the distillation in popular terms of the essence of his moral doctrine of the christian life as the loving response to the saving love of God, and its wider theological context.

The second period, from 1751–68, spans his election as Bishop of St Agatha of the Goths (1762). From this point on, Alphonsus fully accepted his vocation as a writer as an essential form of service to the church. The instinctive response is clarified by a greater measure of serious research and careful thought. From this period of intense literary activity come some of the best-known of his works, including new editions of the *Moral Theology* (1753, 1755), *Praxis Confessarii* (1755), as well as other works intended for the use of confessors. The same concern to develop ideas more systematically can be seen also in the spiritual writings of this period, notably the treatise *Prayer, the Great Means of Salvation* (1759) which is determinedly anti-jansenist in its theology of abundant grace for all, *The True Spouse of Jesus Christ* (1760) which is probably his fullest synthesis of the spiritual life, the *Practice of the Love of Jesus Christ* (1768), the most concrete exposition of christian existence as the loving response in terms of a commentary on Paul's 'hymn to love' in 1 Cor 13.

The final period, from 1769 to 1777, is painful and obscure. It was ushered in by a period of debilitating illness which left him partially paralysed, deaf and more withdrawn from the life both of his own diocese and

2

congregation. There are few works on moral theology, and instead Alphonsus' interest was turned towards the apologetic defence of the faith against what he considered to be the clouds of threatening rationalism and deism. Instinctively, he was right, but the books themselves are defensive. Only in the spiritual writings is there much sign of vigour, and they are marked by an almost total concentration on the twin themes of priesthood and the Passion of Christ.

Sean O'Riordan was born in Tralee, Co. Kerry, on 18 October 1916. Like Alphonsus, he showed marks of precocious learning, but did not wait so long before beginning his apostolate of the pen, his first work, a report on his visit to the Eucharistic Congress in Dublin in 1932, being published at the age of fifteen in his local paper, *The Kerryman*. From his father, a National School teacher, he learned Irish, French and Latin. He received his secondary education at the Redemptorist College in Limerick, having decided at an early age that he wanted to become a priest in the Congregation. He was professed in 1935, and studied philosophy and theology in Esker, Co. Galway. The seminary curriculum of those days was narrow, and undemanding particularly for a gifted student. The Prefect of Students, Fr TJ Regan, recognised Sean's industry and talent and encouraged him to read widely in the well-stocked library of Esker. German and Italian were soon added to his languages, and access to the library at University College, Galway was arranged, with the proviso that he did not spread any new ideas among the other students! There is an unconcious irony here, as the rest of the story will show. After ordination in 1940, he studied Classics and History at University College, Galway. Owing to the war, further studies abroad were impossible, so it was to Maynooth he went in 1944 to complete his theological education, gaining the doctorate in divinity in 1947, with a thesis on the concept of Wisdom in the Old and New Testaments.

From 1947, he taught in the Redemptorist Seminary in Galway, specialising at first in Scripture. Always an imaginative teacher, his course in Hebrew began, not with the traditional grammar, but with a love poem in modern

Hebrew by Hayim Nahman Bialik (1873–1934). In the course of his years in Galway, he taught a wide range of theological disciplines. Pastoral work was not neglected, one particularly significant form of it being in the early ecumenical work of the Redemptorists in Belfast, where he crossed swords with a young clergyman called Ian Paisley. There has always, perhaps, been a latent journalist in Sean O'Riordan; many of his early writings appeared in the Irish language review *Comhar*. In 1950, Dr JG McGarry founded that remarkable journal from Maynooth, *The Furrow*. Sean was a founder member of its editorial board and contributed prolifically to its early numbers, notably in presenting resumés of current thought and surveys of American and continental European reviews. The earliest of these show a marked interest in Eastern Europe, notably Austria and Czechoslovakia. The time in Galway was punctuated by two sabbatical periods in Germany (1952–3) and France (1957–8).

In 1958, he was invited as a guest lecturer to the newly-founded Alphonsian Academy in Rome. The Redemptorists had long hoped to found a specialist institute for the teaching of moral theology. Several attempts had been made in the twentieth century, and with each, the vision became clearer. Fr Leonard Buijs, the Superior General, made a fresh attempt in 1951, setting as its programme 'the work of creating a new moral theology which would meet the immense need of priests engaged in the cure of souls'. With his premature death in 1953, the attempt was abandoned. A fresh start was made in 1957. It was to this new academy that Sean O'Riordan came, dividing his time between Rome and Ireland from 1958 until 1960, when he eventually became a full-time member of its staff. As the Alphonsian Academy expanded its programmes, he diversified his range of theological and moral studies, and acted as director for many of the doctoral students it was beginning to attract from many countries. Those early years in Rome were also the years of the Second Vatican Council, and in the pages of *The Furrow* he reported back to Ireland some of the significant developments which marked each session, a practice continued for the subsequent Synods of Bishops. Both in his articles and courses

4

for his Irish confrères and other priests and religious, he was a significant interpreter of the new directions facing the church. Like Alphonsus, Sean is primarily a pastor's theologian, even if much of his life has been spent in an academic setting.

The 'post-Conciliar' phase of his life, if we may so term it, has been one in which Sean O'Riordan has addressed a wider audience. It has meant lecturing in the USA, South Africa, Australia, the Philippines and Ireland. Renewal courses in theology for clergy both at the North American College in Rome and Nemi have been of special importance. The Redemptorist Pastoral Centre in Marianella, Dublin, owes much to Sean in its founding vision. In today's world, the theologian addresses (and lays himself open to the judgment of) an increasingly sophisticated audience. One of the more tantalising items in Sean's bibliography is a series of articles entitled 'Paradoxes of People Today' which ran monthly from 1977 to 1980 in the Italian periodical *Rocca*, published by the Italian lay community 'Cittadella' with which Sean has been closely involved. It takes up a wide variety of themes, such as 'Prayer in the Desert', 'The Paradox of Sexuality', 'Technology and History'. The word of warning to the young student from his director has (thankfully) been in the main ignored. Redemptorists pride themselves on the charism of their founder of compassion for the spiritually needy. If at times Sean O'Riordan has been misunderstood and criticised for radical or dangerous thinking (either within the Congregation or outside of it), more often than not the criticism springs from a failure to understand that Sean is not interested in new or radical ideas for their own sake. Like Alphonsus, he has sought to express a moral theology which offers hope, rather than discouragement, which places the emphasis on gradual growth into the fullness of moral response, which is a 'theology', in that its starting point is the mystery of the divine compassion.

The contributors to this volume were given their head in the choice of subject. No attempt was made to suggest a theme other than the celebratory, but reflective, nature of the event itself. In the process however, two central themes have emerged, those of history and conscience.

They are suggestive of the origins and development of the Alphonsian tradition. It is characteristic of Sean O'Riordan that the response to any question, whether theological, spiritual or merely a friendly discussion of people and affairs, will begin with an historical prologue which not only sets out the state of the question, but alludes to little-known corners or quaint facts and associations. The historical approach has been his characteristic method in theology. New questions however continue to present challenges to christian conscience, and are an urgent appeal to re-read the tradition afresh.

This, then, is the shape of the present volume. Many people have cooperated in its production, and to them a word of sincere thanks is offered. Without the financial support of the Redemptorist communities in Ireland, it would have been impossible to gather this group of distinguished scholars or to publish for a larger audience the papers delivered at the conference. It is hoped that their publication will be a reminder and an incentive to explore humbly and confidently the tradition of reflective response to changing pastoral needs which gave birth to the Congregation in the first instance. Máire Ní Chearbhaill offered invaluable help at every stage, from planning the congress to the final editing of the papers. In particular, she spent many hours of dedicated research in gathering Sean O'Riordan's extensive bibliography. The community of Marianella and its Pastoral Centre were our hosts and made the final production of this collection possible. Two of the participants, Josef Fuchs and Bernard Häring, have been pioneers in the renewal of moral theology, and have recently retired from the work of teaching, but with vigour undimmed, as their contributions here testify. Others are beginning a like task with confidence for a new generation. All of them, in spite of pressing academic and pastoral work, found time to write these papers. The questions they have suggested will not easily go away. Moral theology is ever on a delicate balance between the fidelity to the tradition, the accumulated wisdom of history, and respect for conscience when it finds itself confronted by new questions springing from its unique historical situation. To them all, a sincere word of thanks. Finally, our thanks to Sean O'Riordan in whose honour we gathered. As a teacher, confrère and friend our debt to him is considerable. This collection is offered as a token of that gratitude.

Raphael Gallagher, CSsR
Brendan McConvery, CSsR

KEVIN T KELLY

1. *The Role of the Moral Theologian in the Life of the Church*

MORAL theology is a branch of theology. Consequently, in what follows I am assuming that statements about theologians in general, especially the Theses of the International Theological Commission on the relationship between the ecclesiastical magisterium and theology (cf ITC Theses 1976)* refer to moral theologians as much as to any other theologians. Naturally, their full significance will need to be explored further in the light of the specific methodology of moral theology.

The phrase 'in the life of the church' is essential in considering the role of the moral theologian. Moral theologians find their very raison d'être within the life of the church. However, it is not simply a matter of the church's needing moral theologians. Moral theologians need the church, as Cardinal Ratzinger insists:

> The theologian who is presumably a believer, is such only in and through the church. If this is not true, if the theologian does not live and breathe Christ through the church, his body, then I suggest we are not dealing with a theologian at all. . . . The church is not, for theology, a demand extraneous or foreign to science, but rather the reason for its existence and the very condition for its possibility (Ratzinger 1986, 765–8).

Later he blends these two emphases together: 'A church without theology is impoverished and blind. A theology without a church soon dissolves into arbitrary theory'

*For key to this and other references, see Notes, p.297

(Ratzinger 1986, 763). Francis Sullivan brings an added dimension to this 'in the life of the church' understanding of the moral theologian when he insists that being a theologian (even a theologian engaged in teaching theology) should not be reduced to a function which can only be carried out by virtue of being delegated by hierarchical authority (Sullivan 1983, 202).

Expectations of the moral theologian

Transmission of teaching. Here the moral theologian shares a common purpose with the hierarchical magisterium.[1] In the common service of the truth, the hierarchical magisterium and theologians share a number of common bonds, viz. the Word of God, the 'sense of the faith' and the documents of tradition (cf ITC Theses 2 and 3, 1976). Thesis 2 stresses that theologians have their own appropriate way of carrying out this service which they share in common with the bishops. Moreover, each branch of theology will attempt to fulfil this service through its own specific methodology. Scientific discernment[2] is the method of analysis which theologians bring to the task. Although it does not produce some kind of 'pure christian teaching', distilled free of all the impurities of any particular age or culture, it helps in the task of distinguishing what belongs to a genuine understanding and living of the Gospel from certain elements in the tradition which are no more than the historical and cultural accidents through which the substance of the faith has been made present. The significance of this has been well brought out in a passage from John Courtney Murray:

> We do indeed stand for the tradition. But the tradition is not simply a thing of the past. It is a tradition of growth, and the true theologian stands on the growing edge of the tradition. . . . He must so present the faith that that which was formerly believed, but obscurely understood, is now believed and understood more clearly, so that posterity may understand and venerate what antiquity has venerated but not understood (cited, Malone 1986, 173–4).

9

All this applies not only to dogmas of the church but also to the core moral truths which guide christian living. Due to historical, cultural and linguistic developments, some of these core moral truths may have lost their meaning in the language and culture of our day. In this field, the task of restoring their full meaning is the responsibility of the theologian.

This could be called the 'pruning' role of theology, cutting away the dead wood so that the main stem can bring forth fresh, healthy growth and thus continue to live. This is a delicate task and requires a deep concern for the main stem and an ability to distinguish it from the dead wood surrounding it. Naturally, it is one of the sources of tension between theologians and the hierarchical magisterium. The latter's specific role inclines it towards being a little over-cautious, anxious lest the main stem be harmed in the pruning operation. This kind of tension is healthy and creative.

Presentation of teaching. The reason why the hierarchical magisterium and the theologians are concerned to safeguard the true teaching of revelation is 'for the service of the people of God and for the whole world's salvation' (ITC Thesis 2). The truths of the christian faith are not mere abstract and theoretical truths—they are *saving* truths. Hence, how these saving truths are presented is of crucial importance. The prime focus of presentation is not to keep these truths safe, locked up in impenetrable formulae from the past. The focus is to make them available and comprehensible for today's hearers so that their saving effect can be achieved. Karl Rahner makes this point very clearly: 'Today it is in the first place never merely a question of repeating the ancient truth, presenting it authoritatively and saying "no" to deviations from it. We are concerned with presenting this truth in such a way that it "speaks" to people and is accepted willingly as being intrinsically true' (Rahner 1972, 86). Saving truth cannot be imposed, it can only be proposed to people. This underlies the theology of Vatican II's 'Declaration on

Religious Liberty' (cf nos 2–3, 10–11). It would be an interesting study to examine whether it is true, as has been claimed, that on social issues the church's teaching is usually proposed, whereas in matters relating to personal and sexual morality it tends to be imposed. In any event, it is of crucial importance that the saving truth of the Gospel be presented to men and women today in a way that relates to their experience so that its richness is allowed to exert its attraction on them.

Development of teaching. Moral teaching can develop in various ways. It develops through the process of refinement and adaptation from one culture and age to another, as referred to above. It also develops as our knowledge and understanding of ourselves as human beings and of the rest of God's creation increases through the advance of the empirical sciences. The Gospel call to be loving, to be peace-makers and community builders and to be prudent stewards of God's creation will take on new dimensions in the light of this increased knowledge. It develops, too, as each age opens out new possibilities for personal and community life. This is especially true in our own age of modern technology with all its applications in the fields of bioethics, health, communications, energy, food, weapons. These new possibilities raise questions about the meaning of being human in today's world.

It is imperative that the moral theologian be in open dialogue with those who are involved in pushing forward the frontiers of our knowledge or in exploring the practical implications of the latest technology. This stance of open dialogue raises a number of issues which need to be examined in exploring the role of the moral theologian.

Moral theology in the public forum

The advances in human knowledge and scientific technology referred to above all occur in the public arena. They are common knowledge and make 'news'. Often they touch on matters which affect human well-being very deeply and so, understandably, the public at large are interested in the major moral questions they raise. If moral theologians are to play their part in the dialogue, they have to be prepared to speak publicly, competently and honestly. Moreover, when they involve themselves in the dialogue, they do not speak as official spokespersons of the Catholic church. That is the role of the hierarchical magisterium or of those commissioned to speak on its behalf: it is not the role of moral theologians. Their role is quite different. It is to explore how this increased human self-understanding might itself be enabling men and women to gain a deeper understanding of God's revealed will for them. Their role also involves offering a christian dimension to the human concern to ensure that new technology enhances, rather than diminishes human-kind's possibilities for living truly human lives. This kind of approach to modern science and technology is high-lighted very clearly by *Gaudium et Spes* (nos 16, 44, 62).

If we are to be in tune with the spirit of our modern age, it is no longer possible to do moral theology behind closed doors or in the privileged pages of some exclusive theological journal. Moral questions are the common fodder of open debate in the mass media. Moral theologians today are faced with a choice. Either they opt out of the dialogue: this might be the recipe for a quiet life removed from any tensions with the hierarchical magisterium but it will be viewed by many moral theologians as a dereliction of duty in their service to the church and world. Or they decide to play their part in the dialogue. If they make this second option, they have no choice but to abide by the rules of the dialogue. And Rule 1 is that they must be prepared to say what they honestly believe. Obviously they can, and usually should, report the authentic teaching of the church, since that is part of the contribution they are expected to make. However, they must also be prepared to query that teaching whenever scientific discernment reveals that it is open to question. To be less than honest or to show a lack of scientific discernment vis-à-vis authentic teaching is to surrender one's credibility in the dialogue; it puts the moral theologian's contribution on a par with that of the party politician. Moreover, such a stance harms the credibility of the church itself, if it is suspected that the reticence of moral theologians might be occasioned by fear of church authorities taking punitive action against them.

Bishop Malone makes a pertinent comment on this delicate issue: 'Bishops and theologians must preserve the faith and share the faith in a culture which values the courage of convictions openly stated, openly criticised and openly defended. . . . The cultivation of ['civilized conversation'] between bishops and priests should be a model for extending the same dialogue into church and society' (Malone, 1986, 174). When moral theologians participate in public dialogue in this way, especially when their contribution involves questioning some aspects of official teaching in the light of scientific and historical analysis, understandably this becomes a further occasion for tension between them and the hierarchical magisterium. Provided, however, that moral theologians who question official teaching in this way are motivated by a real love and concern for the church and its mission as well as for the integrity of its teaching, and do not reject the right of the hierarchical magisterium to teach authentically, then their contribution in the public dialogue should be interpreted as an attempt to help rather than oppose the hierarchical magisterium.

The involvement of moral theologians in public dialogue about the ethical implications of modern science and technology can be interpreted as an important aspect of their sharing in the missionary activity of the church, according to their charism as moral theologians. Thesis 3, no 4 of the ITC brings this out when it insists that 'the scientific character of the theologians' work does not free them from pastoral and missionary responsibility, especially in view of how quickly even scientific matters are given publicity by modern means of communication.' Otto Semmelroth in his commentary on this thesis, stresses this missionary role of theology and agrees that 'it cannot be behind closed doors' (Semmelroth 1976, 13). If, as *Gaudium et Spes* (no 16) insists, 'Christians are joined with the rest of humanity in the search for truth, and for a genuine solution to the numerous problems which arise in the life of individuals and from social relationships', moral theologians would be failing in their missionary role in the church if they refused to participate in this common search by contributing to the dialogue according to their particular charism and competence.

As well as proposing teaching to its own members, the hierarchical magisterium often feels obliged to make a more official contribution to this common dialogue than can be made by individual moral theologians. It is significant that a number of recent statements on moral issues have been addressed not just to Catholics but, at least in part, to all men and women of good will. These statements often try to confirm their teaching by appealing to human reason and by drawing on scientific and empirical evidence. In reality, these pronouncements are doing two things at once. As well as proposing authentic church teaching, they are also, to use the words of Congar and Sullivan (Sullivan 1983, 210), 'doing theology' in public. When these statements concern moral questions, it can be truly said that in them the hierarchical magisterium, as well as offering authentic church teaching, is also 'doing moral theology' in public.

In many ways, this is a welcome development. If the hierarchical magisterium, however, chooses to do moral theology in public in this way, the authority attached to its teaching statement does not automatically rub off on its theological argumentation. Consequently, there is a significant difference between the 'respect' that moral theologians owe to an authentic teaching statement and the respect that they owe to the theological argumentation used in the statement. If the latter is unacceptable or very second-rate, the credibility of the theological enterprise within the church and their own personal theological integrity requires moral theologians to acknowledge this openly and honestly.

The 'ordinary' teaching of the hierarchical magisterium (i.e. teaching not claiming to be infallible) enjoys the presumption of truth. Richard McCormick, the US moral theologian, states this quite categorically and maintains that a moral theologian cannot deny this and still claim to be doing theology 'in the Catholic context'. However, he goes on to insist that this presumption is precisely what

14

the term states, a presumption. Hence it enjoys both the strength and weakness of a presumption: 'More specifically, the pastors of the church enjoy this presumption only insofar as they have appropriately tapped the available resources of human understanding, as the late Karl Rahner so often insisted. When they short-circuit these processes—whether by haste, hubris, pressure, political purpose or whatever—the presumption is correspondingly weakened' (McCormick 1986, 278). Later in the same article, McCormick returns to this notion of presumption when he is describing the quality of respect that can still be present in a moral theologian who feels that a particular church statement is deficient as a proposal of saving truth:

> Such respect is not an assumed public politesse. It flows spontaneously from the conviction that the pastors of the church have a unique, if not the only voice, in our moral guidance. Such respect will translate effortlessly into 1. respect for the office of the teacher; 2. critical reassessment of one's own conclusions; 3. a reluctance (and only that) to conclude to error because one knows that the wisdom of the entire church has gone into the teaching in question, and 4. conduct in the public forum that fosters respect for the teaching office of the church, (ibid 281).

Relationships of the moral theologian

In general, these seem to flow naturally from the role of the moral theologian in the church as outlined above. To avoid repetition therefore, it might be more helpful to pinpoint very briefly some of the problems that can arise in the various relationships in which the moral theologian is involved in the church and in its mission.

The church as a whole. Accepting that moral theology is a service within the church and for the church's mission, moral theologians sometimes feel that what they are doing

15

is being misinterpreted as a disservice. A strong, clear, unambiguous and very authoritative statement on some moral issue (eg abortion, *in-vitro* fertilisation etc) is very obviously likely to make more impact in the public arena than a very qualified one, especially if the latter is simply claiming to be a contribution to an ongoing dialogue and, moreover, a contribution that is open to further revision. Yet this second kind of statement is the sort that many moral theologians are more likely to advocate and welcome. Consequently, such moral theologians can sometimes give the impression of being disloyal to the church and of sabotaging its clear moral witness when they question some of the public moral statements of the hierarchical magisterium.

Moral theologians who find themselves in this situation are in a dilemma. They can appreciate the need for a strong lead on moral issues but at the same time they can see their questioning reaction as the only appropriate response they can offer if they are to be true to the service they are called to give within and for the church. Their stance does not arise from any lack of respect for the hierarchical magisterium nor from any denial of its right to speak on behalf of the church. Rather, it is because they believe that the statement in question is not doing justice to the richest moral insights within the church and may even be misleading as a guide to practical moral action. They are virtually saying that they believe the church has richer and more life-giving teaching to offer the world than what is contained in this statement.

If moral teaching is being directed to the whole church or if it is being put forward to the world as the position of the Catholic church, it needs to be formulated in the light of the best moral thinking that the church can offer. This clearly implies that such teaching should be preceded by an adequate process of prior consultation. Part of that consultation should involve making sure that any proposed statement has benefited from a thorough theological analysis. Moral statements prepared in this way are far more likely to be welcomed by moral theologians as teaching having its own intrinsic authority, and as such far more likely to be fruitful as a proposal of saving truth to believers and non-believers alike.

The local hierarchy. As stressed in the ITC theses, bishops and moral theologians have a common purpose but they have distinct roles in serving that purpose. Communication between them would seem to be a matter of great importance, therefore, for a variety of reasons. Firstly, it would help to create a climate of trust, understanding and collaboration between bishops and moral theologians. Secondly, communication between bishops and moral theologians would seem to be called for when, for example, the hierarchy are preparing a public statement on issues on which moral theologians might be expected to have a contribution to make or on which they might be called upon to offer comment in the public media. Would this kind of communication be helpful when, for instance, a moral theologian is involved in some major public contribution (a book, an important TV programme etc) on an issue which is likely to affect the bishops in their teaching role in the church? Naturally, better communication on these and similar occasions would still not eliminate all tension between theologians and the hierarchical magisterium since the public contributions of each group have a different immediate objective in view and so are likely to be unacceptable to the other group. Consequently for bishops to insist that moral theologians make no public contributions without their prior vetting would be as open to question as it would be for moral theologians to expect the bishops to issue no public statements on moral issues without their prior approval. Thirdly, communication between bishops and moral theologians would also seem to be indicated when the hierarchy or individual bishops are consulted by Rome about the possible content of a projected future Vatican statement on some moral issue. Such communication might perhaps be of greater importance to the church than any Vatican concern for confidentiality. Fourthly, communication between moral theologians and bishops could also form an important element in the ongoing programme of in-service training for each

17

group. Bishops need to be up-dated on a regular basis regarding the latest developments in the field of moral theology. Similarly if moral theologians are to be tuned in at an experiential level, they need to be constantly learning from the bishops about the major moral issues they are encountering in their pastoral over-sight of their people and priests.

Relations with Rome. Being in communion with the bishop of Rome is a hallmark of a Catholic christian. It is equally a hallmark of a Catholic moral theologian. For many Catholics in recent years a mark of their being in communion with the bishop of Rome has been a deep admiration for and devotion to the person of the Pope. The present Pope is a philosopher of repute who has also involved himself in the field of moral theology. One result of this is that, more than previous popes, he is inclined to 'do moral theology' in public. Also he probably involves himself much more personally in the composition of Vatican statements on moral issues. This creates a dilemma for some moral theologians. Although they may feel personally devoted to the Pope in a way similar to many fellow Catholics, they realise that they must not let this interfere with the service they owe the church and its mission in their role as moral theologians. Consequently, there may be occasions when their ecclesial responsibility as moral theologians obliges them to adopt a position which questions some of the moral teaching of the Pope or the moral argumentation he might use to ground such teaching.

To remain silent out of a misguided respect is likely to lead to what McCormick refers to as a 'weakening of papal magisterium'. What McCormick says of bishops in this connection can also apply to moral theologians: if they refrain from speaking their true sentiments, then the Pope is unable to draw on their collective wisdom in the exercise of the ordinary magisterium, with the consequent weakening in papal teaching of presumption of truth which assumes that the ordinary sources of human understanding have been consulted. 'That is why what is called the "enforcement of doctrine" is literally counter productive. It weakens the very vehicle (papal magisterium) that proposes to be the agent of strength and certainty' (McCormick 1987 (2), 102).

Since the Curia exists to offer a service to the church as a whole as well as to the Pope, the relationships of moral theologians to the Curia are in the main adequately covered by the general position outlined above. However, it might be useful to comment specifically on the relationship of moral theologians to the Congregation for the Doctrine of the Faith (CDF).

The CDF seems to believe that moral theologians should never publicly express any disagreement with moral teaching put forward in official church statements. However, many theologians believe that such public disagreement is not only legitimate but also necessary to the life of the church. Ladislas Orsy offers a very helpful analysis of this complex issue. Characteristically, he tries to diffuse the tension by suggesting that dissent is not the most accurate description of what is going on when a theologian disagrees publicly with church teaching.[3] He notes that it is impossible to give an easy or standard meaning to the word *obsequium* used by canon 752. When the search for understanding is at its beginning and the statements of the teaching authority are somewhat tentative (as for example in the case of the early declarations of the Biblical Commission), *obsequium* may not mean more than a respectful listening and reflection on what has been officially stated. At this stage the scope for freedom is great. Orsy goes on to show how *obsequium* is a kind of gradually increasing respect depending on how far the church has progressed along the road to a clear vision. When the search for a full understanding comes close to a clear vision and the minds and hearts in the church converge 'from the bishops down to the last member of the laity', religious respect may well mean submission since the community is on the threshold of a surrender in faith. He also applies this notion of a gradated respect to the issue of non-infallible teaching:

> If 'to dissent' means to offer at that stage any particular insights that are different from the insights of those who are exercising teaching authority, we are not talking so much about dissent as of a contribution towards a common assent that should eventually emerge from the search for 'all the truth'. Should the dissenter claim that he alone has the light, he would deny the communitarian nature of the search. Should the dissenter be unduly silenced, his valuable contribution may be lost.

When the canon states that the faithful should avoid 'what is not congruent with such a doctrine', it is not a call for an assent of faith, but for *obsequium*. 'At times, the voicing of a different opinion can be most congruent because it advances the search and thus helps to clarify the doctrine further. . . . At times, it can be incongruent because it has little positive to offer and it disrupts the church' (Orsy 1986, 398).

The CDF seems to interpret the role of the teacher of moral theology in such a restricted manner that it excludes moral theologians who are unable to assent to all the current authoritative church teaching on moral issues. Yet the methodology of scientific discernment is an essential feature of theology. To exclude this from the theology classroom is to deny students their rightful privilege of being involved in the Catholic theological enterprise. Moreover such an approach can create enormous problems for ordinary Catholics when they are later faced with developments in the church's teaching and practice.

This requirement was one of the main reasons given by the Congregation for its decision that Fr Charles Curranis 'no longer suitable to teach Catholic theology' (Curran 1986, 268). This raises the issue of the comparatively recent notion that a person cannot be a Catholic theologian without receiving a 'canonical mission'. The application of the term 'canonical mission' first appeared in Germany in the mid-nineteenth century and was really a special measure to protect the independence of Catholic teachers from interference by the state. Avery Dulles warns against using this 'historically conditioned manoeuvre' as a 'way of redefining the concept of the Catholic theologian'. He insists that 'Catholic theologian' must not be reduced to a juridical category, for what distinguishes a theologian from other members of the church is skill and competence, normally indicated by factors such as advanced study, publications, a distinguished career as a teacher and esteem by one's peers. He suggests that introducing a juridical requirement like canonical mission before a theologian is allowed to teach theology creates a confusion of roles, and is likely to work to the detriment of both theologians and the hierarchical magisterium, for 'the hierarchy would run the risk of becoming excessively enmeshed in theological controversies and the theologians for their part would find it difficult to maintain the measure of autonomy and critical distance which is desirable for the exercise of their specific role' (Dulles 1983, 122–3).

It is far from certain whether the CDF embarks on any major consultation with moral theologians prior to issuing an official statement on any moral issue. Judging by the statements themselves, it does not seem to be consulting, or at least accepting, the advice of many moral theologians who are highly regarded in theological circles, such as Josef Fuchs, Bernard Häring, Richard McCormick, John Mahoney, Enda McDonagh, Bruno Schüller, Louis Janssens, William Daniel. The impression is given that only one approach to moral theology is being listened to by the Congregation for the Doctrine of the Faith, and its views are being presented as the moral teaching of the church. If this is true, it is tragic, especially since that particular approach, in the eyes of many moral theologians, does not represent the richest and most positive moral thinking of the church. The church's mission as a moral teacher in the world may suffer as a consequence of this.

The issue of authentic declarations of church teaching on moral issues is a legitimate function of the Congregation for the Doctrine of the Faith. However, it is only likely to be a fruitful and constructive exercise if such statements draw on the best thinking in moral theology in the church and if their authors are also open to the moral insights of other christian churches[4] and of all men and

21

women of good will. It might also help if the open procedural method adopted by the US bishops in preparing their pastoral letters on peace and the US economy was followed in the drafting of official Vatican statements. Moreover, as the German bishops noted in their 1967 pastoral letter on teaching authority in the church, it should be openly recognised that some teaching of the hierarchical magisterium is necessarily provisional and open to revision.

Relations with students.   Theology is faith seeking understanding. Submission to God's revelation is a basic stance which moral theologians share with their students. Consequently, they need to heed the warning of Avery Dulles that the prevailing temptation of the theologian is that of 'yielding too much to the pressures of the secular media, seeking novelty at the expense of mystery' (Dulles 1983, 130). That is why moral theologians must encourage their students to see the church's proclamation of the Gospel as their starting point, freeing them to explore the truth it opens out to them.

It is also true however that moral theologians would be failing their students if they neglected to help them develop the methodology of scientific discernment in their approach to moral theology. Although this methodology might lead students at times to question church teaching, these two emphases are not irreconcilable. Cardinal Ratzinger states: 'This vital link between theology and the church must never be allowed to deteriorate to the point where theology goes to the other extreme and idolises church teaching' (Ratzinger 1986, 769).

Relations with society.   Cardinal Ratzinger has emphasised the important role the church has to play within society with regard to moral standards and moral values:

> We see that she performs an essential service in the midst of the turmoil which society is going through. . . . She does have something to do with the moral resources of humanity. We could call these moral resources the most important raw material we have for human existence now and for making

possible a future in which it will still be worthwhile to be a person. . . . One might go so far as to say that the church will survive only if she is in a position to help mankind overcome this hour of trial. In order to do this she must show herself as a moral power. And she must do this in two ways: she must set standards and she must awaken both the will and the power to respond to these standards' (Ratzinger 1984, 4).

In welcoming this statement, moral theologians would want to lay claim to what Sullivan calls their 'divine right' to play their appropriate role in this important aspect of the church's mission to the world. The church's teaching role in the world will be weakened if moral theologians are prevented from playing their specific part in that teaching role.

It may be felt that some moral theologians today are contributing to current tensions within the church by playing a more open and active role in the public debate on controversial moral issues. As the ITC admits, such tension is perhaps inevitable. It might be the price that has to be paid if these moral theologians are to be faithful to their specific charism within the church and to the special part they have to play in the church's mission of proposing the saving truth of the Gospel to the world.

2. *Historicity and Moral Norm*

THE world of the human person is for us, as persons that are subjects, a world that is an object. It exists in space and time, that is, while always being itself, it is not itself in a way that is always the same, nor in an ensemble of elements that is always the same. It is in a permanent state of evolution and change. In this sense, it has a 'history' of its own—a natural history—whether one thinks of the world and the universe as a whole, or of their innumerable individual elements. In this sense, rivers and mountains have their own history, but so, for example, do the various species of animals, in their biological, psychological, and sociological existence, etc, and so do individual beings taken singly. The human person himself, as he considers the world as object, discovers that he too is a part of this world that is an object. He considers himself in the same way as he considers the other realities—including other human persons—and he considers how he acts upon himself. He too has his own natural history, both as humanity or as group or as individual, and as a concrete activity. Self-defence of the group, 'mother-love', etc, are not only phenomena of personal morality, but can at the same time be also sub-personal elements, as in so many animals. One may think not only of the biological and physiological aspects, but also, for example, of the psychological and sociological aspects; one may also think of what the behavioural sciences of recent times teach.

But the human person discovers and experiences himself as historical in another sense, namely as *person and subject*. This means first of all that he perceives and experiences himself as a being capable of reflection on himself, of free initiative, of responsibility, of moral conscience. Such an experience is an absolutely original reality that is not reducible to another element of the reality proper to humanity, ie independently of the problematic of a possible philosophical explanation of this phenomenon. And thus he also understands the other human persons with whom he finds himself in relation.

In that he is a personal subject, the human person has therefore a history different from his natural history, ie from the history of the world as object. Both as humanity and society, and as a personal individual, he not only *has* a history, but he himself *is* constitutively historical. In that he is a subject who is essentially historical and moral, he is always himself: freedom, responsibility, the origin of his own decisions, interpersonal; but he is himself in a way that is always different, as he expresses himself in the multiplicity of the time which goes by and of the space of the world as object that is given to him. While always being himself, he lives and unfolds his existence as person and subject as his own continuous self-development in the multiple particularities of the time and space of his life. The complex of his decisions and personal activities in the world are not the subject himself; they are a continuous and various succession of active personal developments of the world as object. The subject as such is present in them as their source; and he too develops himself in developing the world as subject, himself included. As a consequence of his historicity as subject, the personal human being on the one hand is always himself; on the other hand, in his multiple self-expression in time and space, he continually specifies and changes not only something in the objective world, but truly himself as subject and person—and also the riches of being precisely the human person that he is. It is for this reason that the continuous self-expression in the history of his life never becomes a simple repetition. Since the personal human being must continue to realise himself responsibly as person-spirit-body-world, and this precisely at one determinate point of time and space, it can be seen that the human person as subject is continually confronted with the necessity of discerning what to do and how to decide.

This generates a problem. With the passing of time and of his life, the human person remains the same subject and remains precisely this particular human person with his characteristic specificity; indeed, it is because he has lived his own history up to this point that he has become the human person that he is at this precise point. And from this point onwards, this human person must live his own history, changing himself in changing his world. Since he is called to live his own reality responsibly, the truth that he must seek and that he must live is not only the truth of what it is to be a human person as such, nor only that of being this specific human person, and not even only the truth of the reality that he himself has become historically: it is the truth of one moment of his history in the fullness of the concrete reality.

This call of the individual is indispensable, and it could seem to be an exceedingly difficult call. But both the individual and the society and humanity have already prepared themselves for this inalienable and difficult duty. They have already discovered and formulated moral norms, which can both facilitate the discovery of the moral truth of the concrete case, and also facilitate life together in society, in that they explain what type of behaviour can be expected of individuals in human society. But moral norms, if understood in this way, although their intention is to help, always have necessarily the characteristic of being rather general. This means that they cannot indicate *sic et simpliciter* concrete moral truth for all the moments of the individual or even of a particular community or society—in the course of history.

What problems can arise? Is it certain that all the elements of a concrete problem of a single human person have been sufficiently taken into consideration by a particular norm? Is it certain that all the moral norms inherited in a society sufficiently consider today's reality in its partial changes? Is it certain that the new generations necessarily possess the possibility in every point of evaluating and judging certain human realities in the same way as the preceding generations? They are partially different in their self-perception, in their interpretations and evaluations. And it is certain that the human persons of the new generations will partially change their way of self-understanding, of interpreting and of evaluating, with the passing of time. Finally, is it true that the human person is an historical being, while his moral norms are not historical at all?[1]

The human person as a moral and historical being

Before discussing moral norms directly, it is necessary to continue the reflection on the historicity and the correlative morality of the human person as subject. From this point of view, the human person is not subject to change.

But since the human person is a subject in the continuous flow of time of the world that is an object, his historical and mutable character belongs to the essence of his immutability in this world. Let us leave aside here the question of the hominisation of the human being and humanity; our interest here is rather with the self-perception of the human person that belongs to our own experience.

The human person is always aware of his identity as subject, although he never finds himself at a zero point from which he can begin his history. At every moment, he is aware that he comes from his past, from decisions already made, from a self-realisation that has already begun, and hence from a history of his own that has already formed him; but this, instead of making him come to a halt in the here and now, brings him to a decision about how to continue his own history towards his future, which has its beginning precisely in the passage from the past to the future. The projection towards the future— both as a decision about the immediate next step forward of one's own history, and as a projection that goes further (as is always the case, at least in some manner)—seeks to realise afresh the history that is now past, in order to integrate it in a new way into the future history. Thus, in the historical life of the human person, the subject is always present, while the fullness of his history is never grasped as long as the human person remains a subject in history. But the self-realisation of the human person as an historical person, ie in living his own history, brings him as subject ever nearer to being himself in his historical being, and hence to the fullness of his being a subject and person that is constitutively historical.

The historicity of the human person as subject has its own special importance when we see that the human person as subject and person always perceives himself (I do not say 'recognises himself' in a reflex or explicitly accepted way) as a moral being (moral conscience), ie a being who is always aware of having the moral duty of his own self-development in history. This means a development in the sense of the 'truth' proper to each of its concrete moments — not in an arbitrary manner. It follows that self-projection — together with one's own history that has been lived hitherto — towards the future requires a serious discernment and the will to choose the future path which this discernment identifies. Only thus will the history lived by the personal subject be a true self-development.

The 'future' which the human person projects and lives is to be distinguished from his definitive 'future', which is not determined by himself; rather, he can and must await this and receive it from what is always definitive. The human person perceives that his definitive 'future' is part of the absolute mystery on which depends also, in the same sense, the fact that he is an historical and moral human person and perceives himself as such. The christian calls this mystery God — who, in Jesus Christ and in the Holy Spirit, calls us to the realisation of our history towards our future in the time of human history and, beyond this, to the future that is promised.

Our historical existence in time becomes real in our particular space; it is this space that is often called 'human nature' — although not a nature that is to be understood in an individualistic sense, but rather as essentially interpersonal and worldly (ie, essentially in relation to other persons and to the subhuman world). Man perceives this space, nature, as a given; it is in bringing this to realisation that he realises his personal history in time. The space of nature, almost like an extension of his own being as subject and person, offers him the rich possibility of the construction of a human world, and also, because of 'human' meanings (= meanings for the human person or for humanity), sets limits to our realisation of the construction of the human person and the world. In this sense, it must be said that the human person, to the extent that he perceives himself to be a moral being, also perceives the duty to 'live' the human person as world, ie to 'create' in his history a world of the human person that can be a true development of this world, and to mark it with the sign of the historical human person who operates in the space of the human person as world.

I have said that the reality 'given' to the human person can be called nature; it can also be called, theologically, creation. But we must always bear in mind that this nature-creation was not given to us 'from the beginning' in exactly the state in which we find it today. Rather, it has been given and created as that reality which bore in itself the possibility of evolving and of being developed, in order thus to become the human reality that presents itself to us today. We do not know the zero point from which it started, nor do we know all the potentialities which it holds for our future. And it is the human person himself, along with many other factors, who takes his own initiative in forming the given nature-creation, both as it was in periods long ago, and as it presents itself today. In this sense, it is correct to say that although we know the nature-creation of the human person as world, we know very little about it. The future will disclose ever more about it. Metaphysical reflection on the being of the human person as world offers us fundamental knowledge, but very little knowledge; there is a danger that we may wish to call metaphysical whatever displays itself to us today (perhaps only *de facto*) as a seemingly permanent human reality. It is, accordingly, the reality of nature-creation, as it exists today, that has been given to us together with the charge of interpreting it, of evaluating it and of developing it correspondingly.

But we do not see the reality of nature-creation, as it exists precisely today, in a simply objective vision, ie as it exists *de facto*. We always see it as it has been already interpreted by ourselves. Such an interpretation is subject to the influence of the history of our mode of interpreting the reality of nature-creation, which for its part is not without the influence of our human environment, of our society, and, let us not forget, of our faith and of our ecclesial society.

And just as the nature-creation given to us has always already been interpreted by us, it has also already been evaluated by us in a certain way, both in its ensemble and in its individual elements. It is clear that the evaluation of the reality of the human person as world depends essentially on how it is interpreted; but it does not start from a zero point of evaluation of the concrete reality. Rather, it is in a living relationship with the personal history of the human evaluation of nature-creation, and this is influenced by faith and by the concrete society.

When we think about the problem of moral norms, some relevant points already become clear: the human person as subject is an historical and moral being, who realises himself in the realisation of a nature-creation. This too has a continuous history of its own. Besides this, we never encounter it in a purely objective manner; we have always already interpreted it and evaluated it. It is only if we consider the human person in this way, that it will be possible to perceive and formulate moral norms; it is only in this way that one can grasp how the moral norms are to be understood.

Historicity of moral rightness

The historicity of the human person, as has been shown, concerns both the subject as such, in that this is a person, and the human realisation of the world as object (nature-creation). With regard to normative morality, there has always existed the awareness both of the right realisation of the subject-person as such and of the right realisation of the world-object (nature-creation). On the other hand, this distinction has not always been made in a systematic way; indeed, the two aspects have not seldom been confused, even to the extent that it was no longer clear what was being discussed.

The right realisation of the subject-person is generally (or at least very frequently) today called moral goodness, or even simply personal morality, because it is only the subject-person as such, and his attitudes and his free decisions, as such, that can be called moral in the narrow sense of this word. And with respect to morality as such, one can speak only of personal moral goodness—and of the negation of this, ie of being morally bad, immoral.

The right realisation of the world-object (nature-creation), in order to distinguish this from personal moral goodness, is usually called moral correctness (righteousness, rightness); it bespeaks the appropriate or inappropriate realisation, on the part of the personal human being, of the world-object as nature-creation. The greater number of moral norms speak of this rightness of human conduct. The distinction between the moral goodness of the person and moral rightness in conduct—although, in the strict sense of the word, only the person can be moral—does not mean that the two distinct realities are separate, or without an intrinsic mutual relationship. In point of fact, the rightness of human conduct is to be accepted and assumed in human conduct by personal morality, by the moral goodness of the subject-person, which for its part—precisely because it is goodness—aims to become incarnate in right realisations of the world-object, ie it always wishes what is good, and hence also the good of the world-object of the human person. Has it not always been said that the first moral principle is: *bonum faciendum, malum vitandum*?

The concept of moral goodness has remained basically the same through all the history of moral theology: that one must, for example, aim to realise oneself, to do good, to follow one's conscience, etc. The same cannot be said of the moral rightness of conduct, which has remained problematic. It is true that the rightness of conduct depends also on moral goodness, that is, on the question whether one is ready to accept this; in this sense, one is open and will not seek to close one's eyes to the correct solutions to moral problems. But the rightness itself, as such, depends rather on the reality of the world-object, considered as a human world, ie the world of the human person.

From this last point of view, humanity has not always had the same solutions, nor has them today. The realities of the world change to a certain extent; the results of the sciences of the realities of the world-object may be well-founded for the moment, but despite this they are perhaps only hypothetical and may possibly change; the human interpretations of the facts that have evolved in history are not necessarily identical; nor are the evaluations of the various data necessarily always the same, since they depend much on the vision of the human world (*Weltanschauung*) which one freely assumes. All these elements belong to the given reality, and the moral judgment about the rightness of their human realisation must take them—in their ensemble—into account, for otherwise it loses its objectivity.

The judgment about the rightness of human conduct is not *per se* and in itself a moral judgment (or a moral norm). Rather, it replies in a way that is neutral from the moral point of view to only one question: which realisation of the reality is to be considered humanly—that is, from the point of view of the existence of human beings, appropriate or inappropriate? Such a judgment is nevertheless a judgment of moral rightness, for the sole reason that morality, in the strict sense of the word (ie the goodness of the human person) demands a realisation of the world-object that is not arbitrary, but right. The moral norms of the right realisation of the world-object, therefore, are called moral only because the requirement of (personal) morality and the judgment about right conduct (on its part a morally neutral judgment) coincide in the same subject-person.

If one thinks of the possible variability of the many elements that make up the world-object, which must necessarily be taken into consideration in the formulation of the norms of moral rightness, one will readily see that not all norms can be materially completely the same for all circumstances and for all times. One moral theologian likes to formulate it as follows: *the* moral rightness does not exist.[2] And anyone who would wish to appeal to the 'eternal law', with regard to the norms of moral rightness, must understand that this contains all the concrete solutions for right conduct in the world which is so variable.

Given these explanations, it is already evident that the problematic indicated in the title 'Historicity and moral norm' refers primarily to the norms of moral rightness in conduct in the world-object of the human person. It is interesting to note that this therefore refers to norms which can be called 'moral' only by analogy. It is *per se* superfluous to say explicitly that, in the reflections which follow, moral norms are understood in the sense of norms of moral rightness, except where the text or the context make it clear that the opposite is the case.

Norms of moral rightness

The human person is constitutively historical, but the world-object too is historical, in another sense. The question now is: how can the human person have norms of right conduct in the world, such that these norms express something that is permanent? In order to give a reply to this, we must first ask what precisely is the object of the norms of moral rightness.

Although we do not wish here to enter into the question of hominisation and thus also the beginning of the problem of judgments and of norms of moral rightness, a brief reflection may nevertheless be useful. In the course of his evolution (thanks to the creation of God) towards being truly the human person that we know today, the human person—like other beings of creation—will certainly have had experiences of his own behaviour and will have learned rules of conduct. The more he becomes 'spirit', the more he begins to make nature become also culture. In the final development of a 'spiritual being', he perceives slowly and increasingly that such norms as he has discovered are also moral, ie they are not left up to his arbitrary decision; for example, norms of social, family, sexual, conduct. With regard to the last area, he will sense in some way that the human person is a cultural being, and he will discover and establish taboos which are to be observed. It is well known that various peoples have identified taboos—moral rules—in this area which are very various. To give an example, even today one finds in vast populations of Asia, which are well civilised, the taboo which forbids one ever to touch the genitals, even for urination.

Thus there have been formed, in a manner that is more or less conscious, norms that are based on the knowledge, interpretation and evaluation of the facts (nature) and of lived experiences. It is frequently the élites of the society who intervene to formulate norms that are to be observed in a community or society. But it may be new knowledge or experiences, or likewise new methods of interpreting and evaluating the realities encountered, that intervene, and the result is new norms partially distinct from those that existed previously. The historical human person perceives himself as confronted not only with the historically changing reality of the non-human world, but also with norms which in various ways seek to interpret and judge, from a moral point of view, the rightness of the human realisation of the reality that is encountered and interpreted. The human person who seeks a judgment and a moral norm of rightness for his behaviour thus always finds himself already in the continuity of judgments and norms of a community and society of which he is a part. Despite this, it remains his personal task to discover *his* norm and *his* correct judgment, in the light of the historical continuity of moral norms.

How are the moral norms of rightness, thus arrived at, to be justified? The answer is: by means of a hermeneutical reading of the concrete reality. The results of such a reading are called, in the long story of moral theology, norms of moral natural law. The difficult question, still much discussed today, is: how is this hermeneutical reading to be done? One of the traditional answers is that nature itself teaches us right conduct. This answer is understood more easily in Stoic ethics, which considers nature in a pantheistic way to be divine. Although christianity does not consider nature (pantheistically) to be divine, but understands it as created by God the creator

34

and thus only human, nevertheless christian philosophers and theologians often hold that in many things nature shows or tells us what is morally correct conduct.

In fact, nature-creation does speak to us; but it tells us only what it is, and how it functions on its own. In other words, in nature the Creator shows us what he willed to exist, and how it functions, but not how he wills the human person, *qua* human person, to use this existing reality. It is the human person, as a rational and prudent created being, who must interpret, evaluate and judge the realisation of the given nature from the moral point of view. And it is not a nature considered in the abstract and ahistorically, eg, sexuality, disposing of human life, false statement, that must be judged, interpreted and consequently judged morally, but this nature as it is found now concretely realised in the ensemble of concrete reality; for this consists not only of one determined element-nature (eg a particular sexual activity), but also of various other elements that are real, or to be expected as consequences. It follows that what is to be interpreted, evaluated and judged, not by nature, but by the rational and prudent human person, is the ensemble (as ensemble) of the various realities that constitute a concrete activity—a human act.

In fact, one sometimes notes that in some matters the reflection we have just made is observed, while in other matters it is believed that one can read in a reality of nature the moral norm of right conduct. In 1951, Pius XII held his famous discourse to the Italian midwives on matrimonial questions.[3] *Inter alia*, he spoke of the contraceptive use of matrimony with 'artificial' means and of the use of matrimony from which a sick child was to be expected. Pius XII holds that procreation is the principal natural goal both of the conjugal act and of matrimony itself. Nevertheless, while he considers an artificially contraceptive act absolutely illicit, he does not judge a totally infertile use (with non-artificial means) of matrimony, for proportionally important reasons, in this way. What is the reason for this difference? Nature tends to a conjugal act that is procreative and at the same time unitive; from this, the conclusion is drawn that the human

35

person too has the moral duty to observe this tendency in conjugal life. With respect to the number of children as the fruit of conjugal life, however, nature does not display an unambiguous tendency; therefore the marriage partners morally can and must determine freely and prudently, from the condition of their conjugal life as a whole, the number of children. In the first case, it is held that nature speaks a word that is also moral; in the second case, this is not so. If in the second case it is left to the rational and prudent human person to find a good solution in accordance with the ensemble of the conjugal life, ought one not to seek a parallel moral method for the first case? There is just one difficulty: the idea that the word 'natural' predicated of the individual act is understood, not only in the physical sense, but also in the moral sense—which is a naturalistic fallacy.

In fact, there exists not only a sexuality that is 'natural' in the full sense of the word, but also a sexuality that is rather 'deficient', eg an immature sexuality (tending for example to masturbation), an exclusively homosexual sexuality (not tending to the sexuality that is both procreative and unitive), and a unitive sexuality which can also be procreative only by means of *in vitro* fertilisation: such existing types of sexuality do not *per se* tell us what is the right manner to realise them. It is not nature itself, but the prudent reason of the human person, that must interpret, evaluate and judge this.

To carry this reflection further, it can be important to note that traditionally, within the sphere of marriage, various 'imperfect' sexual activities (without orgasm) are not excluded from a moral point of view, although these imperfect sexual activities, as such, are not procreative and therefore are not natural in the same way as the natural conjugal act. In the same way, it is usual to consider as morally acceptable a conjugal act which is known in advance to be sterile, non-procreative. All this seems to indicate that nature itself offers various types of sexual activity; but if these are morally acceptable or not— as is, for example, the natural conjugal act—it is not nature that tells us this, but rather the rational human person who reflects on the facts, interprets them and judges them from the moral point of view—within the entirety of what it is to be a human person.

The aim of the last reflections has been to indicate that the moral norms of the rightness of our conduct share the historicity of the human person and of his world. Nature itself and its individual elements do not teach morality. Nature is not free of change, nor may it be considered in the abstract, ie only in the individual natural elements; it must be considered in the entirety of a concrete reality. Thus it is the human person himself, rational and prudent, and essentially historical, who can and must make the moral judgment about the concrete reality—the nature/creation that has taken on concrete form in history.

The hermeneutical reading of nature/creation in the abstract and of concrete reality has its own history in the history of the human person who seeks norms and moral judgments about correct behaviour. This is not carried out without a relationship to the normative indications which have been discovered hitherto in the history of the historical human person. There is thus a continuity between the moral norms of the past and the norms of the present. But the specificity of what is normative in the present cannot fail to take account also of the specific discontinuity between what was normative in the past and what is normative in the present. It is only thus that the hermeneutical—historical—reading of nature/creation and of the concrete reality can be valid. And thus there is not only a hermeneutical reading of nature/creation and of the concrete reality itself, but also of the norm inherited from the past.

As christians, we are aware that the reading of nature/creation and of the concrete reality is also carried out in the light of faith, of the bible, of revelation, and of the teaching of the church's magisterium. Not in the sense that these christian realities tell us in a simple manner the morality of correct behaviour in this world; rather, they give us a christian ethos, they give us norms of a correct behaviour which was believed at certain periods to be well compatible with the faith and with the received ethos, they give us a specific vision of the human person and of his world, which makes it easier to attempt to discern valid moral norms of rightness. Thus there exists a strong historical continuity in what is normative for moral rightness.

But even the bible, revelation and the magisterium share in the historicity of the human person. It follows that even the reading of these normative sources must be responsibly hermeneutical, if we wish to find genuine help in them as we seek a morality of moral rightness for today: a reading that is basically fundamentalist will not help.

As for the bible, first we need an exegesis that is scientifically exact: what are we told in the sacred text? One may, for example, think of the recent document of the Congregation for the Doctrine of the Faith on homosexuality. In this we find not only a reading of the bible that is different from the document *Persona Humana* (1975) of the same Congregation, in which there was no reference to the once classical biblical text of the story of Sodom; there is also a failure to indicate that there are serious exegetical problems today with the interpretation of other biblical texts (including Rom 1), and that the text of Gen 1 and 2 has nothing to do with the problem of homosexuality. Second, it seems that it is wrong to look in a fundamentalist way in the bible for formal divine revelations of categorial norms of moral rightness—given the nature both of divine revelation and of such historical and contingent norms; categorial moral truths of moral rightness do not exist in full independence of their genesis in our moral conscience. Third, one must consider what the various biblical authors wished to say for a particular historical situation, and under the conditions of what they understood at that period of the human world, and in terms of the convictions of their culture. Fourth, one must see whether their moral statements intend to be a true moral teaching, or only an exhortation (*paranesis*) in which the moral contents are presupposed, and in this sense accepted, but not taught. Fifth, I do not see how it is possible to think of a 'force of inspiration' which confers a special authority on each and all of the statements of the bible (as some theologians have written); if St Paul states that his advice is only his own (although it is that of a christian and an apostle), inspiration does not alter the fact, affirmed by the apostle himself, that what he says is only advice—and this advice is specifically for his concrete addressees.

With respect to the norms formulated during the history of christian moral theology, hence of the christian tradition, our observations must be similar: we must observe what is truly affirmed, for a well-determined historical situation, and under the conditions and in keeping with the moral convictions of a particular period or of a particular tendency.

Similar questions arise with regard to documents and decisions of the church's magisterium, which are likewise historically conditioned by certain presuppositions and convictions.

After these reflections on the historicity of the moral norms of right conduct, we go on to ask what is meant by the frequently-affirmed objectivity of norms of moral rightness? A first negative reply is that the objectivity does not derive from a formal revelation of such norms, or only from a tradition or from authentic documents of the magisterium. A second positive reply would run as follows: if the norms of moral rightness derive from a process of knowledge, evaluation and judgment, it must be admitted that they are determined not only by the elements of the world-object, but also by elements of the judging subject which necessarily enter into this process. For example, the subject cannot recognise a norm which, according to the self-understanding and interpretation of experience on the part of a human person who is sinful and redeemed, requires more than is humanly 'realisable' (*zumutbar*: K Demmer). The subject cannot make a moral judgment without involving in this his own understanding of the human person and of his world, and his possibilities—likewise conditioned historically—of evaluating these realities. Not all values are always 'actual' (K Rahner). Both the facts and the experience of a particular culture and civilisation, and the system of evaluation of the various realities of these, must enter into a concrete judgment that is to be objectively normative for such a supposed reality. It follows that an ideal intuition is not, as such, *ipso facto* a moral norm. Rather, the norm must say what the ideal can require and intends to require—in view of the object-subject reality in which the abstract ideal is involved and in which therefore it must be realised. It is only in this way that a norm is truly objective—whether it is discerned by a society or by a single person. This does not prohibit a reflex control of the norm, nor does it prohibit the comparison with other norms, in order to see which of these is nearest to the ideal and to the concrete reality. The various norms, understood in this way, are part of the eternal law, in that this implies all that the realisation of the ideal in the various concretisations must be, given the datum of the created human person/world.

The concept of objectivity set out here differs from the concept of objectivity that *de facto* is often employed; the latter usage is accustomed to call objective the norm that is generally accepted in a society, for example in the Catholic Church, or proposed by a competent authority, for example by the magisterium of the church. But such norms, considered objective in this sense, not only can be inadequate or formulated in an inadequate manner, but can sometimes even be shown to be partially or totally erroneous, whether by competent persons or by a general rethinking in later periods. There will necessarily always be fresh endeavours to bring the hitherto accepted norms to a greater objectivity.

These considerations are confirmed in the Second Vatican Council. A formulation finally reached after great struggle says that the moral norms (of matrimonial life) must come from criteria taken *ex personae eiusdemque actuum natura* (*Gaudium et Spes*), ie not only from the nature of the acts. Further, it is admitted that even faithful and truly responsible christians can reach different conclusions of moral rightness, and further that even the pastors do not always have sufficient answers to new moral questions. Finally, the Council considers that the riches of the various cultures manifest more fully human nature and the various paths to the truth; but this seems to include the moral truths that correspond to various elements of such cultures.

The understanding of the objectivity of the moral norms of right behaviour proposed here raises another problem: what does it mean to assert that certain moral norms accepted or taught in the society (eg in the church), or opinions of particular groups or persons, or even certain judgments of conscience in situations can be potentially erroneous? The problem is this: might one not be right to say that such norms, opinions or judgments express precisely the objective moral truth of the concrete object-subject? The usage of speaking rather about conscience and erroneous judgments reflects a different reality, ie that such judgments are not in conformity with the judgments generally accepted in a society, and clearly considered to be true.

The function of the norms of moral rightness

Norms of moral rightness seek to grasp and to express the moral truth, or truths, of the reality of the human person and of his world, in order to help both individuals and society as a whole. It could seem that such norms are discerned and formulated precisely to resolve the problems of being the human persons that we are today; but thus it could appear also that they are fixed only for today, and are in this sense static. However, they ought to be capable of being normative for the essentially historical and changing human reality, which does not give the human person a 'today' or a quiet moment of total stasis. How do the norms of moral rightness serve the historical human person, and how do they function for such a service? There are some theologians who consider such norms as laws that are to be applied 'simply', especially in the case of norms formulated negatively; there are other theologians who see such norms rather as the expression of a reflection made beforehand, and therefore in the abstract: while such norms are certainly highly useful for a concrete moral judgment, they are no more than highly useful, because the norm as such does not refer formally and exactly to the truth of the concrete reality here and now. For the moment, let us leave this difference between these two types of theologians.

Experience shows us that human persons generally live well within the norms of moral rightness, both as individuals and as a society. This depends on the fact that although the human person is in an historical change, this change is neither total nor continually and explicitly observable. Nevertheless, historical changes, both in the reality of the human person-world and in the human interpretation and evaluation, exist, and the human person is in some way aware of them. Application of the norms is therefore not a univocal process, but understands the norm in a hermeneutical reading that takes account of the concrete here and now, precisely in order to know what the norm fundamentally has to say about the concrete reality,[4] ie the norms are applied analogically, and in this sense too they have an historical character.

Since the norms of rightness are essentially human judgments, and therefore historical, existential doubts can arise. Therefore, if everything is historical and changes—even if not totally—problems remain. If some norms were formulated for particular realities fundamentally different from the realities that exist today, or with an understanding of these realities profoundly different from our understanding today, the question arises whether a norm formulated in this way can help us today (ie can be valid), or should not rather be replaced by another norm. If problems never known previously arise today because of new knowledge, for example in the field of embryology or of genetics, how far must or can one resolve them by means of principles or norms that were established without the possibility of taking into account what is known today, norms that were not truly formulated for our new problems? If the norms of rightness are frequently formulated in an inadequate manner, not yet taking account of certain realities and solutions that cause problems to arise, and seemingly unable to give a sufficient answer to such problems—although the norm literally claims to be the solution of the problem—then ought one not to reformulate the norm, at least in part, to make it more adequate?

This would mean, as some propose (for example, Virt and Demmer), using the virtue of *epikeia* in moral theology too. A similar problem could arise in an individual case of a single person, but also in a very common doubt or in a question that is seriously discussed by those who are 'competent'. It is conceivable that, not only in particular cultures very different from ours, but also in subcultures within our more general culture, there could exist convictions and visions of the human person-world which, to the extent that they do exist as such, are consequently the foundation of certain 'objective' moral norms (such behaviour corresponds objectively to such a reality of the human person-world), which must be respected as such,[5] although at the same time they are not acceptable for the rest of us.

When, therefore, we have serious doubts with regard to certain proposed or inherited norms about whether they are genuinely helpful for a solution of our problems, we must undertake a serious hermeneutical reading of the norms in question. If, for example, it is clear that the intention has been to read the norm 'in the nature of things' when it is a clear case of a naturalistic fallacy, the norm is not useful and must be reformulated.

If, on the other hand, a norm is justified, not by a naturalistic fallacy, but 'teleologically', it may be that we must check the evaluation of the various elements involved in the norm. As has just been shown, the cases can be various.

Similar problems are reflected in certain formulations that have been proposed both long ago and recently. Is it not true that Aquinas requires a hermeneutical reading of the norms, instead of an unconditional application, when he says that the concrete norms (unlike the most general principles) *valent ut in pluribus* (and not more)? It may be the case that the principle *praesumptio cedit veritati*, with its origin in law, does not apply in moral questions: if a *praesumptio* that was made at the outset can be falsified, must one not review the norm? Modern English-speaking ethics has introduced the concept of *prima facie* duties; this does not mean that the obligations indicated formulate norms which seem to be almost evident, while difficulties and doubts can be demonstrated in the concrete application, which demand a new reading of an inadequately formulated norm, ie a reading that takes account of all the elements relevant for the solution of a moral problem.

What was the intention of authors such as G Martelet (in a book recommended by Paul VI after the publication of the encyclical *Humanae Vitae*), D Capone (in an article on homosexuality in the *Osservatore Romano*, and in another article on *Humanae Vitae* in the periodical *Lateranum*), P Chirico (in a very interesting article in *Theological Studies*),[6] or the much-discussed instruction of the French Bishops after the encyclical *Humanae Vitae*? All accept the full validity of the norms (documents) in question, but require—in various ways—that the application *in concreto* of such norms should take account also of other elements of the concrete human reality, which are likewise morally relevant, in order to arrive at a true application. Is it not true to say that basically they wish a hermeneutical reading of the accepted norm in a more concrete context? This seems to me to indicate fundamentally that the accepted norm is formulated in a manner that is not totally adequate, in that it makes a valid judgment about only one single element of a reality that is much more complex.

When L Kohlberg discussed the famous question of a growing moral maturity in the life of individuals, he saw the greatest moral maturity of a human person to lie in the ability to find solutions for his conduct in the fact that he has become more and more independent of moral authorities, that is, has become more himself, in his moral judgment. Does not this imply that, in the use of moral norms, the serious hermeneutical reading of these norms must become ever more important and decisive?

The human person is an historical being, together with his world, not excluding his moral norms of right conduct. Thus the moral norms, if adequately understood, are not in tension with the historicity of the human person.

3. *Thomistic and Analytic Philosophers on the First Principles of Morality: A Conflict of Interpretations*

A RECURRENT problem for Catholic moralists has been not only to present the church's natural law tradition rationally but convincingly to a secular world that holds for an autonomous ethic. It appears that the language and logic of the natural law teaching of the Catholic church is quite foreign to those educated in modern philosophies. This is a serious challenge to the church's evangelising mission in the world.

This essay will not concern itself with the church's tradition as such, nor with an exposition of the thought of St Thomas Aquinas.[1] Nor will its focus be the analytic tradition in Anglo-Saxon philosophy as such but that philosophy's attempt to make sense of the first principles of morality. In a certain sense this essay is a narrative that evokes the inner logic of a new presentation of natural law theory.

The story begins with an exposition of the problem of doing moral theology as seen by analytic philosophy, and the problem of first principles. It then moves into a number of proposed solutions and concludes with an overview of the matured theory. It will not be an exhaustive treatment of analytic philosophers on this topic but will be selective both as regards matter and authors.

There is a dialectic that moves through these four stages: a thesis, namely the propositions accredited by the tradition which is, for the most part, St Thomas Aquinas' exposition of the first principles of morality in the *Summa Theologiae*, I-II, 94, a.2; an antithesis, namely the principles of analytic philosophy, eg the 'is-ought' distinction, and modern logic, eg a deduction based on 'natural necessity'; a synthesis between the 'basic goods' and the 'modes of responsibility' which are both key terms in the new theory.

The problem as seen by analytic philosophy

The London *Tablet* of 4 April 1987 carried an article by John Finnis that read like the manifesto of an intellectual movement that had tasted success. Entitled 'The Claim of Absolutes' it was full of self-assurance with clear definitions of its positions and objectives. Its major claim was that it fulfilled the Second Vatican Council's mandate to give moral theology a more scientific exposition.[2] It repeats the accusation that the tradition of the manuals — for example the *Moral and Pastoral Theology* of Henry Davis, SJ — was deficient in its use of Sacred Scripture, that it lacked a synthetic vision of morality within the perspectives of christology, ecclesiology and eschatology. But the most important charge is that it will not stand up to a thorough examination by analytic philosophy, that it is wanting in logical coherence and proof.

Finnis is here reflecting what has been a long-time feeling among analytic philosophers. He noted that this dissatisfaction has been apparent since the 1930s when English-speaking Catholic philosophers began criticising Suarez's account of the natural law which was that most commonly held by Catholics at the time. But a return to St Thomas caused more problems in logic than anybody expected. It was not obvious how the first principles of morality were founded nor how they related to the norms of moral action, that is, how principles, precepts and norms are to be distinguished.

But the disillusionment went far deeper than these seemingly unanswered questions. Vincent MacNamara has listed the following sources of objection to how moral theology is practised: there is an absence of intellectual and logical rigour in moral theology that produces 'rich mines of fallacious argument and unexamined assumptions'; christian ethics is also said to experience 'a relative absence of careful definition, clear statement, or cogent and rigorous argument'; the proclaimed renewal of moral theology since Vatican II has resulted in more confusion than clarity about fundamental moral concepts.[3]

Eric D'Arcy has delved far more deeply into the malaise that exists when Catholic moral theology is confronted with evangelising the moral and ethical thought of the Anglo-Saxon world. He asserts that Catholic moral theory has never had deep roots in English-speaking culture, let alone in English-speaking philosophy.[4]

Some of the cultural facts that underlie this situation are that moral theology has traditionally been done in ecclesiastical institutions preparing candidates for the priesthood; this tradition has emphasised the seminarian's future ministry in the sacrament of penance; the intellectual backdrop to moral theology was Thomism which was neither in sympathy with nor in any realistic contact with the English tradition, eg the objections raised by Hume's famous 'no-ought-from-is' passage; the renewal in moral theology has occurred mainly in terms of the philosophies predominant in the Franco-German area, such as the lines of thought that come down through Kant and Hegel to Kierkegaard, through phenomenology into existentialism and more lately structuralism; in the English-speaking world, however, the predominant philosophical movement grew out of the progress in logic made as a result of the discoveries of Frege, Russell and Whitehead, and the philosophical rationalisings of Russell, Moore and Wittgenstein: it is this discovery of a revolutionary philosophical method whose principal task is the logical analysis of meaning, that has been commonly called 'analytic philosophy'.[5]

D'Arcy notes how moral theologians since Vatican II have been content to treat problems and issues that took the attention of the Franco-German world. This has been a stimulus to English-speaking theologians. However, his concern seems far overstated and even prejudiced when one considers contributions made recently by bishops and theologians in the United States on questions of peace and war, medical ethics and the economy. His point, however, about a lack of awareness of analytic philosophy among moralists is still mostly true.

There are three important disadvantages that accrue in this state of affairs. Firstly, the difference in style. The Continentals are more inclined towards heightened, dramatic intensity and a liking for abstractions in their writing. Words such as 'dialogue' 'commitment' and 'authenticity' have an immediate resonance in a European ear. But Anglo-Saxons are not given to mysticism or abstractions. Our questions are direct, concrete and pragmatic. 'What is it?' 'What does it mean?' 'How do you know that?' 'How does it work?' 'What difference will it make?' These are the questions of the intellectual and of the person in the street alike. These are the terms in which they hear the christian message and in which they need to be evangelised. It is because of this that the church's moral thinking, especially on natural law, needs to be presented in terms accommodated to this mentality and culture.

The second disadvantage concerns topics under discussion. There is no deep interest in the questions of vital interest to the world of English-speaking philosophy: 'It is very hard to find moralists working in Catholic seminaries who contribute seriously to the moral, especially the meta-ethical, problems engaging the interest of analytic philosophers.'[6] The most obvious example is the 'naturalistic fallacy' which is meant to 'subvert all the vulgar systems of morality' and in particular the christian.

The third drawback D'Arcy perceives is that while theologians have learned to utilise modern psychology and sociology, their thinking is still tied to outdated forms of logic. Here we touch upon what is perhaps the major contention of the analytic school. Greater advances have been made in the last hundred years in logic than in the previous twenty-three centuries. This is true with regard to the breakthroughs in formal logic, as it is also true, but to a lesser extent, of philosophical logic. Many problems previously thought to be those of metaphysics or epistemology are now seen and treated as problems of logic, for example, the mind-body problem, or how can one say of Jesus of Nazareth that he is literally divine and literally human at the same time. Analytic philosophers have examined the different logical statuses of rules and of methods for deciding the appropriate 'description under which' an act is to be morally evaluated.[7] These new ways in logic have lead to a revolution in moral reasoning and argumentation.

The problem of first principles

D'Arcy himself has utilised these tools in his book *Conscience and its Right to Freedom*[8] and by his critique opened the door to the contemporary discussion on the first principles of morality. Chapter 3, 'The Problem of Content', is of the greatest importance where he describes the judgment of conscience as the conclusion of a practical syllogism. Its major is provided by synderesis. The whole problem is summed up in these words of D'Arcy: 'It is vexing to find that St Thomas leaves us rather uncertain about the content of synderesis.'[9] The obvious candidate as a first principle is 'good should be done and evil avoided'. But what is the efficacy of this principle? To lead to a moral judgment by being the major of a moral syllogism, or somehow to found and determine our moral choices and decisions, or both? The second choice sees synderesis as 'inciting us to what is good and drawing us back from evil'. In traditional terminology this is the order of finality, the order of the real that realises our intentions. D'Arcy and the analytic school with him take the first choice which sees in synderesis the major premise of a syllogism. It is purely a problem of logic in which we demonstrate the necessary relationships whereby 'from its first principles we proceed to new ones, and pass judgment on these when we reach them'. (*S Th* I, 79. 12c). In this sense synderesis is a 'purely formal principle',[10] logically parallel to the principle of non-contradiction.

The analytic school, consistent with the ideals it set itself of purifying and clarifying language, has chosen a certain reading and interpretation of St Thomas. Analysts' interest is wholly in the logic of propositions. It should be noted that while they are reluctant to deny the medieval synthesis, they have sundered the most important elements in its ethical and moral vision. The medievals saw logic as a mental discipline whereby the knowing subject could explore the real in knowledge. It was an instrument for articulating knowledge in order to be able to reach into the inner structures of the real. Synderesis for the medievals, following the Stoics, was the human disposition to be moral, to seek goodness and avoid evil. As a disposition, and therefore belonging to the order of the real, it was regarded as the essential *inclinatio naturalis* of a human being. As a real principle it is the source that generates our moral being in action. Now this principle and what flows from it can be understood in a logical manner. Synderesis is thus the capacity to recognise basic principles of morals, a disposition 'containing the precepts of the natural law' (*S Th* I-II, 94, a.2.). The sundering of the real and logical orders in the medieval synthesis will lead the analysts to propose another distinction based on modern logic in order to explain the content of synderesis, ie, that between the 'basic goods' and the 'modes of responsibility' as I shall explain later.

One of the reverberations of this emphasis on logical coherence is the question of whether the first principles of natural law are 'general principles or primary precepts'. A good example would be 'perjury is wrong'. This serves well as the major of a syllogism but how does it pertain to synderesis? How is the conclusion deduced? For HLA Hart along with St Thomas, there is a syllogism that obeys the laws of logical validity. Hart, however, departs from St Thomas in that he holds that first principles are value-judgments that are a matter of choice. Thus the choice of first principles is not a case of self-evidence. CL Strawson on the other hand assaults the assertion that the first principles of morality are self-evident on the ground that the connection between the reasons for an action and the action is not logical but causal. We come back to the above-mentioned point: the connection between logic and causality that characterised the medieval synthesis has been irreparably ruptured.[11]

The analytic school has been able to make a very powerful case against the traditional conception of self-evidence as the foundation in logic and epistemology for first principles. St Thomas affirms that the precepts of the natural law, like the first principles of speculative science, are self-evident. They are *per se notum*, of which there are two types. A proposition may be self-evident *secundum se* if its predicate is 'contained in the notion of the subject', ie once the terms of the proposition are understood the predicate is seen to be necessarily contained in the subject, for example 'all criminals are law-breakers'. A proposition may also be self-evident to us, *quoad nos* when we understand the meanings of the terms in the proposition. Many propositions are obvious 'only to the wise', who have studied the subject in question, for example every octagon has eight sides. Now the first principle of practical reason corresponds to the first theoretical principle, that of non-contradiction. This type of self-evidence maintains that a proposition cannot be reduced to more primitive elements. This is important for Aristotle and St Thomas for the reason that we cannot prove every statement without either committing ourselves to infinite regress or to a vicious circle. So there must be some propositions that are known with certainty and without inference.

The analytic school has been able to demonstrate that St Thomas did not sufficiently distinguish between what is logically primitive from what is psychologically obvious. It is possible for both to fall under his concept of 'self-evidence'. As Strawson pointed out, if the connection between the reasons for an action and the action itself is causal, then self-evidence is idiosyncratic to each person, depending on an individual's psychological attitudes.

There have been two developments in the conception of self-evident propositions suggested by analytic philosophers. As regards logic, there is a new understanding of the starting-point in any system of logically connected propositions. Not only must there be some such irreducible propositions but these are not always necessarily the same propositions. That is, what is essential to the system is not the axioms which can be various but the conditions or rules that ensure that correct conclusions result and are drawn from these premises. This insight is due in particular to advances in modern systems of geometry. DJ

O'Connor has observed, 'We need rules to develop consequences from the axioms (a point that Aristotle and St
Thomas did not fully appreciate)'.[12] 'The modes of responsibility' correspond to the rules of deriving moral norms
for drawing a correct judgment of conscience from a major
premise provided by the basic goods.

As regards the psychological aspect of self-evidence, a
self-evident proposition must be obvious to someone. The
distinction between propositions self-evident, *in se* and
quoad nos obscures this truth. Analysts point out that false
propositions often seem obviously true, that self-evidence
depends on factors other than logic, and that 'truth'
cannot be applied univocally to propositions of different
types.

This raises the greatest difficulty for the analytic school
when dealing with the traditional presentation of the first
principles of morality. Does not St Thomas when he
speaks of 'law' in natural law confuse two senses of that
word? Law as a moral rule or even as a socially established
ordinance has a prescriptive 'ought' sense, since it is
designed to bring about a certain type of conduct. Law can
also mean a regularity in nature, eg the law of gravity, and
in this sense law has a descriptive 'is' sense.

The 'is-ought' distinction is modern but St Thomas was
not altogether ignorant of its force. Now it must be
appreciated that St Thomas furnishes us with a theological
tract on law that is philosophically coherent and consistent. Natural law is the rational creature's participation in
the eternal law. It is what is naturally and immediately
known by man as a moral being. He explains that a thing
can be subject to eternal law in two ways: 1. by awareness
of what is, ie by personal governance of one's own life; 2.
by way of an internal motive principle. Man as rational is
subject to eternal law in both these ways. Any thing obeys
the eternal law by following its natural inclinations. But
since it is a part of human nature that man 'act in
accordance with reason' he is following his most fundamental tendency to self-fulfilment when he acts reasonably and rationally. Thus for St Thomas the two senses of
law, prescriptive and descriptive, have a common origin

in natural inclination. However, modern analysts do not accept this conception of a providential God who planned and guides the universe as a primary axiom in their ethics. They conceive ethics as an autonomous science that must critically found and justify its own first principles. Germain Grisez has steadfastly maintained that St Thomas' approach can be seen to be open to the charge of defying the 'is-ought' distinction of reducing moral principles to physicalism or biologism—to mere facts. Cut off from the vision of a provident God establishing purpose in the universe and order among man's natural inclinations there is no necessary order among the first principles of morality, as in St Thomas, but Grisez maintains that each first principle is then logically equally necessary and equally morally binding. They are incommensurable one with another. In an autonomous ethic it is more than ever necessary to demonstrate when a moral object is intrinsically evil and therefore absolutely prohibited and never to be sought as an accomplishment of human fulfilment. This position is an unavoidable consequence of the exercise of an autonomous logic in this type of ethics. Given the premises of equally binding principles this conclusion cannot be rationally escaped. The validity of this new theory all swings on the correctness of its primary premises, the 'basic goods', and their meaning. The problem is how to specify these incommensurable or basic goods.

To summarise this section, analysts discern a common problem as regards the first principles of morality. The tradition and St Thomas as its most brilliant exponent, cannot adequately demonstrate the logic of the transition from first principles to the judgment of conscience. Nor has the traditional approach been able to show how it logically determines the major of this syllogism which pertains to the content of synderesis and the primary principles of natural law. The problem is that the content of synderesis is uncertain and undetermined for the analysts.

D'Arcy charges that 'The complaint stands that St Thomas' terminology is not consistent',[13] and that he has not overcome the difficulty raised by Hume of making an invalid prescriptive inference from descriptive premises. O'Connor has perceived the same 'gap' in St Thomas' reasoning:

> Either moral rules are derivable from the general precepts given in *synderesis* or they are not. If they are, we require to see the derivations, since what is provable can be proved. If they are not how are they to be justified?[14]

Suggested solutions by analytic philosophers

There have been a number of insights as to how this 'gap' might be filled.

Herbert McCabe, OP takes the whole argument face-on directly and interprets St Thomas in such a way that synderesis is not just a set of premises from which moral truths or moral norms are deduced. Rather it provides the terms within which and in the light of which a moral argument is conducted. For him the moral syllogism is very flexible since the minor — the concrete — situation and circumstances, are always open and can be added to, so that the judgment of conscience does not result in a way that corresponds with a mathematical type of logic but connaturally. His vision is really one of prudence which mediates the meaning of action for us and closes the 'gap'.[15] He seems to have provided a reading that leaves St Thomas' meaning intact and integral, lifting the discussion above the merely logical and concentrating on the dynamism of the moral agent. However he gives no satisfactory account of what St Thomas means by 'derived' in *S Th* I-II, 94, a.6.

Alan Donagan believes that St Thomas' version of natural law has much to offer secular ethicists. The stumbling block to this contribution is that St Thomas' theological vision does not sit well with the doctrine of the autonomy of ethics. Yet St Thomas does seem to imply the autonomy of ethics because he derives, says Donagan, the first precept of the natural law, 'good is to be done and evil avoided', from the metaphysical statement that good is what all beings seek. This raises all the difficulties foreseen by Hume but it also establishes that ethics has its own autonomous first principles. In this St Thomas is of one accord with Kant: ethics can be philosophically established in its own right. Thus 'natural law is a set of precepts the binding force of which can be ascertained by human reason.' Donagan then goes on to his central point that 'no adequate scholastic *philosophy* of natural law has yet been elaborated'.[16] He uses the precept against lying to illustrate the 'gap' already observed by O'Connor. St Thomas is too dependent, he thinks, on Aristotle's idea of the natural end of the faculty of speech to formulate a valid prescriptively normative argument. How then can a precept such as 'it is wrong to tell a lie' be derived from moral first principles and justified? The argument from the frustration of nature is unconvincing today. St Thomas was mistaken in taking Aristotle's natural philosophy as the way of specifying the goods we should seek, says Donagan. 'But nothing in his definition of natural law obliges him to make that mistake.'[17] Donagan's insight is that St Thomas' doctrine that 'man is the end of the whole order of generation' (*Summa contra Gentiles*, III, 22, 7) essentially corresponds with Kant's principle that 'man ... exists as an end in himself, not merely as a means for arbitrary use by this or that will'.[18] Kant's principle is therefore viewed as being implicit in St Thomas. It provides as it were the 'missing link' with which analytic philosophers can cross the gap between first principles and concrete moral norms. It is a way of specifying moral goods and evils. Thus it is wrong to lie because this involves using another human being merely as a means. Donagan has purified Kant's insights and attempted to fit them into the Thomistic framework of natural law in his major work, *The Theory of Morality*.[19] He derives moral norms from necessary 'a priori' principles by a deontic line of reasoning.

The mature theory

The author who brought together the diverse lines of thought so far described, criticised them and propounded a new theory was Germain Grisez. His work has been highly praised and has taken the imagination of many Catholic authors with an analytic background.

He approached his task with some basic convictions. Firstly that there is an objective moral order. He would have no part of Hume's subjectivism. Morality consists of objective truths, objective goods to be achieved and lived. Eric D'Arcy has lauded the move to objectivity in Anglo-Saxon philosophy since the 1950s as a grace-filled chance for the evangelisation of that culture.[20] Grisez is the one who has grasped this opportunity by presenting natural law in terms acceptable to analytic philosophy. His second conviction, as is obvious, was that analytic philosophy is the most appropriate tool with which to explore these moral truths.

Among his many studies the one which is of interest to us here is 'The First Principle of Practical Reason: A Commentary on the *Summa Theologiae* 1-2, Question 94, article 2'.[21] It is one of his two attempts at Thomistic exegesis and must be rated as an important breakthrough for our topic. His contribution is in being able to identify and specify the basic goods that serve as the major in a moral syllogism. These are the 'missing links' sought by the analysts which lay hidden within St Thomas' reasoning, according to Grisez. With them it is possible to found and justify moral norms. He is not interested in an historical study as such but in theology and philosophy. He, therefore, is not slow to part company with and criticise St Thomas even though he was originally inspired by him.

He begins by criticising the Suarezian account of natural law. Moral norms are derived this way according to Suarez: man discovers a divine imperative written in his conscience, eg 'do not steal'. If this corresponds with what man perceives in his essence as not befitting him then stealing is morally prohibited. The moral norm is thus deduced from the metaphysical nature of man with the help of divine commands. But Suarez failed to discern the nature of practical reason. 'Practical reason is the mind working as a principle of action, not simply as a recipient of objective reality.'[22] The mind plans and charters what is to be; it is not a record of reality as in speculative knowledge. Out of our experience the mind formulates a plan for our lives and the norms of action. Practical reason establishes the possibilities of action by proposing ends-to-be-sought to the mind. The precept thus gives an orientation or direction to action since it expresses the attractivity of the end to-be-sought. This of course is based on the finality of the natural inclinations. These inclinations reveal the possibilities or range of human action, that is the goods-to-be-sought. The key to Grisez's interpretation is in these goods-to-be-sought. 'To be sought' signifies, according to Grisez, not a command to act but a precept that can guide deliberation and action. He takes this distinction from analytic philosophy. 'To-be-sought' has the force of a noun: it betokens an object which serves as the end of natural inclination and action. By understanding this object, which since it is an end is a good, we set up the rules of deliberation that precede decision. The good so defined in nounal form becomes a first principle of practical reason from which we can generate the concrete norms of action. The first principle is formulated as 'Good is to be done and pursued, and evil is to be avoided'. This gives a direction and orientation for the mind to follow: it is a plan of action in the mind and not a command for the will to execute. According to Grisez it is cognitive and not volitional. 'To-be-sought' is not envisaged in its verbal form whereby the action or tendency of the natural inclination is dynamically incorporated into our conception of seeking the ultimate good of human fulfilment but as the good sought.

Contrary to Suarez, Grisez begins in human experience and not in an abstract concept of human nature or in a divine command. Here is the great advantage in his reformulation. He shows how norms are rules for action and not for essence or human nature. However, this is not sufficiently followed through: the inclination to sinfulness, for instance, is not incorporated into his principles of morality in a very coherent way. 'Is to be sought' has a verbal, dynamic force for St Thomas which is the reason that it always appears in propositional form. Grisez by treating it as a noun reifies the human tendencies and inclinations into objectified goods or ends separate from decision and action. His ethics thus loses contact with ontology. Is this type of objectification of human tendency and potential too high a price to pay to find a means of justifying moral norms? As it were, Grisez has pulled St Thomas' sentence apart, dispensed with the verb, and minutely analysed the object of the action. The type of logic he uses leads to the sundering of inclination, action and end from each other and from the agent. God has put them together in a rational pattern in the divine design of nature, and our logic should respect that. This truth is valid even for an autonomous logic. Grisez's motivation for so proceeding has been to avoid the objection that he falls foul of the 'is-ought' distinction. His theory thus has two parts. A descriptive section which is a type of phenomenology of the basic goods. These provide the major of the moral syllogism. This could be said to be his value-theory. John Finnis lists these goods as life, know-ledge, play, aesthetic experience, sociability, practical reasonableness and religion in *Natural Law and Natural Rights*. The second part is prescriptive and consists in the modes of responsibility which specify how these goods are to be sought morally. This is ethics properly so called and furnishes the minor in the moral syllogism which having moral content allows us to draw a moral conclu-sion to our reasoning.[23] Finnis has formulated the 'modes of responsibility' thus: 1. reasonableness structures our pursuit of every good; 2. a coherent plan of life; 3. no arbitrary preference among values; 4. no arbitrary prefer-ence among persons; 5. detachment and commitment complement each other; 6. consequences represent ef-ficiency in action and have limited moral relevance; 7. every basic value is to be respected in every act; 8. the common good is to provide the conditions for human fulfilment and flourishing; 9. conscience must be adhered to apart from passion or social pressure. In the major Grisez seeks out the intelligibility of the goods-to-be-sought; in the minor he specifies *how* this good is to be attained rationally, morally and humanly. The conclu-sion is the action to be done. Thus, 'the primary precepts of practical reason concern the things to-be-done, that practical reason naturally grasps as human goods, and the things to-be-avoided that are opposed to those goods.'[24]

While it is impossible to describe all the details and the evolution of Grisez's theory, we must note how he used one of the discoveries of philosophical logic that descends from Frege, namely 'natural necessity'. From contingent human affairs it is possible to draw necessary philosophical conclusions. A richer logic is needed than heretofore. As Herbert Hart said:

> It is a truth of some importance that for the adequate description not only of law but of many other social institutions, a place must be reserved, besides definitions and ordinary statements of fact, for a third category of statements; those the truth of which is contingent on human beings and the world we live in retaining the salient characteristics which they have.[25]

This led HLA Hart to restate 'the core of good sense in natural law theory'. It has led John Finnis and Joseph M Boyle Jr to develop the logic of natural necessity, and so, along with Grisez, to expand the horizons of natural law thinking. The point of arrival of Grisez's reformulation of the first principles of morality may be seen in this new definition in terms of basic human goods that integrally fulfils man as his natural beatitude:

> In voluntary acting for human goods and avoiding what is opposed to them, one ought to choose and otherwise will those and only those possibilities whose willing is compatible with integral fulfilment.[26]

The ideas of these authors are the source of much thought and debate,[27] and their legacy of a natural law theory based on analytic principles is secure.

Father Sean O'Riordan, in whose honour this paper is being presented, has been a keen scholar of both natural law and analytic philosophy. The authors studied here have used the modern techniques of analysing a logical system into axioms—the basic goods, and valid modes of inference, that is, the modes of responsibility—in order to throw a fascinating new light on an ancient tradition.

4. *Reciprocity of Consciences: A Key Concept in Moral Theology*

IT is perhaps the most distinctive characteristic of the moral theology of St Alphonsus that, in contrast to the manuals of his day, he did not begin his *Theologia Moralis* with an abstract tractate on the ultimate end, but with one on conscience, and that in cases of conflict between law and conscience he gave priority to the latter. I would place the life-work of Father Sean O'Riordan squarely within this tradition. In this commemorative volume in his honour, I have therefore chosen to discuss the theme of 'reciprocity of conscience' and its relevance for the present state of moral theology.

I see conscience (Greek *syneidesis*, Latin *con-scientia*) as a knowing of one's self and the world in company with others. Con-science comes to its full flowering when it implies knowing one's self and one's interrelatedness with others in the sight of God, knowing that we are 'known' by God, and viewing ourselves and our relationships with others from that vantage point.

In French, *réciprocité*[1] has two meanings, but both are strictly related. With the wisdom of the French as my starting point, I will discuss in the first place the mutuality or reciprocity of consciousness, and its psycho-social implications before proceeding to a discussion on its ethical meaning, conscience strictly so-called.

One example of reciprocity of consciousness we find is the process of *mimesis*,[2] the imitative 'aping' of apes. The ape's 'intelligence' and socialised 'memory' spring from its capacity for imitation. Mimesis compels the ape to try to have what another ape has and enjoys. From the process of mimesis however, conflicts will arise. Experience, for example, warns the ape that it would be dangerous to attempt to take something from another ape that has much greater power and capacity for violence.

Human reciprocity of consciousness develops on this same mimetic level. For example: if parents educate mainly, or even exclusively, by means of sanctions (whether pleasurable rewards or unpleasant punishments),[3] the child interiorises this approach, and develops a corresponding *super-ego*. Since it has learned to act mainly, or even exclusively, for pleasurable reward or to avoid unpleasant sanctions, the child's consciousness can become a fertile ground for manipulation, in Skinner's sense, through pleasure and pain. Where the more pleasurable sensations are the stronger, the super-ego will transmit the message, 'I will follow my parents' example.' When, on the other hand, up-bringing has been associated in the main with the experience of punishment, the super-ego may indicate 'That's the way it should be done' or, more frequently, 'I don't want to become like my parents.' In either case, we find a form of reciprocity of consciousness which is broadly that of mimesis, the 'aping' process of apes.

In a repressive society in which the privileged cling to the status quo which supports their unjust privileges, many of them may be acting simply on the basis of a consciousness which says 'That's the way it's to be done.' Aping the powerful and wealthy, many may easily confuse this kind of consciousness reinforcement (the super-ego) with conscience. This means that they are imprisoned in a superficial reciprocity of consciousness and, in consequence, lapse into a kind of pseudo-innocence. The exploited and oppressed can similarly fall into the trap of wishing to imitate the wealthy and the powerful if given the opportunity. On the one hand, they accept the situation with an apathy that asks 'What can we do about it?' while on the other, they frequently interiorise the destructive range of values of the powerful. They are thus caught in a double bind. We shall return to this problem when we consider the healing and liberating power of non-violence as a truthful reciprocity of consciences.

One particularly burning example of destructive reciprocity of consciousness is the spirit and the system of apartheid in South Africa. The ruling white class constantly confirms its members in the belief that, in virtue of being white and successful, they are a superior kind of people. (In a perverted religious language, this can even be expressed as being 'the chosen people'.) In a myriad of ways, they tell one another that they have the right and duty to use all available means to keep law and order, in other words, to maintain their own privileged status. They can become the prisoners of the reciprocity of consciousness of their class to the extent that they do not even question oppressive measures, including violence or torture, in the maintenance of law and order. As long as the black and coloured population accepted this as unchangeable, they were doubly imprisoned, firstly within the reality of the society itself and secondly within a form of 'reciprocity of consciousness' which has made them look up to the successful class. But by breaking the cycle, becoming proud of being black or coloured, and not part of the oppressive system, they have broken the most dangerous fetters. They no longer see themselves with the eyes of their masters, but with a new self-respect.

It can happen (and often did in the past) that the oppressed are so impressed by the efficiency of the violent strategy of the oppressors that they can conceive of no other way of obtaining justice than by counter-violence. If however, in groups and communities, they live in free mutual exchange with the gospel message of non-violence and come to see that the solidarity of non-violence can be the stronger force, they have broken the strongest fetters that the violent can place upon them. They no longer accept the given model as a kind of super-ego, but find instead their true selves, their dignity as persons and communities. It follows then that one of the main goals of a non-violent strategy and spirituality will be to help the members of the oppressing classes to make a breakthrough from an aping reciprocity of consciousness to a genuine encounter with the conscience of the non-violent. While affirming with conviction their own rights and dignity, the non-violent can convey to the oppressors and their supporters the message that they too can recover their dignity, their conscience, their freedom in the pursuit of justice and a community which excludes no one.

Many years ago, when I was lecturing regularly in South Africa, I told the supporters of apartheid:

> If you look down on the black and coloured people, you will only know yourselves as people who are not coloured; if you look down on the poor because of your own economic success and higher social status, you will know yourselves only as economic animals. But if you really begin to honour the poor, the less successful, people of a different colour, then you will have made a wonderful discovery. You will begin to know yourselves as persons, having broken the fetters of a poisoned reciprocity of consciousness, and discovered instead a reciprocity of conscience with the poor, the downtrodden. And if you are really touched by the moral strength of the non-violent who affirm with dignity not only their own rights but the rights of all to live in a just society, then you will have discovered your own most precious inner resources. Then you will live no longer on the level of aping, of bare mimesis, but on the level of a true and enriching reciprocity of consciences.

Two kinds of solidarity

Those who live on the level of mimesis without moral discernment are bound together by a similar kind of consciousness. It unites them when it happens to reinforce the selfish goals of the group, but leads to opposition when an individual or group wishes to possess what the others have. To live at the level of aping behaviour, acting under the stimulus of pleasure or pain leads to a degrading form of solidarity. The biblical concepts of 'the sin of the world' and '*sarx*' (deeply-rooted individual or collective selfishness) can shed some light on this. There is no exit from this form of slavery except through conversion to saving solidarity, which implies a genuinely respectful dialogue, shared reflection and discernment along with a great respect for the consciences of others. I discover the dignity and strength of my own conscience through a profound respect for the conscience of my neighbour, and indeed for the conscience of every other human being. A genuine reciprocity of consciences is founded on freedom—freedom of love, freedom to listen to each other, freedom to help one another discover the innermost resources of truth, goodness and justice.

Church history provides us with many examples of the two kinds of reciprocity we have been discussing: on the one hand a genuine reciprocity of consciences in saving solidarity, and on the other a group cohesion based on the process of reinforcement. The saints, for example, spoke to the hearts of others since they had already found a high level of reciprocity of conscience with the Lord; not merely did they seek in all things to please him, but they also lived on a high level of genuine dialogue, shared ideals and mutual respect. From this form of reciprocity of consciences sprang new communities with shared ideals, striving in solidarity to preach the gospel, heal the sick, honour the poor. In evangelising the poor, they were in turn evangelised by them from the mere fact of living with them on the level of a genuine reciprocity of consciences.

The church knows the terrible danger of in-groups bound to one another by a whole system of reinforcements, eg promotion, adulation, sanctions. One example of this can be clerical groups whose almost exclusive interest is their own concern for promotion, pay, exclusion from, or access to, the centres of influence. One of the temptations sometimes present in such in-grown groups is a strange competitiveness to out-do one another in public manifestations of an orthodoxy far removed from the inclusive truth of the gospel. Groups like these can build up their own survival system, often in the form of a permanent suspicion of those who think and act differently. It may serve to keep the group together for a while, but inevitably, it will recoil upon the group and its members, blinding them to the dignity of conscience of others, and consequently, to their own.

St Alphonsus was aware of this, and introduced into his congregation a vow neither to seek nor accept ecclesiastical honours and offices. Saving solidarity and genuine reciprocity of consciences can only blossom in an atmosphere that sets a premium on sincerity and where unselfish love for one another and for the church excludes any attempt to manipulate either one's own conscience or the consciences of others.

Natural law and reciprocity of consciences

In the Letter to the Romans, Paul explicitly discusses natural law in the context of encouraging mutual respect between Jewish and Gentile christians. He expects the Roman community to display mutual respect for one another, in spite of the diversity of backgrounds, for such mutual respect is a fruit of the gospel of reconciliation and will in turn promote the evangelisation of the Gentiles.

> God has no favourites. . . . When Gentiles who do not possess the Law carry out its precepts by the light of nature, then, although they are their own law, they display the substance of the law inscribed on their hearts. Their conscience is called as witness, and their own thoughts argue the case on either side, against them or for them, on the day when God judges the secrets of the human heart through Christ Jesus. So my gospel declares (Rom 2:11-16).

In the writings of Paul, there is no doubt that the substance of the Law is love of God and of neighbour, and this will be the basis of judgment at the coming of Christ (cf Mt 25:31-46). People learn to discern what is in accordance with the law written in their hearts, 'arguing the case on either side', and this not in a merely intellectual dialogue, for the demands of mutual love are discovered by shared experience and reflection, by treasuring traditions and revitalising them in new experiences, and handing on new insights to a new generation.

The Pastoral Constitution on the Church in the Modern World of Vatican II (*Gaudium et Spes*) refers explicitly to Rom 2:15 when speaking of conscience, and then continues to discuss reciprocity of consciences in relation to christians and others: 'In fidelity to conscience, christians are joined with the rest of humanity in the search for truth, and for genuine solutions to the numerous problems which arise in the life of individuals and from social relationships.'[4]

The very nature of the person is dialogical. Love of neighbour is not something added on to his/her nature. The human person comes to self-identity in openness to the Other and to others. Human life which has discovered its fulfilment is a kind of *perichoresis* in the we-thou-I reality (or thou-I-we reality) according to the image of the Triune God; the Father is himself through giving all his fullness to his Word (his Son) and the Son is this divine person by receiving and returning himself to the Father in the power of the Holy Spirit who is the eternal event of mutuality. Conscience is the innermost core and sanctuary of the human person, where he/she comes to fullness in openness to the neighbour, in the process of giving and receiving, in ongoing sharing. As a consequence, natural law, the law written in the heart, exists through shared experience and shared reflection, arising from and leading to shared action. It is simply unthinkable that a human person can be faithful to conscience without a constant openness to others in the search for vital truth and truthful solutions to human problems.

The logic of this is expressed in the next sentence of *Gaudium et Spes* no 16: 'Hence the more that a correct conscience holds sway, the more individuals and groups turn aside from blind choice and strive to be guided by the objective norms of morality.' This holds for both christians and non-christians, and we can remind ourselves of the words of the apostle: 'God has no favourites' (Rom 2:11). No individual and no group has a monopoly of existential truth. No one can remain faithful to conscience without joining 'the rest of men' in the search for more light.

Historicity and reciprocity of conscience

Conscience can never be guided by an unchanging code of norms claiming to express natural law. What is written into the heart (conscience, the innermost core) is not 'a code but the dynamics of thou-I-we in ongoing history.

Humankind lives from the wealth of experience and wisdom of past generations, but it constantly has to address new situations and new problems. Each culture and sub-culture has its own share of experiences, and human wisdom will grow the more that individuals, groups and cultures enter into earnest dialogue in the shared quest for light.

It is unnatural, therefore, and shows a lack of faithfulness to conscience if one group imagines that it knows it all and that it does not need the process of shared learning. If churchmen think they have no need to listen to women, or if European church leaders and teachers select their information only from the store of European history, it is not only a contradiction of the worldwide solidarity of a church with a universal mission of evangelisation, but it is also a sign of a deformed conscience.

The human person is a history, has a history and shapes history, but these are also moments of a single history of God with humankind. Our conscience must be inserted into the search for wisdom and the learning process of all humanity. Remote applications of a basic natural law written into the heart were, and are, time-bound. Anyone who would choose to declare them as absolute and applicable under all historical circumstances is not being faithful to conscience, to their own nature itself or to the Lord of the one history of salvation. If the horizons of history widen through every historical event, then the church catholic in particular must enter into a world-wide reciprocity of consciences and thereby become an ongoing learner if she is to be a wise teacher for all nations in all that concerns natural law. No meaningful talk is possible about the relationship between magisterium and theologians unless all parties are willing to take part, as far as possible, in a world-wide process of ongoing learning arising from the depths of conscience and marked with a great mutual respect.

Moral theology cannot be computerised for all time. Morally speaking, it is impossible to pull answers to new problems out of the archives of the inquisition, or indeed, out of any other archive. Past wisdom must be treasured. But the true virtue of wisdom does not lie in self-sufficiency. Instead, it draws one into the process of ongoing mutuality, in which one shares from the depth of conscience and for the sake of fidelity to conscience.

Magisterium, theologians and the rest of men

The assistance of the Holy Spirit does not bypass the process of reciprocity of consciences. The higher the religious authority, the greater is its duty to listen to how the consciences of others find expression. It should foster within itself an authentic conscience with is able to listen, appreciate, discern, respond, while at the same time, expressing its own expectations. One of the most noble tasks of moral theology, and also one of its most demanding ones, is that of hearing all who have a stake in some issue, and of discerning and integrating into its response what their conscience manifests. Theologians must, of course, be attentive to the teaching of those in authority, to the fact that their conscience too is alert to the needs of the age. But they must also transmit to the magisterium what they have perceived in their own consciences. Everyone needs to cooperate in the creation and preservation of an atmosphere in which conscience can speak to conscience. When both magisterium and theologians as theologians speak and teach, their main purpose is not the transmission of norms so much as a manifestation of the greatest art and gift which is to know Jesus Christ, to know the Father in the love which the Holy Spirit pours into our hearts and so to know the true 'countenance of redeemed and redeeming love'. In this way, reciprocity of consciences of believers and ministers of Christ comes into being and develops. They should never assume that they have nothing to learn from the 'rest of men'.

While it is true that the Lord promised his Holy Spirit to the church and to her guides in a very special way, such assistance does not come in an automatic fashion, but in the measure of our docility and our fidelity to the reciprocity of consciences, in the measure of listening, learning, and even, when there is need, unlearning.

Faithful dissent in matters concerning natural law

There are many matters upon which the church has given the best possible response *in illo tempore*, that is, with the knowledge then available and in the light of the cultural and historical circumstances then pertaining. Moral theologians would render a poor service to the magisterium and to the people were they merely to cling to such formulations of doctrine in all their details even under quite different historical circumstances. If they offer new solutions in the light of differences of culture, new needs or new knowledge, this should not be called 'dissent'. It belongs rather to the *obsequium religiosum* due to authority, that they contribute to the discussion all the new knowledge that is available to them. It belongs to them to widen the horizons. For example, certain formulations were made in view of what pertained in one country, or from a cultural experience which was solely European or Mediterranean; to impose such in a rigorous manner would render any serious attempt at inculturation impossible, and would be merely another form of the error of the Jewish christians who wanted to impose their traditions on those coming from the Gentile mission.

It has also happened that in the past church doctrines, even those taught by popes, bishops and the Roman inquisition, were downright false, but in the climate of papal centralism and inquisition of the day theologians had not even the courage to think critically, much less the courage to speak courageously. Accordingly, unchristian doctrines and practices such as the torture and burning of witches continued for centuries. Vatican II on the other hand has encouraged frank speaking: 'An individual layman, by reason of his knowledge, competence, or the outstanding ability which he may enjoy, is permitted and sometimes even obliged to express his opinion on things which concern the good of the church.'[5]

In the chapter 'on the proper development of culture' in *Gaudium et Spes*, great emphasis is placed on the spirit of freedom and frankness as a necessary condition for genuine cultural development. The whole chapter ends with an appeal: 'Let it be recognised that all the faithful, clerical and lay, possess a lawful freedom of enquiry and of thought, and the freedom to express their minds humbly and courageously about those matters in which they enjoy competence.'[6]

It sometimes happens that those in high authority have learned moral theology from moralists of a particular school or of a certain cultural background. It is alarming, for example, when a bishop who openly admits to never having opened a book on moral theology for thirty years, dares to condemn a moral theologian whose writings he has never read. This extraordinary case has actually occurred. But even under normal conditions, it would be dangerous for the prestige of the magisterium if only men of an older school received a hearing and were permitted to share in the preparation of doctrinal texts on matters dealing with natural law. Even under circumstances such as these, every moral theologian will give proper attention to texts written from a world view and in a language he cannot share, and will try his best to understand and accept what is really meant. He can then try to the best of his abilities to communicate it in language more intelligible to his/her readers and listeners. There is however no place for an atmosphere of suspicion in which theologians, clerical and lay, are expected to confine themselves to a mere repetition of formulae, and be expected to conceal their own inmost convictions.

There are numerous historical occasions recorded where holy men and women expressed their dissent to those in authority, even on matters which concerned something more important than some remote application of natural law. Some, like Cardinal Newman, had to suffer for a long time before finally seeing themselves honoured for their contribution. Others were suppressed for a lifetime. I have met several people whose deep wounds never healed, or at least did so only after a very long time. It is clear, however, that so-called dissent is truly an *obsequium religiosum* when the theologian, priest or lay, has gone through a painstaking process of reflection, dialogue with other competent theologians, and when he or she speaks

70

with serenity and in a constructive manner. And, may I add, if someone decides to offer his 'dissent' as *obsequium religiosum*, they must also be prepared to suffer. Under the rubric 'suffering' I do not mean simply the fact that they might never be promoted. *Obsequium religiosum* in the form of 'dissent' can only be expected from people who have made up their minds not to expect honours and promotions in the church. On the other hand, if it should come about that only 'yes-sayers' are honoured by those in authority, then the process of reciprocity of consciences would have broken down completely, at least on the part of those who favour and practise such an attitude.

It is disconcerting that after the Council's strong appeal for frankness and liberty as the hallmark of Catholic theology, the new Code of Canon Law treats dissent regarding non-infallible doctrines as a crime to be punished unless the author makes formal retraction (Can 1371, cf Can 752, cf Can 812). There is no distinction drawn between constructive and destructive dissent. This penal law, which would outlaw any dissent, was introduced at the last moment and without the cooperation of the commission which prepared the new code. It is a law which can be applied without entering into a dialogue about arguments or reasons for dissent. I see it as jeopardising the reciprocity of consciences. In 'fidelity to conscience' those in authority might receive and give help towards a greater understanding of the issue and thus avoid the danger of scandal. Grave scandal is given if those who call for sanctions seriously distort the dissenting opinion and thus spread abroad the impression that a dissenting theologian would justify any kind of immorality.[7] It is even worse if those who judge the case point in a similar wrong direction in an attempt to justify the sanctions they have imposed.

Natural law is characterised as 'open to the eyes of reason'. Therefore the cases must be argued on either side (cf Rom 2:15). And if no convincing reasons can be found for norms derived from remote applications of the basic law inscribed in the heart, the law of love, then it appears to me that the best solution would be to allow each party to follow their sincere conviction. Doubtful reasons are not sufficient to impose heavy burdens on others.[8] But if it is a matter of particular relevance, then dialogue, as an expression of reciprocity of consciences, must be continued in a way that respects the sincerity and fidelity to conscience of both sides.

5. *Moral Theology and Transformative Justice*

THE original title for this contribution to the conference in honour at once of two remarkable Redemptorist theologians, St Alphonsus Liguori and Father Sean O'Riordan, was: 'Does Moral Theology Exist?'. Clearly in the context of such a distinguished gathering of moral theologians for a great moral theological occasion, it was intended to be sharply provocative. But not only so. Since I was first appointed to teach moral theology almost thirty years ago, I have been haunted by a theological version of Pritchard's question in 1904, 'Does Moral Philosophy Rest on a Mistake?' Not for quite the same reasons of course. And the astonishing changes in the method and matter of moral theology since my appointment at Maynooth in 1958 might be fairly urged in support of a strongly affirmative answer to my own question. And no doubt it could be very persuasively urged by other contributors to this volume, including such outstanding pioneers as Bernard Häring and Josef Fuchs, who have done so much to develop these changes. Three of their achievements are relevant to my further concerns here: the restoration of the theological dimension of moral theology, particularly by return to its biblical roots; the exposing of the historical dimension of morality both in its theoretical understanding and in its practical expression; the emphasis on the personal subject rather than the individual action. These three achievements at least have enabled moral theology to transcend its manual exposition which dominated the Catholic theological world from about 1600 to 1960. And such basic developments are by no means at an end.

Moral theology: achievements and reservations

My reservations, however provocatively expressed, relate directly to these three positive achievements. Moving in the reverse order, I find in the extraordinary richness of the development of person as subject an almost inevitable tendency to overshadow the community dimension of morality and moral theology. Of course one might respond by recognising that the person is always perceived in relationship with other persons and in community. Still, the location, perception and expression of morality is discussed primarily, if not exclusively, in personal terms. Personal awareness, personal understanding, personal decision and personal activity: these are stuff of moral analysis for philosophers as well as theologians. Community awareness and understanding, decision and activity are not analysed in similar ways. For all the genuine community concerns of moral theologians, community remains extra and extrinsic to their primary analysis.

A possible central reaction to this would be parallel to the current moral theologian's reaction to the manualist's preoccupation with individual actions rather than with person-in-act. It is intrinsically incomplete and so unreal. Preoccupation with the person as distinct from the person-in-community and as, more obviously, not placed in balance with community-of-persons is intrinsically incomplete and so unreal. I have dealt with morality/moral theology as based on both persons-in-community and community-of-persons elsewhere in more general terms. In this paper I will be concentrating on a particular aspect of it under the rubric of justice.

The second important achievement instanced earlier was the discovery or recovery of the historical dimension of morality in theory and practice. In terms of moral theology itself this has been an important advance. Natural Law, which has been fundamental to moral theory in the Catholic tradition at least since Aquinas, has been seen more recently to incorporate the historical dimension of humanity, human culture and human morality. This has in parallel, if not always directly related fashion, influenced moral theology's understanding of the person as developing and historical. It may be too much to say, given, for example, the theological stress on conversion (Häring *et al*) and the philosophical stress on fundamental option (Fuchs *et al*), that continuity has been stressed at the expense of discontinuity. Yet much moral theological discussion of person and community seems to take the evolutionary, gradually developing sense of history more immediately into account than the eschatological, transformative sense of history. Creation, as in the debate about the specifically christian ethic, is more directly and clearly at issue than new creation.

Incarnation is more significant than redemption or resurrection.[1] This I take to be more clearly applicable to *social* morality and its theology than to *personal*, where certainly for Häring, Curran and others, conversion and discontinuity have played an important role. Indeed the fuller dimensions of continuity and discontinuity between Creation and New Creation involve person, community and cosmos.

All of which argument moves towards the final question and first assertion about the 'new' moral theology. How biblical and theological has it become? Is it more directly derived from or at least more substantially influenced by the judaeo-christian tradition than its manualist predecessors? Is the biblical-theological language and reference in the end no more than a veneer on the naturalistic, legal ethics rather narrowly expressed in the manuals? Or is there a genuine sense of the gospel at work in the shaping of moral theology and in its more particular discussions whether of special areas of christian living such as sexuality or of concrete decisions such as the use of *in vitro* fertilisation?

Answers to these questions and to the earlier ones raised on person, community and cosmos, as well as on history and eschatology demand much more lengthy and delicate re-evaluation of the meaning and task of moral theology than is possible in this paper. However, the originating question, 'Does moral theology exist?' will continue to disturb.

A theology of justice and its morality

The strategy adopted here, not primarily as evasion of the deeper and more comprehensive question, is to examine the role of justice in current theology and its discussion of morality. The phraseology is, for the moment, quite deliberate as justice, like other moral concepts such as truth, freedom and peace, have much wider theological ramifications today than even contemporary moral theological writing might suggest. And theology's discussion of morality leaves open for the moment the difficulties alluded to about the phrase 'moral theology'.

The return of justice to a central place in theology in the seventies and eighties has been no doubt for a number of different reasons. Dominant among these may be the emergence of various 'liberation theologies'. Hitherto justice had been the exclusive concern of manual moral theology or, more marginally in its social implications, of Catholic social teaching. Even with the gradual theologising of papal social encyclicals and other christian social documents in the sixties and seventies, the heart of Western systematic theology remained untouched. It is seldom remarked how seriously the doctrinal tradition in theology has suffered from the impoverished theological condition of moral theology, manual and renewed. Central doctrines of God, Christ, Holy Spirit, Salvation, Grace, Church and Sacraments have suffered from aridity and distortion by their distance from and lack of challenge from the living concerns characteristic of moral theology.

A theology of meaning, however related to the cultural, philosophical movements of its time, risks unreality unless it is closely integrated with a theology of living. The one theological ideal of the great scholastics, if no longer capable of such systematic unity in elaboration and expression, must for the sake of the doctrinal as well as the moral theologians, operate as stimulus to dialogue, critique, correction and conversion among the many specialised theologians. A doctrine of the trinity which has not confronted theological thinking about marriage and society and a moral theology of truth which ignores the

76

great christian doctrine of revelation and saving truth are both reduced and distorted.

Justice, as I have been suggesting, offers a singularly important and illuminating example of this disjunction and impoverishment. Its manual and even scholastic history were not illuminatingly theological and christian. The influence of Aristotle as opposed to that of Amos, of the philosophical as opposed to the biblical-theological tradition, ensured a clear analysis of justice as dealing with claims between individuals, as exchange/commutative or restorative justice with the important extension for distributive justice on regulating claims of individual citizens against the *polis* or state. All this was considered in the context of a general virtue of justice which might be interpreted as the most generally virtuous condition of the good person. It provided for Aquinas *et al* as cardinal virtue a principle of organisation for a whole range of subordinate virtues, including that regulating the relation of human beings to God, religion.

There was a clarity here in one-to-one relationships, in giving the other his due which remains essential to the maintenance of ethical human relationships and the survival of society. It was balanced by an acceptance of distributive justice within society and qualified by important exceptive situations such as urgent need (*evidens, et urgens necessitas*, Aquinas, *S Th*, II.II. 66.6). There was, then, an openness to larger considerations and possibilities of development which were, however, largely overshadowed by the dominantly individualist concerns and the focus on the possession, dispossession and restitution of property. Manuals of moral theology, in 350 years' reign, could scarcely escape from this. The gradual growth of Catholic social teaching, initiated by Pope Leo XIII, at once retrieving an older patristic tradition and developing a contemporary one, were not regarded as hard-nosed moral analysis of the kind on offer in Noldin-Schmitt or Aertnys-Damen. And neither manual, down to 1960, was particularly interested in the central truths of theology.

The integration of individualist and social morality and the emergence of some theological concern (cf Synod of

Bishops 1971) have at least made important connections. It would be too much to say that these developments have in ethical terms truly integrated personal and social justice, made it a unified virtue affecting the relations of persons, communities and cosmos. It would be even more misleading to see these moves as exposing the deeper doctrinal/ theological meaning of justice, as revelatory of God and of God's saving work in Jesus Christ.

Renewing the justice tradition

A quite different line of theological development, that of liberation theologies, has, as I mentioned and despite its title, taken 'justice in society' as a central theological theme. The connections between justice and liberation have obvious historical, social and political dimensions. The emergence of human rights as criterion of justice in society clearly provides a bridge-concept between right as basis of justice (Aquinas) and right as freedom (Locke to UN Declaration). Theologically, liberation is the equivalent of salvation, redemption and justification, in that genuinely theological sense of the justice of God transforming unjust human beings into *the just*. (The Reformation debates as to the meaning of justification and its distinction from sanctification, for example, are, I believe, no longer relevant here.)

The Aristotle-Aquinas tradition, which dominated justice discussion for so long and, in an attenuated form, shaped the manuals of moral theology, was rich and subtle. This was evident in Aristotle's reflection on how the just human being behaves as critical: in their shared division of justice into the general virtue as characterising the good person over all, restorative (Aristotle) or exchange justice and distributive justice. The definition as the constant inclination to give every person his/her due with right (*jus*) as the object of justice was all the more developed in Aquinas but on the basis of Aristotle. Pride of place in this tradition went to exchange justice between individual human beings involving 'exact' equality. Distributive justice as between state/society and the individual did not seem quite so significant although it provided a basis in the later manuals for a rather weak presentation of taxation and welfare laws. The purely penal law attitude to taxation laws, so prevalent in moral theology until recently, fitted into this weaker sense of distributive justice. Real justice, for moralist and confessor, involved an obligation of restitution on violation. Only violations of exchange, or commutative justice involved such obligations.

The potential of this tradition was of course much more fully realised later. Catholic social teaching did extend many of its central ideas into the idea of just wages and conditions for workers, an extension of exchange/contract justice and special care for the weak and deprived, an extension of distributive justice. Meantime a secularised version of the tradition which held that right was the object of justice (Aquinas), moved into natural rights, rights of man and human rights. These in turn found their natural place in late Catholic social teaching (*Pacem in Terris* etc).

This was then a developing, open tradition in many ways. The natural law in its background and ultimately its basis was not a closed, unhistorical idea. Later influential theories about justice in society such as that of John Rawls, belong within this larger tradition with social contract dimensions.

Between Aristotle and Amos

Yet recent theological concerns have exposed some of the limitations of this tradition. For christian theology, human dignity, based on creation in the image of God and new creation as daughter/son of God, has given respect for and response to persons and their human rights a depth and urgency which purely secular theories finally lack. More significantly the recovery of the biblical tradition of justice has thrown much revealing light on this historic phenomenon.

For the biblical as opposed to the 'philosophical' tradition, justice (*sedaqah*) is primarily a characteristic of God in his/her dealings with the covenant people of Israel. Yahweh/God is at once the origin and standard of *sedaqah*, rendered in the Septuagint as *dikaiosune*. This justice of God is not so sharply differentiated in Hebrew as in Greek and later Western vocabulary. It overlaps with fidelity, loving-kindness and mercy. Hebrew monotheism clearly plays a role in Hebrew understanding of the unity and overlapping at this transcendent level of the qualities manifested by Yahweh in his dealings with his people Israel. An isolated justice which might become simply vindictive as in 'an eye for an eye' hardly seems faithful to the God whose justice and mercy were so deeply intertwined. In his clarification and development of mercy and forgiveness in the Sermon on the Mount and elsewhere, Jesus was being true to the deepest thrust of his own Hebrew tradition.

The transcendent origin of *sedaqah* and its role as standard for Yahweh's people involve also, of course, their gracious God in providing a divine enablement. If they were to be just, as God was just, they must enjoy the presence in power of that God. The biblical tradition knows of human weakness in justice as in other areas in ways which the philosophical tradition can only touch on post-factum. Enablement from God and for Israel is included in the challenge of covenant justice. The awesomeness of justice as transcendent in origin is balanced by the intimacy of justice enablement as immanent to the people.

Neighbourly relations within the people of Israel have individual aspects analagous to the great philosophical traditions. This is evident in the Decalogue, for example. Yet the great prophetic tradition stemming from the eighth century BCE exposes the essentially social character of covenant justice in ways that are scarcely developed or even discernible in philosophers before Marx. Amos seems in this respect to stand in great contrast to Aristotle. It is the injustice of the society as a whole which is the object of his denunciations. This is specified by his attacks on society's officials, the judges, for their acceptance of bribery to render false judgments; in the extravagant behaviour of wealthy women, and generally in the neglect and exploitation by the wealthy and powerful of these by now traditional categories of the oppressed in

Israel, the poor, the widows, the orphans and the strangers. (He has his own version of class description, if not yet class analysis.) For this the religious assemblies of Israel are unacceptable. For this their society, like neighbouring unjust societies, will be destroyed.

These features of injustice in society as a whole, the unjust behaviour by wealthy, officials and powerful, the exploitations of particular weaker groups, recur in the other great prophets. It was this tradition which Jesus inherited and developed in his teaching and ministry, in his denunciations of the rich and powerful and in his fellowship with the weak and excluded.

The biblical tradition then offers a much stonger sense of justice in society than simply justice between single individuals. It takes as a final criterion the treatment of the poor and the weak, the sick and people with handicap, isolated women and strangers or immigrants. But it does not leave it at that. Amos, in some ways the angriest prophet, urged by the priestly leader to go back to his village and his shepherding, has a vision too of a new society and a new justice. The promise, which undergirds the whole history of Israel of justice and peace flourishing in a society and cosmos transformed, keeps open the hope of Israel in God's power to bring about a new kingdom. It is that trust in the transformative power of God, in the transformative justice of God which sustains the people until the Messiah should appear, the time be fulfilled and the kingdom come.

The Jesus Way

Jesus' paradoxical way of meeting these promises left many in Israel perplexed. Yet the time was at hand and the kingdom had come. The new Israel and new creation in Paul's phrase ensured the justification of all. The transformative justice of God was at hand and at work. The end time had begun. Justice and peace should reign. The gift of God's justice and mercy was available in the gift of the Spirit through the risen Christ. History must still continue its ambiguous way, but the final, eschatological breakthrough of God in justice had occurred. The human

81

task was to let that justice take root in person and community, in relationship and structure. What Amos had foreseen was to be realised, if still partially and fitfully, but still effectively as the transformation of human beings and human society.

The vision of such a just society, the gift of it on offer and the power or the grace to achieve it which summarises the judaeo-christian tradition of justice seems rather remote from the more careful and calculated analysis of an Aristotle or even an Aquinas. It may have been Karl Marx, undoubtedly drawing on his Jewish prophetic roots but unable to accept their essential connection with a transcendent God of justice, who restored to the philosophical tradition of justice something of the vision and fire-power of transformative justice. In this the liberation theologians are following and going beyond his work to its truly biblical and transcendent roots.

From managerial to transformative justice

Of course the Aristotle-Aquinas tradition has never been simply individualist and never been closed to developments in the social area. These developments have been for the most part incremental, adapting to various changes in society rather than inspiring or generating them. This would be true of various contractual theories also, many of which—including such sophisticated and fair ones as that of Rawls—do offer ways of at least improving society in justice terms.

I believe that these forms of justice are therefore essential to the management of society. They constitute, to invoke a much-used analogy in moral and theological discussion, the grammar of personal and social relations. Without them our everyday and much longer-term dealings could not operate fairly and, in the true human sense, fruitfully. The sustaining of social life like the sustaining of conversation depends on observing the rules of grammar embodied in the regulations of what I might call managerial justice.

It is, I think, a useful phrase as long as it is not used in a pejorative or dismissive sense. And as long as it is not understood as simply static or paralysing of the status quo. It has its own openness to gradual change like all rules of grammar.

However, much of the injustice confronting the modern world requires a more visionary kind of justice. Justice, because the people concerned, races, impoverished countries and classes, women, people with handicap and so on have rights to an entirely new quality of life, relationship and structure. Visionary, because slow, incremental improvements based on present structures will simply not prove effective or timely. That kind of vision to meet that kind of need requires transformative justice, a justice that sees such transformation in a particular way as the right as well as the need of the particularly deprived.

The example of international debt

There are a number of areas where one could illustrate the importance of both managerial and transformative justice. A particularly acute current set of problems is that of international debt. Within the accepted range of managerial justice much of this debt of Third World countries could be recognised as already paid or as to be written off or as to be drastically rescheduled by Western countries and financial institutions in ways that are fair and indeed of mutual benefit. The Economic Summit in Toronto in July 1988 seemed to be making moves along these lines. They are to be welcomed by all anxious to redress the fundamental injustice underlying first world-third world economic relations and the particular injustices to third world countries involved in many of these loans. (First world institutions were handing out money in the seventies often to national leaders who had no popular mandate and had clearly no interest in anything but their own enrichment.)

However, such welcome expressions of managerial justice do not attack the underlying structures. A new economic order has been proposed frequently enough in the last fifteen or twenty years. The requirements of justice, transformative justice, include such a transformation of the world economic order. It is no longer to be treated as an utopian dream or neglected in favour of occasional exercises of overdue managerial justice as at Toronto.

Other examples, such as women in society or race relations or the place of particular groups in particular societies, travellers, people with handicap, unemployed, enable one to see the value and limitations of a progressive managerial justice and the final necessity of transformative justice.

Transformative justice, with its origins in God's self-giving in covenant and finally in Jesus, with its divine summons and divine grace or enablement, transcends but does not displace the managerial justice which has been the main preoccupation of the philosophical tradition. This may be a paradigm for the relationship between christian faith with its implicit morality and what is sometimes described as human or secular morality. It could, therefore, offer a way into a genuinely theological moral theology. And en route it could allow a further exploration of the God who is justice and the God who is love as a way of establishing a more satisfactory relationship between justice and love than hitherto available even in renewed moral theology.

6. Official Catholic Social Teaching and Conscience

THIS study will explore how the social teaching of the universal church and the recent pastoral letters on peace and on the economy proposed by the United States bishops treat some aspects of conscience. Conscience will be understood in the classical sense as the judgment about the morality of an action to be done or omitted and limited to antecedent conscience. It is obvious that social teaching or social ethics in general does not directly and systematically discuss the nature or the function of conscience, for such a treatment belongs to general moral theology. However, the social teaching of the church cannot ignore the reality of conscience which plays so central a role in the moral life.

From within the Catholic perspective perhaps the most characteristic and distinctive aspect of the understanding of conscience in Catholic social teaching is the recognition of the freedom of the conscience of the individual christian and the diversity of concrete judgments which can exist on social matters within the church. While recognising such freedom and diversity, the social teachings try to influence the formation of conscience. In addition, church social teaching does give some indication of how the judgments of conscience are made even though there is no systematic or in-depth development of how individual consciences make concrete judgments and decisions. Official universal Catholic social teaching and the more recent social teaching proposed by the United States bishops will be examined for what they say about these two aspects of conscience.

Universal social teaching

Official universal Catholic social teaching is generally associated with the papal encyclicals beginning with Pope Leo XIII's *Rerum Novarum* of 1891 and including conciliar and other documents of the universal church down to the present. At first sight it might seem surprising, but the most significant aspect of the understanding of conscience mentioned in this teaching is the freedom of conscience and the possibility of pluralism and diversity within the Catholic church on specific questions of social morality. This position has been consistently upheld in the tradition, and there is no appreciative development in the statement of the position even though, as will be pointed out in the next section, there seems to have been development in the reasons behind the position. This thesis will be proved by examining the documents themselves, by the testimony of the commentators on these documents, by pointing out in reality the pluralism and diversity that have existed in the area of social morality within the church, and finally by proposing the reasons why such a freedom and range of diversity must exist within the Catholic church.

The documents forming the tradition explicitly recognise the legitimate freedom of conscience and the possibility of diversity within the church on specific judgments in the social realm. An excellent illustration of this position has been the attitude of the tradition to the best form of government. Traditionally, church documents have been reluctant to claim that there can be only one form of government and all other forms are morally bad. The documents have generally stressed the principles of justice that should be present within any political society no matter what its particular form, for example, monarchy, democracy, or even dictatorship. Over the centuries the church has existed with all different forms of political government and has been hesitant to condemn a particular form. There are indications, especially in the last forty years, that the official teaching is more open to democratic forms of government, but it is interesting that one-person rule or one-party rule has never been condemned as such. The Pastoral Constitution on the Church in the Modern World of Vatican Council II explicitly states that the Church 'is bound to no particular form of human culture, nor to any political, economic, or social system'.[1]

The official documents of the universal church both insist on and indicate the duty and right of the church to teach authoritatively on moral aspects of the political, social, and economic orders; but at the same time these documents also recognise the limits of the church's authoritative teaching in these areas. In explaining and praising what his predecessor, Leo XIII, had done, Pope Pius XI in his encyclical *Quadragesimo Anno* in 1931 characterised Leo as relying solely on the unchangeable principles drawn from right reason and divine revelation.[2] In his encyclical on atheistic communism the same Pius XI described the function of the teaching church as proposing the guiding principles which are susceptible of varied concrete applications according to the diversified conditions of times, places, and peoples.[3] Both the competency and the limits of the church intervention in the social order are determined by the unchanging moral principles derived from the natural law and revelation. Pope John XXIII in *Mater et Magistra* made the same distinction between norms or principles and their application. In applying these principles the pope recognised that even sincere Catholics may have differing positions.[4] More recent documents also maintain the diversity of specific judgments and actions within the church. *Octogesima Adveniens*, the 1971 letter of Pope Paul VI, explicitly recognises that it is neither the pope's ambition nor his mission to put forward solutions which have universal validity.[5] Thus, the documents themselves, both in what they actually propose and in what they explicitly say about what they propose, give great freedom to the individual christian in concrete decisions in the social realm.

The commentators on the papal teaching have universally recognised that official church teaching allows for a pluralism of specific decisions and approaches. Calvez and Perrin are typical of the pre-Vatican II commentators in describing the roles of authoritative church teaching and of the conscience of the believer in terms of unchangeable principles and changing applications. The church teaching defends and promotes values which are unchangeable. The competency of church teaching extends to essential determinations of the natural law and the fundamental conditions of action comfortable to the law of charity. Beyond this realm of unchangeable natural law, the church recognises the freedom of all in the realm of application precisely because of the changing circumstances involved.[6] Post-Vatican II commentators recognise that the solutions to particular problems can only be proposed on the basis of a discernment done on the local level.[7]

The life of the Catholic Church well illustrates the diversity and pluralism of approaches in the areas of political, social and economic institutions. As already noted, the church has existed with, and continues to exist with, many different types of social structures and institutions. The difference between unchanging principles and changing applications which was heavily emphasised in the pre-Vatican II times, is well illustrated in the principle of subsidiarity and its applications. According to this principle the state should encourage individuals, families, and other lesser associations and groups to do what they can and should do within society while the state should intervene only when no other institution in society can effectively deal with the issue. This principle has been interpreted differently by different people. Catholics in most of the western world have often differed over what is the proper role of the state. In the United States, both democratic and republican proposals, both liberal and conservative approaches, have appealed to the principle of subsidiarity.[8] Within the Catholic community in the United States there have been what can accurately be called conservative, reforming, and even radical approaches to the social order but all claiming to be based on Catholic social teaching.[9] Thus the Catholic reality bears out the diversity and pluralism which can exist within the context of official Catholic social teaching. While insisting on the legitimacy of authoritative church teaching to guide the social realm, the church has also insisted on the limits of its teaching and thereby recognised and protected the freedom of the individual church member in making concrete judgments and decisions in the social order.

What are the ultimate reasons why the church recognises a diversity of specific judgments, decisions, and actions in the social realm within the parameters of its general moral teaching? Ecclesiological, theological, and epistemological reasons all support the theory and practice of the church in recognising a pluralism of such concrete judgments and actions in the social realm. From an ecclesiological perspective, the church claims a universal mission to all people and all times and in all historical and cultural circumstances. As a result the church cannot ally itself to just one political or economic system. The universality of the church demands an openness to all approaches while insisting that all social structures and institutions work toward greater justice. There are naturally limits on what the church can and should accept, but its universal mission argues for a great latitude in structuring the social, political, and economic orders.

From a contemporary theological perspective the gospel must have something to say about human existence in the social order. However, faith and the gospel must always be mediated through the human and especially through the data of all the human sciences involved and through all the relevant facts. The gospel and faith do not provide a substitute for or a way around all the complexities of the human. Some would argue that the church has no competence to teach on social questions primarily because the church cannot claim to have expertise in this area. It is true that the competence of the church is based on the gospel, but the gospel must become incarnated in particular situations, institutions, and choices. Gospel values must influence particular facts and judgments. However, the gospel is mediated through the human and in the midst of human complexity one must recognise that it is impossible to claim that there is only one possible christian approach.

This theological reason based on how faith and the gospel must always be mediated through the human is intimately connected with the epistemological reason for recognising the possibility of pluralism and diversity on specific decisions, structures, actions, and judgments. The more specific and complex the reality, the less the possibility of certitude. The principle of logic maintains that the possibility of certitude decreases as specificity and complexity increase. On the level of the general and the formal, one can have a great degree of certitude; for example, injustice or murder is always wrong. But whether or not the particular action involves injustice is a much more complex matter and often there will be a legitimate diversity of opinion. Ecclesiological, theological, and epistemological reasons support the position that within the social realm the church must recognise the possibility of diversity and pluralism on specific judgments and hence recognise and protect the legitimate freedom of the believer in these areas.

The second important aspect of conscience considered in the traditional Catholic social teaching is the generic understanding of how individual conscience functions. Church teaching in the social realm has the purpose of forming the conscience of believers while at the same time safeguarding a legitimate freedom of conscience. One should not expect an explicit, systematic, in-depth, theoretical development of how conscience works, but the documents must be working with some implicit understanding of how conscience does function and how the individual makes decisions. The primary purpose of the social teaching is to form the consciences of the individual christians so that the documents must reveal some concept of how conscience works and operates.

In the developing tradition of Catholic social teaching there seems to be some change in the understanding of how conscience operates. This change generically can be described as the shift from classicism to historical consciousness. Classicism moves from the abstract and the general to the concrete, emphasises the immutable natural law principles, and tends to be more deductive. Historical-mindedness does not begin with the abstract and the general but rather with the particular and the concrete, emphasises the changing character of history, and tends to be somewhat more inductive in its approach. There can be no doubt that the documents in the tradition do recognise such a change although Paul VI is much stronger on historical consciousness than his successor, John Paul II.[10]

The language of the earlier documents and the language of the earlier commentators emphasise the unchangeable principles and the changing applications. Natural law is understood as the unchanging given which is then applied in particular circumstances. The function of the individual conscience is to apply the principles to the changing situation. This classicist understanding of conscience coincides well with the manualistic understanding that conscience at least implicitly follows the method of the syllogism in arriving at its particular conclusions. However, in *Mater et Magistra* conscience is described in a way that does not necessarily have to be understood in a totally classicist vein. Here Pope John XXIII adopts the approach of Catholic Action to the functioning of conscience. The Catholic Action movement spearheaded especially by Joseph Cardijn proposed the famous three steps of see, judge, act. This approach by its very nature can break away somewhat from the abstract and totally deductive approach of a classicist understanding of conscience. Pope John XXIII still understands this threefold approach, however, as adapting the traditional norms to the circumstances of time and place.[11]

However, beginning with John XXIII one can note incipient changes in the development of historical consciousness. *Mater et Magistra* in a major part of the document called for a reconstruction of the social relationships in truth, justice, and love.[12] Two years later Pope John XXIII, in *Pacem in Terris*, has added an important element to this trinity — truth, justice, love, and freedom.[13] *Pacem in Terris* ends each of the four major parts of the encyclical with a description of the signs of the times. The Pastoral Constitution on the Church in the Modern World in its discussion of five subjects or issues of concern in the second part of the document begins each one of these chapters with a discussion of the signs of the times. There is a definite move from beginning with the abstract to beginning with the concrete, from an emphasis on the unchanging to an emphasis on the historical.

Without a doubt, *Octogesima Adveniens*, the 1971 letter of Pope Paul VI to Cardinal Roy, is the best illustration of historical consciousness found in the documents of the tradition of the social teaching of the Catholic Church. *Octogesima Adveniens* begins by recognising the diversity of situations facing the contemporary world. In the midst of such widely varying situations the pope insists it is neither his mission nor his ambition to propose a unified message or to put forward a solution which has universal validity. The local christian communities themselves in the light of their situation, the gospel, and the social teaching of the church must come up with their own solutions to these questions (par 4).

The emphasis on history and historical change contrasts with the approach taken in the earlier documents. Other documents did recognise changes which had occurred since the previous pope had spoken on the subject, but the insistence on change and new developments in *Octogesima Adveniens* is marked. Pope Paul VI speaks about very rapid and profound changes and points out special problems in the areas of urbanisation, youth, women, workers, victims of change, discrimination, emigrant workers, the need to create employment, the media of social communication, and the environment (par 8–22).

The older emphasis on the immutable and the unchanging is gone. In the midst of these rapid and profound changes the human person discovers one's self anew and questions one's self about the meaning of personal existence and collective survival (par 7). This letter does not deny permanent and eternal truths but one cannot easily deduce from these how one should act.

Octogesima Adveniens describes the church's social teaching in a very historically conscious way. With all its dynamism, the social teaching of the church accompanies human beings in their search for answers to the urgent problems of today. The dynamic nature of the social teaching is spelled out by describing it as drawing on the rich experiences of the past, continuing its permanent preoccupations, and undertaking the daring and creative innovations which the present state of the world requires (par 42).

The letter ends with a call to action and insists that amid the diversity of situations, functions, and organisations, each one must discern in one's conscience the actions that he or she is called to share in (par 49). In the description of how conscience functions, this letter avoids the description of conscience as applying abstract and immutable principles to concrete situations. The word used to describe the function of conscience is discernment — not the application of principles to concrete cases (par 35 ff). The pope appeals to utopias — the first such appeal in the history of the tradition of the social teaching of the church. Utopias are not abstract and immutable principles. Utopias as criticisms of existing societies provoke the forward-looking imagination to perceive in the present the disregarded possibilities hidden within it and to direct itself toward a fresh future. Utopias sustain social dynamism by appealing to the inventive powers of the human heart and mind. The Spirit dwelling within the christian urges the believer to go beyond the limits and restrictions of every system and every ideology. This emphasis on conscience as discernment and the role of utopias recognises that at the heart of the world there dwells the mystery of the human person discovering the self as God's child in the course of an historical and psychological process in which constraint and freedom as well as the weight of sin and the breath of the Spirit alternate and struggle for the upper hand (par 37).

The description of conscience in *Octogesima Adveniens* differs markedly from the earlier emphasis on the application of immutable and absolute principles to changing circumstances. One cannot expect this document to give a detailed and systematic treatise on the nature and function of conscience, but the more historically-conscious, concrete, and inductive characteristics of conscience are clearly present in the description of conscience as well as in the employment of the concepts of discernment and utopias.

Social teaching of the United States Bishops

The first part of this study has examined the social teaching of the universal church to see what is said about the legitimate freedom of the conscience of the believer in social matters and what is said about the nature and function of conscience. The second part will examine the social teaching of the United States bishops, especially the two recent pastoral letters on peace and the economy, to see how they treat the legitimate freedom of the conscience of members of the church and how they understand the role and function of conscience.[14]

The most characteristic aspect of the two United States pastoral letters is the greater specificity found in them and the more particular judgments made there in comparison to the documents of the universal hierarchical teaching office. The United States documents do not go against the teachings of the universal hierarchical magisterium, but they go beyond the universal documents in the sense of being much more specific. The pastoral letter on peace and nuclear war, for example, makes the judgment that the first use of nuclear weapons is wrong.[15]

How do the United States documents look at the legitimate freedom of the conscience of the individual Catholic? By being more specific it would seem that these documents might actually give a lesser role to the freedom of the individual Catholic in social matters.

The two pastoral letters were not written in a vacuum. The United States bishops had been speaking out on social issues in a more specific way for quite some time, and this became even more pronounced after the Second Vatican Council.[16] The impetus for such an approach also came from the acute social problems that were being faced in the United States during this time. There can be no doubt that the national debate over the Vietnam war put pressure on the bishops to make some specific judgments about that war. Particular judgments were also made on many other current social problems facing the United States. There

94

has been some debate among Catholics in the United States about the wisdom of the bishops making such specific and concrete judgments, but this has been the accepted approach of the bishops themselves.[17] From the very beginning it was recognised that the pastoral letter on peace and the nuclear question would make such specific moral judgments.[18]

The ramifications of some of the specific judgments made in the first drafts of the pastoral letter on peace and the nuclear issue created attention. An informal consultation was held in Rome in January 1983, involving representatives of the United States Bishops' Conference with representatives of many Western European Bishops' Conferences and with the Vatican (Cardinal Ratzinger presided at the meeting) to discuss questions arising from the second draft of the pastoral letter. A summary of the meeting was prepared by Archbishop Roach and Cardinal Bernardin on 25 January and shared with the committee writing the pastoral letter. A longer memorandum written by Father Jan Schotte, secretary of the Pontifical Commission for Justice and Peace, summarised the meeting in greater detail. These two memoranda were sent to all the United States bishops with a covering memorandum by Archbishop Roach and Cardinal Bernardin on 21 March 1983.[19] The covering memorandum said that perhaps the crucial point of the exchanges was 'to focus attention on the need to distinguish clearly between moral principles and their application to concrete realities—that is, between principles on the one hand and, on the other, specific applications of these principles via the assessment of factual circumstances'. This distinction is necessary to avoid attaching an unwarranted level of authority to prudential, contingent judgments in which the complexity of the facts makes possible a number of legitimate options.[20]

The longer Schotte memorandum maintained that a clear line must be drawn between a statement of principle and practical choices based on prudential judgment. The need for this differentiation comes from the need to distinguish very clearly the different levels of teaching authority in the letter. This distinction will respect the freedom of the christian as to what is binding and what is not binding and will safeguard the integrity of the faith so that nothing is proposed as the doctrine of the church which merely pertains to prudential judgments.[21]

The third draft of the pastoral letter on peace issued shortly thereafter and the final document approved in the next month clearly make this distinction. In the very beginning the final version of the peace pastoral distinguishes different levels of ethical discourse with correspondingly different levels of teaching authority. Universal moral principles and quotations from universal church teaching involve the teaching authority of bishops as such. However, at times the pastoral letter applies moral principles to specific cases which involve prudential judgments that can be interpreted differently by people of good will. The bishops themselves give as an example here their judgment about no first use of nuclear weapons. These judgments made in specific cases are not binding in conscience, but they should be given serious attention and consideration by Catholics. On the level of the application of principles, there can be a legitimate diversity and pluralism within the Catholic church.[22]

The pastoral letter on the economy continues in the same general direction. The letter maintains that in teaching the fundamentals of christian faith, church teaching, and basic moral principles the bishops are proposing norms which should inform the consciences of the members of the church. On the other hand, the recommendations about specific policies for decisions in the economic sphere involve prudential judgments and different conclusions are possible even among those who share the same moral principles and objectives.[23] Thus, even though the United States pastoral letters do make specific policy recommendations, they safeguard the legitimate freedom of the believer's conscience on specific, complex issues and policies.

The second question to be investigated concerns the understanding in the pastoral letters of the United States bishops on how conscience operates. As mentioned above, the January 1983, Rome meeting insisted on the need to distinguish the various levels of moral teaching with the correspondingly different levels of authoritative teaching and described these levels primarily in terms of universal principles and the applications of these principles in particular historical circumstances. 'The Challenge of Peace: God's Promise and Our Response' likewise uses the terminology of universal principles and their application to point out that on the level of application there can be a legitimate diversity within the church. The economic pastoral distinguishes the various levels of moral teaching, moves from principles to policies, but shies away from describing its practical judgments as applications of principles in discussing the different levels of its teaching.[24] There seems to be some change here.

The pastoral letter on peace claims to be following the methodology and the teaching of *Gaudium et Spes*, the Pastoral Constitution on the Church in the Modern World of Vatican II. The pastoral thus begins with a recognition of the signs of the time, especially in terms of the threat of nuclear destruction of the world. However, in general the structure of the document goes from the more general to the more specific. A scriptural understanding of peace is followed by a theological approach to the relationship between the kingdom of God and history. Then the document discusses the just war criteria and non-violence. The judgments about nuclear weapons and nuclear deterrence in the second chapter are made in light of the just war principles of discrimination and proportionality in governing the way in which war is to be waged. The impression is given that these principles are applied to the present situation to arrive at the specific judgments made in the letter.

Is it legitimate, then, to conclude that the pastoral letter on peace understands the function of conscience as moving from the abstract and general to the particular and concrete, and proceeds by way of applying universal principles to specific circumstances? Although the document definitely gives the impression that it understands conscience to function in this way, the case can be made that as a matter of fact in the letter itself specific judgments of conscience are not necessarily the result of the application of universals to specific circumstances and are not based on a process of going from the abstract and the general to the particular and the concrete.

In my view there is a very specific judgment that has influenced many of the other specific judgments and even affected some of the principles proposed in the pastoral letter on peace. This important judgment apparently was not and could not be made by the application of a general principle to particular circumstances. Unfortunately, the final version of the letter itself does not explain this particular judgment in great detail, nor does it explicitly recognise how important this judgment is in the overall development and structure of the pastoral letter. However, the case can be made to prove the centrality of this judgment and its influence on many of the other judgments and even on some of the theoretical principles proposed in the pastoral letter itself. I refer to the judgment or conscience decision not to demand total unilateral nuclear disarmament at this time. In reality this judgment is much more central in the pastoral letter than appears on the surface. In the course of the development of the document through its various drafts this judgment or conscience decision remains constant while other changes on a more theoretical and general level were made to accommodate the continued conclusion about not demanding total unilateral nuclear disarmament at this time. The historical development of the document thus indicates the importance and centrality of the existential judgment about no unilateral disarmament.

If one makes the judgment that there should not be immediate and total unilateral nuclear disarmament at this time, then one must have reasons to justify the morality of nuclear deterrence at the present time. The history of the drafts indicates a continuing search for such a rationale which is needed to shore up this very significant existential judgment. The changing rationale proposed indicates that the non-negotiable aspect throughout the development of the letter was the particular judgment itself and not the rationale which was proposed for it.

In the first draft of the letter the bishops developed a two-tiered approach to deterrence. Through five different steps they build up the justification for a barely justified deterrent. Here the draft accepts the principle that one cannot threaten to do what one cannot do. Since it is wrong to attack cities and civilian targets, it is wrong to threaten to attack them as part of a strategy of deterrence. The draft does not categorically condemn the use of nuclear weapons in response to the first use of nuclear weapons by others if these retaliatory weapons are restricted to military targets. This position is the basis for a barely justified nuclear deterrent involving counterforce nuclear weapons. However, the draft goes further by willing to tolerate as a lesser evil what is understood to be the present United States deterrence policy involving counterpopulation deterrence. This type of deterrence can be tolerated as long as there are hopes that such deterrence will be a step toward the reduction of nuclear arms.[25]

The second draft drops the two-tiered consideration of deterrence. The document recognises the moral and political paradox of deterrence, which by threatening the use of nuclear weapons has actually seemed to many to have prevented their use. The draft understands United States policy as directed against targets of value which either include civilian populations directly or involve killing large numbers of civilians in an indirect manner. The draft then tolerates this deterrence provided steps are being taken to reduce the overall nuclear strength and eventually to phase out nuclear deterrence and the threat of mutual assured destruction. The second draft sees this toleration as another way of expressing what Pope John Paul II said to the United Nations in June of 1982: 'In current conditions deterrence based on balance, certainly not as an end in itself, but as a step on the way toward a progressive disarmament may still be judged morally acceptable.' There are limits and conditions on nuclear deterrence, but the draft does not call for unilateral nuclear disarmament.[26]

As time went on the drafters became aware of a problem in their ethics. One cannot tolerate one's own intention to do evil. You can tolerate what some call non-moral evil, but you can never tolerate your own intention to do moral evil. By the time of the third draft the committee also had in its possession a document from William Clark, the National Security Advisor, stating that 'the United States does not target the Soviet civilian population as such'. In the light of these developing understandings the third draft and the final version pose their position on deterrence. To prevent nuclear war from ever occurring and to protect and preserve the key moral values of justice, freedom, and independence, a conditional, limited acceptance of some counterforce deterrence is acceptable at the present time. A major condition is the need to see deterrence not as something permanent but as a step on the way to progressive disarmament. Many limits are proposed but above all such deterrence must be limited to counterforce deterrence and not countercity or counterpopulation deterrence. Other conditions and limits are also expounded.[27]

A fascinating development occurred when the bishops voted on the final document in May 1983. The proposed document condemned all counterpopulation use of nuclear weapons, the first use of even the smallest counterforce nuclear weapon, but did not categorically condemn the retaliatory use of all counterforce nuclear weapons. A motion was made from the floor and passed by the body of bishops to condemn all use of nuclear weapons. The logical conclusion of this resolution would be that the letter would then have to demand unilateral nuclear disarmament. If you are not able to use any nuclear weapons, then you are not able to threaten to use any such weapons in a strategy of deterrence. Without developing the rationale totally, Cardinal Bernardin later in the meeting strongly urged that the bishops retract the amendment they had earlier adopted which condemned all use of nuclear weapons. Ultimately the body of bishops did change their mind on this amendment, and thus the document did not condemn all use of nuclear weapons.[28] The reaction by Bernardin and others at this time indicates how significant was the judgment that there should be no call for unilateral nuclear disarmament at the present time. There are also strong indications from this discussion that not all the bishops realised how the rationale for this position was developed.

There can be no doubt that the drafters of the pastoral struggled over the theory of deterrence, but from the very beginning through to the end they were clearly opposed to demanding unilateral nuclear disarmament at the present time. This judgment never wavered even though more theoretical considerations and principles were changed. The judgment about not demanding unilateral disarmament at the present time is a central part and even a cornerstone of the pastoral letter on peace and is not merely deduced from a more general principle. This comparatively long analysis has tried to prove that the pastoral letter on peace does not necessarily understand the judgment of conscience to be made in a deductive way by applying principles to particular cases.

It will not be necessary to do as protracted an analysis of the drafts of the pastoral letter on the economy to determine how it understands conscience to function. As already pointed out, the letter recognises the different levels of moral principles and particular judgments and moves from principles to policies, but does not explicitly describe the specific judgments as formed by applying principles to the particular historical circumstances. The principles interact with empirical data with historical, social, and political realities, and with competing demands on limited resources.[29]

The first draft of the pastoral letter on the economy structures itself by moving from the more general to the more specific. The first and most general consideration is a christian vision of economic life, which for all practical purposes is a biblical vision. The next section proposes the ethical norms that should govern economic life and institutions. Part Two involves policy applications, and in separate chapters treats the five specific issues of employment, poverty, food and agriculture, collaboration to shape the economy, and the United States and the world economy.[30] Archbishop Weakland, the chairman of the committee drafting the economic pastoral, tried to respond to critics who found difficulty in what Weakland called the highly deductive nature of the first draft. As a result, the second draft avoids the strict division into the two parts of theory and application and presents in a first chapter a descriptive focus on the signs of the times.[31] The final document follows the same basic approach and thus tries to avoid the deductive approach of the first draft.

Conclusion

The conclusion of this analysis looks both to the past and to the future. In the recent past it seems that both the documents of the universal church social teaching and the recent pastoral letters of the United States bishops have attempted to safeguard the legitimate freedom of the conscience of the believer on specific, concrete social judgments and actions. Although the United States pastoral letters do make many prudential and specific judgments on policies and institutions, they recognise that others in the christian community might disagree with them.

In their understanding of how conscience functions, the older documents of the universal church teaching office often indicate that conscience works by applying universal principles to particular circumstances, by going from the general to the particular, and by strict deduction. Later documents, especially as illustrated in *Octogesima Adveniens*, show that conscience decisions are not made by applying universal principles to particular circumstances or by moving rigorously from the more general to the more particular.

There are many indications that the pastoral letter of the United States bishops on peace understands the decision of conscience to be made by the application of universal principles to particular circumstances. The document refers to the different levels of principles and the applications of principles. The content of the letter spells out the just war criteria and then applies them. The letter definitely moves from the more general to the more specific. However, in reality it seems that a very significant judgment of conscience on not demanding unilateral nuclear disarmament at the present time was made by the bishops in a non-deductive manner. In fact, more general theoretical aspects and principles were even changed in the various drafts to make sure that this particular judgment could still logically be made. The second draft of the pastoral letter on the economy does generally move from the more general to the more specific, but avoids speaking of specific judgments of conscience as the application of principles to changing circumstances and attempts to blunt the criticism that the first draft was too deductive. The final document follows the same approach. It seems to me, that in following the directions from the January 1983, Rome meeting to distinguish clearly between the level of universal principles and the level of application and by structuring their document by going from the more general to the more specific, the pastoral letters give the impression that judgments of conscience are formed deductively by moving from the abstract and the general to the concrete and the particular. However, as a matter of fact, these documents do not see conscience as always or even often operating in this fashion.

For any future pastoral letter which makes such specific judgments and decisions on policies and actions, it is important to continue to safeguard the freedom of the believer. To safeguard this proper freedom it is necessary to recognise that on more specific and complex matters there exists a possible pluralism and diversity even within the church. Not only from the ecclesiological perspective but also from the perspective of systematic moral theology there is some merit in recognising different levels moving from the more general to the more specific. However, it should also be explicitly recognised that in the existential reality concrete judgments and decisions of a specific kind about the social order do not very often involve deduction or the movement from the abstract and general to the concrete and the particular. Discernment of conscience involving specific judgments is the most specific level of moral discourse and must logically be related to the more general levels, but such judgments are not necessarily made in the existential order by moving from the more general to the more specific. Logically such judgments must cohere with the more general understanding of perspectives, values, virtues, and principles but such judgments in the existential order are formed in a more connatural and inductive way which does not follow deductive logic or a move from the abstract and general to the concrete and particular.

7. Sterilisation: The Dilemma of Catholic Hospitals

IN a report in the *Washington Post*, 22 May 1977, the Worldwatch Institute called sterilisation 'the contraceptive phenomenon of the 1970s'.[1] In one-third of all married couples in the United States trying to avoid conception, one or other partner has undergone sterilisation. Sterilisation now exceeds any other single preventive family planning measure. Bruce Stokes, author of the report, stated that the figures for the United States were based on a 1973 National Survey of Family Growth by the National Center for Health Statistics of the then Department of Health, Education and Welfare (DHEW).

How do Catholics fit into these trends? Writing in *Family Planning Perspectives* (1977), Charles F Westoff and Elise F Jones, both of Princeton University, Office of Population Research, stated, on the basis of comparative figures for 1970 and 1975, that 'within several years, even sterilisation will probably be adopted by the same proportion of Catholics as non-Catholics. . . .'[2] After noting that three-fourths of the women surveyed are using some form of contraception (79.9% for non-Catholics and 76.4% for Catholics) they presented the following results on sterilisation for 1975:

	Non-Catholic	Catholic
Wife sterilised	13.9	9.8
Husband sterilised	12.4	9.9

Dr Conrad Taeuber and Dr Jeanne Clare Ridley of Georgetown University have provided even more recent (1976) statistics similar to those of the Westoff-Jones study. Using a computer tape file from the nationwide

Family Growth Survey carried out under the direction of the National Center for Health Studies, the researchers note that 'the conclusion that there has been a significant increase in the contraceptive use of sterilisation since 1970 is clearly established, and there is little doubt that the rate for Catholic couples has increased more rapidly than the rate for couples identified as non-Catholic.'[3] This conclusion supports the Westoff and Jones prediction that 'sterilization . . . will probably be adopted in several years by the same proportion of Catholics as non-Catholics, judging from recent trends.'

The Westhoff-Jones prediction appears to be on target when evidence of another kind is assembled. For instance, in a 1986 letter to American bishops on the 'Charles Curran affair', John F Kippley, president of the Couple to Couple League and an advocate of natural family planning as the only morally acceptable form of birth regulation, noted that 95% of Catholic couples are using 'unnatural, immoral methods'.[4] Only 2–3% of non-pregnant newly-weds start their marriages with some form of natural family planning. Another indication is the Notre Dame Study of Parish Life entitled 'Pastors and People: Viewpoints on Church Policies and Positions'.[5] Opposition to *Humanae Vitae* was reported as very strong, especially among the better-educated and those under fifty. Support for the encyclical was found only among pastors *as a group*, with large numbers dissenting.[6]

This trend presents a real dilemma for at least some, possibly very many, Catholic hospitals. The problem is above all tubal ligation, the severing of the fallopian tubes to make meeting of sperm and ovum impossible. Vasectomy, male sterilisation, is not necessarily a hospital procedure. There are repeated instances often involving so-called medical indications, like renal or cardiac disease, when both the woman and the physician judge that another pregnancy would endanger the life or health of the mother or the foetus. They therefore judge that sterilisation is the only solution and is in the overall best interests of the woman, her marriage, her family. Thus, in a survey of Catholic hospitals, published in the *American Journal of Obstetrics* and *Gynaecology*, 20% (66 of 336 responding) permitted sterilisations for medical reasons.[7] This number would be higher had all hospitals responded and had some hospital personnel realised what constitutes a prohibited sterilisation, as I note below. Forty-seven per cent of the 270 not permitting sterilisation reported that their medical staffs were interested in doing sterilisations. In my own discussions with Catholic physicians and health care providers throughout the country, I have found that heavy majorities believe that sterilisation is at times a justifiable response to a critical medical problem.

I have also discovered a great disparity of practice and no little confusion. For instance, some hospital administrators assert that they follow the *Ethical and Religious Directives for Catholic Health Facilities* (1971) and therefore (!) allow sterilisations only for medical reasons. Others report that they tolerate only so-called indirect sterilisations, but further discussion reveals that they sometimes understand this as one 'required by the health of the mother'. Some assert that they 'have no problem with sterilisation' since they do not allow them at all, and yet a significant number of such responders preside over obstetrical services that are heavily underused, constitute severe financial burdens and whose very existence is threatened.

In the face of such diverging practices, the National Conference of Catholic Bishops (NCCB) issued a document (3 July 1980) repeating traditional Catholic teaching on sterilisation.[8] The document summarises and applies, somewhat more rigidly at one point, the response of the Sacred Congregation for the Doctrine of the Faith given 13 March 1975.[9] It does this 'since we note among Catholic health care facilities a certain confusion in the understanding and application of authentic Catholic teaching with regard to the morality of tubal ligation'. It was this same 'confusion' that led the NCCB to seek a clarification of the matter from the Congregation for the Doctrine of the Faith in 1974, a request that led to the 1975 response noted above. For instance, G Emmett Carter, then bishop of London, Ontario, concluded in 1973 that there was enough theological support at that time to allow sterilisation under certain specific conditions.[10] The same conclusion had been reached by other bishops. Quite a few have told me so personally. Indeed, the practice of a notable number of hospitals, the opinions of a significant number of bishops, theologians, physicians and administrators lead me to believe that what the NCCB document identifies as 'confusion' is more likely straightforward disagreement with the absoluteness of the traditional formulation.

To dispel the confusion the NCCB reasserted: 1. the objective grave immorality of every direct (contraceptive in purpose) sterilisation; 2. the invalidity of the use of the principle of totality to justify it; 3. that any material cooperation, which is said to be an 'unlikely and extraordinary situation' is justified only by grave reasons extrinsic to the case, not by the medical reasons given for the sterilisation. In other words, if pregnancy would threaten the life or health of the mother or risk a seriously defective child, that is insufficient reason for a Catholic hospital to tolerate the procedure.

The doctrine of the NCCB document and of the Congregation for the Doctrine of the Faith is not new, except perhaps that the NCCB doctrine seems stricter on material cooperation. Indeed the overall teaching is utterly traditional. Some theologians argued that direct sterilisation was condemned in Pius XI's *Casti Connubii* when it all-inclusively referred to 'any use whatsoever of matrimony exercised in such a way that the act is deliberately frustrated in its natural power to generate life is an offence against the law of God and nature'.[11]

The Holy Office was asked 'whether the direct sterilisation of man or woman, whether perpetual or temporary, is licit'. Its reply (24 February 1940): 'In the negative; it is forbidden by the law of nature.'[12] Pius XII made this very clear in his address to the Italian Society of Urologists on 8 October 1953. He denied the application of the principle of totality—the principle allowing for the disposal or mutilation of a part of the body for the good of the whole person—to cases where the danger to the woman originated in pregnancy itself. As he put it:

> In this case the danger that the mother runs does not arise, either directly or indirectly, from the presence or the normal functioning of the tubes, or from their

influence on the diseased organs—kidneys, lungs, heart. The danger appears only if voluntary sexual activity brings about a pregnancy that could threaten the aforesaid weak or diseased organs. The conditions that would allow the disposal of one part for the good of the whole by reason of the principle of totality are lacking. It is therefore not permitted to interfere with the healthy [fallopian] tubes.[13]

This same teaching was repeated very clearly in Paul VI's *Humanae Vitae*:

Equally to be excluded, as the teaching authority of the church has frequently declared, is direct sterilisation, whether perpetual or temporary, whether of the man or of the woman.[14]

The pope explicitly rejected the use of the principle of totality to directly sterilising interventions.

It is no wonder, then, that the *Ethical and Religious Directives for Catholic Health Care Facilities* (1971) exclude direct sterilisation. To have done anything else would have been to disagree with explicit papal teaching.

There have been several analyses of this absolute prohibition. For instance, some theologians like John C Ford, SJ, and Gerald Kelly, SJ, who argued in their *Contemporary Moral Theology II*, that the 'generative faculty . . . has a unique, inviolable character, because it is given to man principally for the good of the species rather than for his personal good'.[15] Others varied this slightly by urging that direct sterilisation is direct interference with the sources of life, and as such must be rejected, quite as vigorously as taking life itself. Again, in a commentary accompanying the NCCB document, it was argued by William E May of the Catholic University that contraceptive sterilisation involves us in 'acting against' the power to give life. It deprives 'a person of a good properly pertaining to him or her'. That is 'to do moral evil'.

Let me give an example here. I know a prominent (non-Catholic) pediatric surgeon. He and his wife had eleven children. The last was slightly retarded, so the wife had a tubal ligation performed. The couple then adopted three more children, an Indian, a black and a retarded child. Anyone who argues that the tubal ligation involved this couple in 'acting against' the power to give life or the 'procreative good' is arguing from a mountain top that is thickly insulated from the real world by a coronal mist. If human actions must be tested by moral principles, it is no less true that moral formulations must be tested and purified by clinical complexity and the messiness and unpredictability of real life. I have the unavoidable impression that some more fundamentalist Catholics are more concerned with defending past formulations than with critically testing them in new circumstances.

A significant number of theologians have therefore found these arguments insufficient to establish the absolute prohibition of direct sterilisation. Such arguments either beg the question—by assuming what is to be established, that is, that sterilisation is always a *moral* evil—or absolutise a biological aspect of the human person by equating the unequatable: human life and the sources of human life. Depriving a person of life is one thing; depriving oneself of the power to procreate is a remarkably different thing and ought not to be treated in an identical way ethically. For instance, Paul Ramsey, who agrees that we may never directly take human life because this involves us in 'turning against the good of life', does not view sterilisation as always involving our acting against the good of the power to procreate. Many would argue that in some cases the physiological condition of the mother has already negated or severely compromised procreation as a good in her case. To say anything else is to absolutise physical integrity. Again in *Contemporary Moral Theology II*, Ford and Kelly wrote in 1963: 'One cannot exaggerate the importance attached to the physical integrity of the act within papal documents and in Catholic theology generally.'[16] Many theologians reject such an emphasis. Similarly, given Vatican II's rejection of the notion of procreation as a primary end, the argument that the generative faculty is given principally for the good of the species loses persuasiveness. Pope Paul VI stated in *Humanae Vitae*: 'We believe that the men of our day are particularly capable of seizing the deeply reasonable and human character of this fundamental principle' (the inseparability of the unitive and procreative aspects of sexual union).[17] That has not happened, at least as a principle without exceptions. Gerald Kelly wrote that the argument is to a great extent intuitive: 'One either grasps it or one does not.'[18] Very many theologians have not. Indeed the appeal to intuition could easily be viewed as a reflection on the weakness of the arguments.

Thus, the so-called 'Majority Report' of the Papal Commission on Population, the Family and Natality concluded: 'Sterilisation, since it is a drastic and irreversible intervention in a matter of great importance, is *generally* to be excluded as a means of responsibly avoiding conceptions.'[19] This remains the conclusion of at least very many theologians today. Concretely, they assert that direct sterilisation is not intrinsically evil. There are times when it can be justified. Walter J Burghardt, SJ, a prominent theologian and editor of *Theological Studies*, spoke for many when he wrote in the *New York Times*: 'Rome should not expect that every official document calls for the same degree of acceptance from every Catholic. A reaffirmation that Jesus really rose from the dead makes a legitimate demand for a single response. But do not question my faith or fidelity if I choke on the Congregation's arguments condemning all direct sterilization.'[20]

In *Medical Ethics*, moral theologian, Bernard Häring, CSsR, puts it as follows:

> Whenever the direct preoccupation is responsible care for the health of persons or for saving a marriage (which also affects the total health of all persons involved), sterilisation can then receive its justification from valid medical reasons. If, therefore, a competent physician can determine, in full agreement with this patient, that in this particular situation a new pregnancy must be excluded now and forever because it would be thoroughly irresponsible, and if from a medical point of view sterilisation is the best possible solution, it cannot be against the principle of medical ethics, nor is it against the 'natural law' (*recta ratio*).[21]

I agree with that conclusion, as do many Catholic theologians. Such agreement is not a rejection of the church's substantial concern where sterilisation is involved. Nor is it a promotion of sterilisation as some less careful, usually quite fundamentalist, commentators would have us believe. Sterilisation, it can and should be argued, is not a neutral intervention, much less a desirable one. As 'drastic and irreversible' it has the character of a last resort, much as in its own domain violent self-defence, whether personal or national, is to be viewed as a last resort. That is why many theologians refer to sterilisation as an *evil*, although pre-moral or non-moral until more is known of the circumstances in which it occurs. It is something to be avoided in so far as reasonably possible. But just as not every killing is murder, not every falsehood a lie, not every taking of another's property is theft, not every war is unjust, so not every sterilisation is necessarily unchaste. Where evils are potentially associated with conduct in conflict situations, the Catholic tradition has been by and large one of vigorous and reasoned control, not of absolute exclusion. Why not here too?

But where does that leave Catholic hospitals? In a genuine dilemma. On the one hand the official teaching continues to state that sterilisation for contraceptive purposes is *always* (inherently) wrong. On the other, this formulation is not accepted by a large segment of the theological community, and, I would add from my own contact with bishops, a significant number of the episcopal community.

There are three possible hospital policies. First, allow tubal ligation on an individual and carefully controlled basis, that is, for medical indications as an instance of the principle of totality. Second, allow sterilisation as a form of material cooperation in the face of outside pressure to do so. Third, do no sterilisations at all.

There are problems in all three. If a hospital adopts the first policy, it is in dissent from official church teaching and will often be in trouble with the local bishop. Furthermore, there is the difficult problem of establishing the criteria for line-drawing. How is it possible to draw the line at medical indications? Cannot economic and other factors threaten the stability of a marriage and family via pregnancy, as Pius XII conceded?

If the second policy is adopted, the hospital still is in trouble with the authorities for the NCCB insists that toleration (material cooperation) of sterilisation under the only circumstances allowable will be 'an extraordinary and unlikely event'. Many hospitals do not experience the pressures leading to sterilisation as 'extraordinary and unlikely'.

If the third policy is adopted, the hospital will be in the position of denying to desperate women what is widely regarded as both good medicine and good morality. My concern here is not primarily the gradual abandonment of obstetrical-gynaecological services, with possible threats to the very viability of the Catholic hospital, though that is increasingly a possibility and a tragic one. For Catholic hospitals to forfeit obstetrical-gynaecological services in a culture where abortion is rampant and at a time when foetal therapy may well come into its own would be a regrettable dereliction. My own concern is above all the overall well-being of the patient and patients. If reputable theologians believe that direct sterilisation cannot be absolutely excluded morally, then one has to question whether the hospital is pursuing the true overall good of the patient if it adopts a policy that is based on an absolutist moral position.

This is not to suggest that Catholic health care facilities ought to adopt a laissez-faire attitude or policy. Not at all. There are many reasons for being extremely cautious in this area. Sterilisation has been and is widely abused. As the *Washington Star* (22 June 1986) noted: There is growing evidence that as many as two-thirds of the hospitals across the nation are ignoring them (Federal Regulations on Sterilisation).[22] Thousands of indigent women have been sterilised 'in the best interests of society'. In Maryland, Virginia and the District of Columbia, 11,000 Medicaid patients were sterilised during the period 1975–80. Joseph Califano told me, during his tenure as Secretary of DHEW (1977–9), that he was shocked to learn of the number of patients sterilised at government expense. Not only is there abuse, there is the fact that today's exceptions become tomorrow's rules or habitual practices. There is the fact that in a technologically-oriented and comfort-conditioned culture many will seek sterilisation where it is objectively unjustified. There is the genuine danger of coercion in many situations. And so on.

A stringent policy of control is assuredly called for, not least as a symbol to a society increasingly anti-natalist. Reasons such as these lead me to believe that a Catholic hospital is justified in limiting its toleration to serious medical indications. It is only the absolutism of the present moral teaching and subsequent policy that is a cause for concern and is at the heart of the Catholic hospital's dilemma. What we have here is a confusion of policy with moral theology. There are many reasons for a cautious, even strict policy. But such a policy need not root in the highly dubious contention that every direct sterilisation is morally wrong.

Behind this practical dilemma is, of course, the doctrinal problem. The church is still divided, and deeply divided, on how it ought to formulate its genuine concerns in the area of birth regulation. But the division has hardened. Trenches have been dug deeper. True conversation has all but ceased. We exist in a stalemate. Those who endorse the official formulation are said to be 'loyal', those who do not, 'disloyal', 'deviant', 'unorthodox'. Cardinal Joseph Ratzinger recently chastised such dissenters as captives to a 'middle-class' morality.[23] On these questions, consultation is increasingly limited and pre-programmed. The Catholic health care facility is trapped in the intransigence of the moral question. I have heard this again and again from truly responsible health-care providers.

They state their concerns in terms of the couple at high risk for a congenitally defective child, of the woman whose life or life-span could be seriously threatened by a pregnancy, of the woman whose life-preserving medication would seriously affect any foetus's health. These are situations where a pregnancy would be, as Father Häring notes, 'thoroughly irresponsible'. Discovering whether natural family planning 'works' means running an irresponsible risk. To demand that a couple forego sexual relations altogether is very often to threaten the marriage, as Vatican II noted when it said: 'But where the intimacy of married life is broken off, it is not rare for its faithfulness to be imperilled and its quality of fruitfulness ruined.'

This is the dilemma of Catholic hospitals as I experience it over and over again around the country. The problem is not going to go away. Indeed, it will only be exacerbated by a simple repetition of a traditional exceptionless formulation, as if the formulation were truer and truer the more often it is repeated. Perhaps that is why *Commonweal*, after high praise for the Vatican document on euthanasia, argued that the sterilisation edict 'promises to reduce rather than increase respect for traditional teaching'. *Commonweal* continued: 'It will create bureaucratic problems for Catholic hospitals, but for most Catholics it will only add to the church's unfortunate loss of credibility in all matters of sexual morals.'[24]

What has happened, at least in not a few places, is that the dilemma has been taken underground. That is, at least some Catholic hospitals quietly and without publicity or fanfare allowed to happen what is officially prohibited. That is not a healthy situation, not least of all because it increasingly distances leaders in the church from actual practice. That is a tragedy, particularly at a time when research and medical practice need the strong value-infusion that should be expected from Catholic leadership.

I have no solutions to this practical problem. But I do have a suggestion: the conversation must continue. And the conversation ought to include all with a genuine competence and stake in the matter: bishops, physicians, married couples, theologians and others, much as the Birth Control Commission included these specialities. When a question is the object of a genuine dispute in the church, the very worst thing to do is to close the conversation, decree a solution and select as consultants only those who will support it. This is what happened in a recent convention of moral theologians in Rome in April, 1986. Only those who adhered to a 'Roman line' were invited. They were addressed by the pope and several cardinals in what can only be called a recrudescence of 'court theology'.[25] That is to abort the learning process in and of the church. If the conversation is considered closed, if difficult problems are handled by mere repetition of traditional formulations, if finally Catholic hospitals go underground, I believe that the leadership of the American church will be exposing itself to some painful and unnecessary self-inflicted wounds.

The case of the Sisters of Mercy

Regrettably a 'closing of the conversation' is precisely what has happened. In the remainder of this paper I want to detail how this occurred as a kind of object lesson as to how it should not occur.

In 1978 the Sisters of Mercy of the Union, sponsors of the largest group of non-profit hospitals in the country, began a study of the theological and ethical aspects of tubal ligation.[26] The study resulted in a recommendation to the General Administration of the Sisters of Mercy that tubal ligations be allowed when they are determined by patient and physician to be essential to the overall good of the patient. The General Administrative Team accepted this recommendation in principle. In a letter dated 12 November 1980 to their hospital administrators, the General Administrative Team reported the results of the study and indicated a desire to draw concerned persons into dialogue on the issue. They did not, as was inaccurately reported to the bishops of this country, mandate a policy.

Copies of the original study, the position statement of the General Administrative Team, and the letter to the hospitals somehow fell into the hands of officials in Rome and of the Committee on Doctrine of the NCCB. One thing led to another until finally a dialogue was initiated between a committee of five bishops (James Malone, chairman; Raphael M Fliss; William H Keeler; James D Niedergeses; William B Friend [Bishop Friend attended none of the meetings]) and six Sisters of Mercy (M Theresa Kane, Emily George, Mary Ellen Quinn, Helen Marie Burns, Norita Cooney, M Roch Rocklage). Both groups had theological consultants, Msgr Richard Malone and

John R Connery, SJ, for the bishops, Margaret Farley and I for the Mercy sisters. Two meetings were held, in September and December 1981. These were largely exploratory, get-acquainted-with-the-problem meetings. At the December meeting it was decided that the next meeting (March, 1982) would enter the substance of the problem. The sisters were to present a single-page position paper stating why they thought that not all tubal ligations were morally wrong. The episcopal committee was to do the same, showing why they were.

During the first week of March, Archbishop John Roach (President of the NCCB), just returned from Rome, informed Sister M Theresa Kane that 'after consultation with church authorities in the United States', the Holy See had concluded that the dialogue had 'not met with success' in convincing the sisters to accept the church's teaching on tubal ligation. The dialogue was off. In its stead Rome had appointed a Committee of Verification (composed of three bishops, James Malone, William Keeler, Paul Waldschmidt). The purpose of this committee was to verify the Administrative Team's answer to two questions: 1. Does it accept the teaching of the magisterium on tubal ligation? 2. Will it withdraw its circular letter of 12 November to its hospitals?

Parenthetically I must add here how shocked I was at this turn of events. Just as the dialogue was to turn to the substantive issue, it was cancelled and replaced by jurisdictional muscle. I wrote to Bishop Malone protesting this. For reasons that are perhaps understandable—what response *could* Bishop Malone make?—I received no answer.

On 11 May 1982, The Administrative Team addressed their response to Pope John Paul II. The pertinent answers read as follows:

1. We receive the teaching of the Church on tubal ligation with respectful fidelity in accord with *Lumen Gentium 25 (obsequium religiosum)*. We have personal disagreements as do others in the Church, including pastors and respectable theologians, with the formulation of the magisterium's teaching on sterilization. However, in light of present circumstances, we will

not take an official public position contrary to this formulation.

2. We withdraw our letter of 12 November 1980 and will notify the recipients of the letter of such withdrawal.

The letter concluded by urging 'continued study and consultation within the Church on this issue'.

This response was drafted with meticulous care. The Administrative Team was aware of the fact that the *obsequium religiosum* asserted by Vatican II does not exclude the possibility of dissent. They were also aware of the fact that, according to traditional theology, all the church could demand of them in response to the teaching on tubal ligation was *obsequium religiosum*. Therefore the Administrative Team correctly concluded that they had an airtight response.

The Committee of Verification seemed quite pleased with the response. The Apostolic Delegate, Archbishop Pio Laghi, phoned Sister M Theresa Kane on 17 June to inform her that the Holy See had accepted the Administrative Team's response. The archbishop told Kane that he wanted to meet personally with her to convey the good news. On 24 June, Laghi met with Kane and Sister Emily George reiterating the approval of The Holy See and expressly mentioning John Paul II, the Sacred Congregation for Religious and Secular Institutes (SCRIS) and the Sacred Congregation for the Doctrine of the Faith (SCDF). The matter seemed quietly put to rest.

However, the sisters received a letter dated 30 August 1982 from E Cardinal Pironio, Prefect of the Congregation for Religious and Secular Institutes. In part it stated: 'In light of all the sentiments expressed in your letter of May 11, as well as your letter of withdrawal, dated 17 May 1982, your reply is not considered fully satisfactory and, indeed, your interpretation of the *obsequium religiosum* is judged incomplete.' The sisters were told by Cardinal Pironio that a 'subsequent response' would be coming from the congregation.

This subsequent response was a letter from Cardinal Pironio to Sister M Theresa Kane dated 21 November. The letter insisted that the religious submission of mind and will (*obsequium religiosum*) 'calls for the Catholic not only not to take a public position contrary to the teaching of the Church but also to direct his or her efforts, by an act of the will, to a more profound personal study of the question which would ideally lead to a deeper understanding and eventually an intellectual acceptance of the teaching in question'. The letter also requested the sisters to write another letter to their hospitals 'clearly prohibiting the performing of tubal ligations in all the hospitals owned and/or operated by the Sisters of Mercy of the Union'.

A letter dated 6 July 1983 was drafted by Sister Theresa Kane to the chief executive officers of the Mercy Sisters' hospitals and forwarded to Cardinal Pironio. It read as follows:

> On 21 November 1982, the Sacred Congregation for Religious and Secular Institutes (SCRIS) requested that we write you stating our re-evaluation of tubal ligation and clearly prohibiting the performance of tubal ligations in Mercy hospitals owned and/or operated by the Sisters of Mercy of the Union.
>
> As requested by SCRIS to re-evaluate, we, the Mercy Administrative Team, have spent additional time in study and consultation on tubal ligation. In obedience to the magisterium we will take no public position on this matter contrary to Church teaching. As you face pastoral problems regarding tubal ligation, we ask that you continue to work in close collaboration with your local ordinary in implementing Church teaching.

The Congregation for Religious responded to this draft in a letter to Bishop James Malone dated 22 August. The congregation insisted that the second and third sentences of paragraph 2 be changed to read as follows: 'In obedience to the magisterium we will continue to study and reflect on Church teaching with a view to accepting it. We, therefore, direct that the performance of tubal ligations be prohibited in all hospitals owned and/or operated by the Sisters of Mercy of the Union.' If any sister does not accept this, she is to specify the dissent in writing and with signature. Furthermore, Bishop Malone stated that 'upon enquiry I have learned that the letter from the congregation is indeed a "formal precept" to you.' That was specified to mean that 'no further compromises or word changes . . . will be entertained by the congregation'.

The sisters recognised both the rock and the hard place. Failure to comply might, indeed assuredly would, lead to consequences that would compromise or nullify their important work in many other areas. Accordingly, on 26 October 1983, Sister M Theresa Kane sent the required letter to the Mercy Hospital administrators. On 16 January 1984, Cardinal Pironio wrote Kane: 'We are pleased that you and the sisters of the Administrative Team have accepted the decision of the Holy See and we pray that as you continue to study and reflect on the magisterium of the Church you will embrace it in its entirety.'

Above I referred to these events as a 'closing of conversation' and as an 'object lesson as to how it should not occur'. I put the matter that way because of the heavy theological implications that invite explication. One such obvious implication is the powerlessness of women in the church. This has been noted by others. I want to point out three others here.

First, in the exchanges over a two-year period, the substantive issue was never discussed. Indeed, at the very point (March 1982) in the dialogue where the substantive issue (Is direct sterilisation intrinsically evil?) was to be discussed, Rome (SCRIS) intervened to terminate the dialogue and appoint the Committee of Verification on the grounds that 'there is nothing to be gained by further dialogue on this issue'.

Is there really nothing to be gained by further dialogue? That would be the case only if it were antecedently clear and certain that the magisterial formulation was absolutely and unquestionably accurate. Yet, how can one sustain this in light of the very widespread theological questioning of that clarity and certainty? I have discussed this matter with very many established theologians throughout Europe and the United States and can report that most would endorse the approach and analysis of Johannes Gründel.[27] Surely this fact needs discussion, unless we are to exclude in principle the relevance of theological analysis. In my judgment that is exactly what has happened here.

The second theologically pertinent issue is the notion of *obsequium religiosum*. The Mercy Administrative Team had responded that 'we receive the teaching of the Church on tubal ligation with respectful fidelity in accord with *Lumen Gentium 25 (obsequium religiosum)'*. The Congregation of Religious responded to this by saying that it was incomplete because a Catholic must also 'direct his or her efforts . . . to a more profound personal study of the question which would ideally lead to a deeper understanding and eventually an intellectual acceptance of the teaching in question'.

This raises a host of interesting issues. First, the assumption seems to be that the members of the Administrative Team have not so 'directed their efforts'. But what is the evidence for that? Surely it is not the simple fact of dissent. That would rule out dissent in principle and elevate the teaching to irreformable status — both theologically untenable. More positively, surely a group that has conducted a three-to-four-year study, consulting opposing theological viewpoints and a variety of competences, has satisfied the demands of *obsequium religiosum*. If not, what more is required? Is this 'direct his or her efforts' a duty with no time limit? Does it go on forever with no discernible *terminus*?

Next, the congregation uses the word 'ideally' of the outcome of such directed efforts. What if it does not turn out that way? Furthermore, what if a group such as the Administrative Team discovers that many competent and demonstrably loyal theologians throughout the world have had similar problems? Are these simply regrettable but ultimately irrelevant failures? If magisterial inaccuracy or error is possible and if dissent is the vehicle that reveals this, is there not a point at which obligations begin to return to and weigh upon the proponents of the disputed formulation? Specifically, must they not re-examine *their* position if it is truth and not juridical position that is our dominant concern? To say anything else is to discount the significance of personal reflection in the teaching-learning process of the church. In other words, it is utterly to juridicise the search for truth.

Finally, the 'Mercy Affair' seems to have all the characteristics of an 'enforcement of morals'. Bishop Christopher Butler, OSB, distinguishing between the irrevocable and provisional in church teaching, states of the latter: 'To require the same adhesion for doctrines that are indeed taught by officials with authority but to which the church has not irrevocably committed itself is to abuse authority, and if this requirement is accompanied by threatened sanctions it is also to abuse the power of constraint.'[28] I shall leave to readers the judgment whether these words fit this case. But if they do, their true theological importance should not be overlooked. One effect is to relieve bishops of their collegial task. An immediate implication of that relief is the undermining of authority in the church. If the bishops cannot report the experience and reflection of the faithful, or if, when they do, it is brushed aside, then clearly the presumption of truth that ordinarily accompanies authentic magisterial teaching has been undermined. For that presumption roots—as I think history shows—not simply in the naked juridical claim that the church has been commissioned to teach in the area of morals, but above all in the fact that in discharging this responsibility it has unparalleled means of overcoming the obstacles that threaten most individual human discernment. Those who treasure the magisterium as a privilege must view such a prospect, because of its generalisable implications, with profound sadness.

8. *Basic Ecclesial Communities and Moral Theology: An Introduction to the Brazilian Experience*

SINCE the aim of this paper is to establish a relationship between basic ecclesial communities (BEC from here on) and moral theology it is necessary, however briefly, to describe the origins and development of the BEC in the Brazilian church.

The BEC, which emerged in Brazil in the mid-nineteen sixties, principally in rural areas, must be seen against a background of poverty and deprivation, not only because the vast majority of its members are poor but also because the reality of a third world country signifies severe suffering and marginalisation for a large proportion of its population. While, in the intervening years, there have been some spectacular advances in industry, technology and telecommunications it is also true that the rich have become richer at the expense of the poor who have become poorer.

The stark contrast between rich and poor has become more accentuated. The increasing concentration of land ownership illustrates this point: in Brazil 1.2% of the properties correspond to a total of 45.8% of agricultural land, while 50.4% of the properties correspond to a mere 2.4%. The tendency is towards further concentration. This statistic says nothing of the many farm workers who do not possess any land. It should not be presumed that this process of concentration is by peaceful negotiation. Threats, corruption and the bullet are some of the tactics used to push small holders and squatters who have legal rights off the land.

Like other third world countries, Brazil has been grappling with development plans and a huge foreign debt.

The former are designed to attend to the latter, which illustrates the dependence of a third world country on the first world. Huge inflation rates, especially since the late seventies, have left poorer people in an even more dramatic situation. In 1983 food prices increased by 213.6%, while in the same period wages increased by 142.4%. In the five years to 1984, the population of Brazil increased by ten million but the consumption of milk and meat fell by 30%.[1]

Due to the land concentration process the rush to the cities has been accelerated. The result has been a significant increase in the number of slum-dwellers. In the city of Fortaleza, capital of the north-eastern state of Ceará, six hundred thousand of its one million seven hundred thousand inhabitants now live in shanty towns. It is amongst these people that unemployment rates are highest, and of course there is no unemployment benefit. In Brazil 42% of workers earn one minimum legal salary (45 US dollars per month) or less. In the north-eastern region this figure rises to 62.6%.[2]

This rather frightening situation has not happened by chance. While corruption and inefficiency cannot be discarded as contributory factors, the principal cause is to be found in the social and political structures which shape society. By structure is meant the ground rules which determine relationships in a society. In Brazil, as in Latin America generally, these ground rules have created an ever-increasing gap between rich and poor, to the point that the quality of life of the latter is constantly threatened and in many cases could hardly be called human at all. Therefore, they are clearly unjust structures. And not only that. They are also such that it is extremely difficult, if not impossible, for the poor who are their victims to demand a change because of the way in which society is organised. In this case one can speak of structural injustice as that which produces human misery and effectively impedes anything being done about it.

One can point to a number of events in church life which contributed to the emergence of the BEC in the mid sixties: the strong religious sentiment of the Brazilian people; the catechetical movement in Barra do Piraí; the radiophonic schools in Rio Grande do Norte; the Catholic Action groups which were very active right through the fifties and into the early sixties; the launching of the First National Pastoral Plan (1964), and of course the Second Vatican Council and the Conference of Medellín. These events contributed in different ways towards clarifying the importance of the Word of God in the life of the church, the role of the laity in the church's ministry, and the church's mission in the world.

The formation of the BEC signified something new in the religious experience of its members. There was not a complete break with their previous experience but something new was added. This could perhaps be best described as people's growing awareness that they are called by God's word to be a community called church which gives witness to the gospel, not only at liturgy but also in day-to-day living. Faith and life must interpenetrate one another. Gradually it was becoming clearer that faith is experienced in a community context and has to do with the totality of human existence.

The ecclesial status of the BEC has been debated at some length for example in the works of Leonardo Boff. The central question is whether they are in fact church or whether they simply possess some ecclesial attributes. Opinions vary, but the greater weight of evidence and opinion recognises the legitimate ecclesial status of the BEC. They are church because they are faith communities, committed to the gospel; they celebrate word and sacrament; they are in communion with others and with their pastors; they serve the world in which they live and give witness to the point of martyrdom. The magisterium of the church has also indicated its recognition of the BEC as church.[3]

In the trajectory of the BEC one can identify different ecclesiological models, principally three: 1. the church as People of God; 2. the church as community, sign of liberation; 3. the church as prophet, instrument of liberation. It would be wrong to imply that these experiences of church are exclusive of one another, either chronologically or theologically. Rather they must be understood in a dynamic and progressive unity.

The church as People of God becomes a more concrete community experience in the BEC which seeks to promote the participation of its members in a liberating way, and acquires a clearer notion of its mission when prophetically it identifies itself with the oppressed in their struggle for justice. A church community that is both sign and instrument of liberation is really a sacrament of God's Kingdom. As they put it themselves at their sixth national congress (1986) the BEC are an 'experiment' of God's Kingdom.

The church's *raison d'être* is the work of evangelisation.[4] The BEC are increasingly aware of this challenge, and also that it must be carried out in the historical context in which they live.

Vatican II and the encyclical *Populorum Progressio* had a big influence on the conference of Medellín (1968), which is a turning point in the Latin-American church's understanding of its mission. The conference was an application of Vatican II to the Latin-American continent, or perhaps more correctly, an interpretation of Vatican II from a Latin-American point of view. The conference[5] stressed the close and necessary relationship between humanisation and evangelisation; the church's mission to be at the service of people, as they are in Latin America; the conflictual nature of Latin-American society; the need for structural change — it is not enough to simply call for more love and greater virtue from individuals; the struggle for justice as an essential element of the church's mission; that people are called by God to be subjects of their own history and justice will come about only if they struggle to liberate themselves from oppression.

These principles have had a profound, though not immediate, effect on the church's pastoral practice. Broadly speaking, these insights have been endorsed by the magisterium.[6] In a very clear way they were upheld by the conference of Puebla (1979), and this is synthesised in its preferential option for the poor.[7] It is important to note that the Puebla option was made in the light of the pastoral experience gained in the intervening years. A large part of this experience was gathered by the BEC.

Increasingly the pastoral thrust of the BEC is seen in the perspective of 'liberation of the poor'. The regular and continued evaluation of their life and work has helped the BEC to clarify and deepen their understanding of liberation. To be an effective sign and instrument of God's kingdom in a world where liberation and oppression are in dialectic tension, they must commit themselves to the liberation of the oppressed.

Liberation has three levels of significance, distinct but closely and necessarily interrelated:[8] on the social, economic and political level, whereby oppressed peoples seek to free themselves from unjust structures which here and now are death-provoking, and thus aim to create a new relationship with their fellow humans as equals; on the broader historical level, whereby people strive to determine their own destiny, and thus create a relationship with the world as its master; on the redemptive-salvific level, whereby people are freed by Christ from sin, which is the root of all oppression and injustice, and thus create a new relationship with God as children.

It would be naive to presume that all the BEC in Brazil have a clear theoretical understanding of these three levels of liberation and their accompanying dynamic relationship. What can be said is that the pastoral thrust referred to above is related to, and in part due to a greater understanding of reality, and thus to the need for a praxis of liberation. It is commonplace at BEC meetings to try to discover the causes of the problems experienced by poor people. No longer are they satisfied that it is God's will, or that it is a passing phase due to the malfunctioning of some mechanisms in society. The christians who participate in the BEC speak more and more of the structures which determine the quality of life, or more to the point, the lack of quality. This has led them to taking a greater interest in social, economic and political questions, and also to taking concrete steps towards a transformation of society, for example, in the question of land reform, or work conditions, or educational and medical opportunities. The praxis of liberation is ever more clearly directed towards life issues, that is, survival and the prospect of a more human existence. It is important to recall at this point that the BEC carry out this praxis in the light of their faith which impels them to deal with such issues.

The BEC are a relatively new experience in the Brazilian church, or put in another way, they are a new way of being church in Brazil. This causes tensions within the ecclesial body because not all christians, either lay or cleric, are supportive of the BEC, and indeed some are quite vociferous in their opposition. In spite of these tensions and difficulties the BEC can be envisaged as a source of renewal and transformation of the whole church in Brazil.

Questions raised for moral theology by the BEC

The BEC raise questions for moral theology for the reason that the latter is necessarily elaborated in a community context. To be true to its own nature moral theology must dialogue with the christian community, of which the BEC are an important expression in Brazil. In summary the questions raised can be reduced to two, method and content, which are interrelated topics.

Method is a fundamental and constitutive element of any science. Theology in the wide sense and moral theology as a more specific task cannot ignore this fact. Moral theology as a normative science aims to work out and justify norms for human behaviour.

The experience of the BEC forces one to face such questions as 'what is the most adequate method to be used with a view to elaborating a moral theology which is meaningful in the context of oppression-liberation?'. Obviously this is a very complex question and only some of the more salient aspects can be referred to here.

The need for an organisational principle, or basic reference point, is indispensable if one is to avoid arbitrary or dispersive argumentation. This principle must be such that it gives unity to the project proposed by moral theology, and opens up the possibility of establishing other principles. For a faith community challenged by the reality of the impoverished what principle can give cohesion to moral theology?

To make the elaboration of norms a viable project one must discover sources, those 'places' (*loci*) which supply information and guidance for the task at hand. There is also the very important challenge of using these sources correctly. For christians, like those in the BEC, who establish a close link between evangelisation and liber-ation, what are the necessary and most important sources and how should they be used?

Much emphasis is given to the idea of community in the BEC. Are individual persons underestimated or over-looked in this desire to emphasise the community context of christian living? What is the relationship between individual and community? Who is the thinking subject, individual or community? Where does responsibility for moral decision rest, with the individual conscience or with the community consensus?

The christians who are active and committed to the BEC must be considered mature people, unless and until there is evidence to the contrary. Can they formulate (moral) theology? What is the relationship between people and academic theologians in the task of elaborating and justify-ing norms? What is the meaning of *sensus fidei* and *consensus fidelium* for moral theology in the BEC?

The BEC emphasise their pastoral mission, ie the task of evangelisation in a structurally unjust society. Does moral theology have merely a pastoral application or is its relationship with pastoral matters more dynamic and more central to its own nature?

Christian living must be rooted in and nourished by spirituality. Otherwise it withers. How can moral theology contribute to an ever-deepening faith? Can the BEC look to moral theology for help in its efforts to live a more profound and a more coherent gospel life?

The BEC signifies something new in the religious experience of its members without representing a com-plete break with the past. The same can be said about the moral issues raised. It has been suggested above that a change in theological and moral method has been taking place in the Brazilian church and that the BEC have contributed to this process. This means that issues are being dealt with in a different way, using a different organisational principle or using different sources or using these differently. It does not necessarily mean that the issues being analysed are different because the same ones could be treated in a plurality of ways. However, one can state that a new methodological stance can open up issues which otherwise may not receive very serious attention or may not be considered at all. As the preferential option for the poor gained ground and as the BEC became more socially and community conscious the issues raised reflected this process.[9] It is also true of course that new issues can force one to look for a more adequate methodology. This serves to illustrate the close connection between method and content and the BEC experience has underlined this.

The ethical issues raised by the BEC are very much in the area of social ethics. An exhaustive list would not be possible here but one can point to examples such as: property and use of land; human rights (to education, to housing and living conditions, to health services); work (conditions, wages, unemployment); foreign debt; marginalisation (of poor, blacks, women, Indians); violence, class warfare, political systems and structures, sin (personal, social, structural). It is interesting to note the specific *'disputationes'* referred to in a recent publication by a leading Latin-American thinker. They are the ethics of work, capital, dependence, transnational companies, international credit and arms, class warfare, violence and revolution, socialism, ecology and culture.[10]

The response of moral theology

In order to appreciate more accurately the response to the moral questions raised by the BEC it is necessary to situate moral theology in some overall theological approach and in this particular case in the context of the theology of liberation.

Since the theology of liberation has already been widely divulged it will suffice here to indicate some of its more important attributes. Vatican II reminded christians that they ought to be in dialogue with the world, that their mission of evangelisation, to be effective, must take note of reality. The conference of Medellín repeated this but did so from the point of view of the Latin-American continent. Here reality is strongly characterised by poverty which

130

initially may be explained as part of the process of underdevelopment but later is understood as a necessary consequence of the process of dependence. To be church in Latin America one must be open to the plight of the impoverished. To them the Good News must be announced and it is liberating in the face of the dependence to which they are subjected. The theology of liberation is thus in line with the tradition established by Vatican II, but within the context of and from the perspective of the poor.

The theology of liberation postulates that the poor are both grace (meeting place with the Lord) and challenge (the misery imposed by dependence repudiates the gospel); incorporates the preferential option for the poor; is inductive, ie it seeks to build on the human and faith experience of people;[11] dialogues with other sciences in order to better understand reality; seeks to judge reality in the light of revelation and theological tradition; seeks to help christians to discover more authentic ways of living the gospel in a third world situation; seeks to establish the necessary and adequate relationship between orthodoxy and orthopraxis.

'Liberate the poor' has emerged as the principle which best expresses the ethos contained in the praxis of the Latin-American church, and in particular in the praxis of the BEC.

The liberation of the poor is undoubtedly one of the greatest challenges facing humanity. While economic development and technological progress may present some success stories it is also true that in Latin America, as in the third world generally, the plight of the poor is worsening. It is an inescapable fact that millions exist in sub-human conditions. Some examples have already been given; one more should suffice to illustrate the trend: in 1985 three hundred and sixty thousand children died of hunger in Brazil. Unless serious action is taken to reverse the process of which this statistic is symptomatic or, in other words, unless conditions and opportunities are created for all of humanity to live in dignity and freedom then the future is bleak. Not to liberate the poor is to run the risk of condemning all of humanity to a future of greater division and misery. If the minimum attention is to be paid to the principles of justice and human solidarity then it is imperative, in view of the situation that presently obtains in the Third World, to liberate the poor. The liberation of the poor is a necessary condition for an adequate transformation of society. The changes it envisages for human co-existence refer not to an inversion of roles within the present structures of domination and oppression but rather to the creation of new structures which incorporate and promote justice for all in a spirit of solidarity. 'Liberate the poor' can be the touchstone for a new phase in the process of healing the divisions of humanity. Whilst economic poverty is not the only form of human deprivation, undoubtedly liberation refers in a special way to those whose very existence is threatened to the point where survival becomes an increasingly daunting task. In summary, the present historical experience of the Third World points clearly to the inescapable duty and necessity of liberating the poor.

From a christian point of view to 'liberate the poor' is best understood in the context of discipleship of Christ and, therefore, of commitment to the Kingdom of God. The christian life, understood as personal and community response to the proposal of Christ, recognises that he is the authentic way, and thus discipleship is obligatory and not optional. Christ is the *norma normans*. His praxis, of which liberation of the poor is a constitutive element, is normative for all christians.

Much recent literature in christology stresses Christ's relationship to and commitment to the Father's Kingdom.[12] The announcement and bringing about of the Kingdom are central to Jesus' own life. The Kingdom of God is Good News, especially for the poor and the marginalised who now have real hope that their cause will be attended to. To them Jesus announces the Kingdom not only as future but also as already present.[13]

Jesus' commitment to the Kingdom put him on a collision course with all forms of domination and oppression, which are signs of death. His God is the God of life and thus Jesus opposes everything which dehumanises or humiliates people. To liberate the poor is to value and esteem human life, both at the personal and social levels.

From a theological point of view 'liberate the poor' puts one in the context of discipleship of Christ, of concretisation of the Kingdom, of ecclesial awareness, and it is firmly rooted in the Bible, is a call to conversion, thus paving the way for a reconciliation which must be founded on justice.[14]

To liberate the poor is a partial stance but it opens up perspectives of universal fraternity. It can be a way to practise the commandment of love for all.

Within the parameters of the theology of liberation what are the sources used for moral reflection? People are situated in an historical reality, which is social, economic, cultural and political. It is also religious but that will be considered later. Human conduct cannot be properly understood and evaluated without taking into account the principle of historicity. After all, human beings are not pure nature. The mediation of the human and social sciences is therefore a fundamental element for moral reflection. It is true that the liberation debate has been giving more attention to the social sciences and immediately the question arises 'which social sciences?'. Theological reflection in Latin America has opted for a dialectical-structural rather than a functional type analysis, because the former elucidates (as opposed to stifles) and explains (as opposed to describes) more clearly the problems of the poor. This is a choice that must be justified from a scientific and from an ethical point of view. As an Argentinian author puts it:

> Dialectical sociologies express a vision from 'below', from those sectors to which society appears inadequate, badly structured, full of conflict and in need of transformation. If this observation is correct, at least in its fundamental outlines, I would claim that the christian is not without orientation for the choice that must be made.[15]

This social analysis is important for an understanding of the first level of liberation already mentioned. It is a pre-theological moment, but necessary for theology.

No serious theological reflection is possible without a philosophical mediation. If it is true that people are situated in historical circumstances, it is also true that they are capable of questioning the meaning of their existence and of projecting something new. The mediation of history is also important in this regard. The combined study of philosophy and history contributes to establishing a diachronic analysis of reality. They help us discover what people are capable of being and the kind of society that they are capable of constructing, even though they may now be submerged in a world of misery and dependence. From a christian point of view, the ultimate meaning of life is to be found in God who reveals himself and does so in a definitive way in the person of Jesus of Nazareth. Thus, the task of moral theology in Latin America must necessarily take into account these four factors:

1. The faith-moral awareness and lived christian experience of the community, because it is through an analysis of the living and committed response to God's call that one can more accurately gauge not only the issues which are decisive for a given community in a given time and place, but also the norms which can guide the community towards a more faithful response.

2. Scripture, because it is a privileged form of Revelation, is normative for christian moral evaluation. In Latin America there has been serious work to establish a proper hermeneutical analysis of scripture.[16] The use of scripture in the BEC has been instrumental in this process.

3. Other theological disciplines, systematic and pastoral, contribute to the process of formulating norms for action not only because they help situate moral theology in an overall theological approach, but also because they help discern what the Spirit is saying to the churches. In the particular case of liberation theology the moral discourse has been especially attentive to christology, ecclesiology and spirituality. Because a new moral analysis depends, in part, on a new scriptural and theological vision, one can understand why the theological ethics of liberation have not been as systematically organised and articulated as some other theological areas.

4. The teaching of the magisterium is another source for the elaboration of norms. In practice it is the social teaching which has been more widely used. Since this teaching arises in historical circumstances a proper hermeneutic must be used to discover its authentic value for christians who live the effects of dependence and domination.

In the past, moral theology has been principally concerned with the individual person, with perhaps insufficient attention given to the importance of relationships for a proper human development. More and more, with the help of the human sciences, it is clear that relationships are important both for personal identity and for personal growth.[17] In the BEC the relationships between persons are clearly influenced by the commitment to be witnesses to Christ in a society which in its very structures repudiates the gospel. A deep community commitment inevitably has consequences for moral reflection and analysis.

In the perspective of the theological ethics of liberation the agent of the moral life is the ecclesial community, sacrament of communion with God and of reconciliation among people and more specifically it is the poor ecclesial community which is called by God to be builder of his people and his kingdom.

Community is not something superimposed on persons. Rather it is a necessary expression of their personhood. It is the context in which their individuality is best understood and can best develop. Community and person need one another. Community is an indispensable source where the individual conscience finds elements for the decision-making process. The sacredness of the individual conscience is in no way diminished by its relationship to a community-ecclesial consciousness. Rather it is enhanced because it is in community that the individual person acquires true identity. To say that the ecclesial community is the moral agent is not to say that moral decision-making is determined by majority voting, but stresses that the community is, in the first place, responsible for christian witness and that the individual christian must pertain to some community. If it is correct to ask 'what ought I to do?' and 'who am I capable of becoming?', it is also valid to ask 'what ought we (community) to do?' and 'who are we (community) capable of becoming?', and these questions are not unassociated.

Conscientisation, that is, a process of growing awareness and understanding of reality in the broadest sense and thus an element for self-identity at both the personal and community levels, is a striking characteristic of the life of the BEC. The formation of the individual conscience is always a search and is necessarily influenced by community participation. The relationship between conscientisation, community consciousness and personal conscience is a complex one but necessary if we are to understand more clearly the significance of the community as moral agent and the possibility of communally discerned norms.

The role of the theologian

The academic theologian is first of all a christian who seeks to live a more profound gospel life, whose baptismal vocation is paramount and implies that he/she belongs to a christian community. While the modality of community experience may vary, many academic theologians in the Latin-American church have contacts and are in dialogue with the BEC.

The function of the moral theologian is one of service to the community, helping it acquire a more criticial understanding of its faith, and more specifically his function is one of collaboration in the task of elaborating and justifying norms. Thus the moral theologian does not unilaterally announce the truth, but seeks to discover it with the community.

How do theologians exercise this function? In the BEC it is imperative that they situate themselves in the perspective of the preferential option for the poor. Otherwise it is not possible to establish a meaningful dialogue. Theologians listen to the community. If it is true that the experience and moral consciousness of the community is a source for moral reflection, it is also true that the community must be considered capable of analysing its own moral experience, and thus of being theologian. This point must be stressed. For too long the community's ability and responsibility in this regard have been underestimated. If we are to have vibrant christian communities then their ability, and indeed vocation, to be theologians must be developed.[18] It is the Spirit acting through all christians who guarantees unity in faith. To listen helps the academic theologians to be sensitive to the process of moral growth in the community, the influence of culture on moral conscience, the issues that are of greater concern to people, the need for an adequate terminology, and their own need to learn from the poor.

When they speak, theologians avoid the extremes of simply endorsing everything people say and of manipulating their opinions to advance their own theories. Rather theologians analyse with the community its process of elaborating and justifying norms. To this end they challenge and question the community, reminding it of factors which it may be leaving aside, consciously or unconsciously. The theologian does not sell short the fundamentals of faith but insists on the central role of revelation and of Jesus Christ in the theological process. While giving due recognition to the role of ideology in human life the theologian is sensitive to the need of establishing a proper relationship between faith/ideology and theology/ideology.

The closer contact with the BEC has helped many academic theologians to rethink and rediscover their role in today's church.

The tension between gospel ideal and the humanly possible is familiar to all who have pastoral experience, and helps one understand that the task of evangelisation is better seen as a process than as something instantaneous. In this context the task of elaborating norms gives due and necessary recognition to the historicity of the work of evangelisation. In other words, unless moral theology is sensitive to the pastoral realities of the people to whom it addresses itself it runs the risk of enunciating only universal type norms which undoubtedly have value, but which may have little impact on day-to-day living.

In current Latin-American moral theology, and especially

through the influence of the BEC, emphasis is placed on something more specific, that is, norms which translate faithfully and adequately the gospel demands for christian communities which live in a structurally unjust society. Because of its commitment to justice and the cause of the poor the ecclesial community seeks to establish and justify norms which both help and challenge in its mission of working towards integral liberation. In other words, moral theology is closely related to the pastoral life of the community.

While the pastoral life of the community may not be reducible to its moral norms, these are necessary for an adequate programme of evangelisation and are more efficacious when elaborated in the light of the pastoral experience and the pastoral potential of the community. The closeness of the theology of liberation to the people has been both remarkable and beneficial. This closeness has helped towards a greater awareness of the cultural values of the poor, and some point to the BEC as possibly the most appropriate context for an adequate inculturation of the gospel in Brazilian society.

'Spirit' as it appears in the Bible tends to be opposed to inactivity and not to material or corporeal things. The Spirit of God impels people to create fraternity, justice and solidarity. For the christian therefore spirituality is defined primarily in terms of obedience to the will of the Father. In the Latin-American context and within the parameters the theological ethics of liberation spirituality is rooted in the conviction that the poor are a mediation of God's word which must be constantly discerned.[19] The praxis which seeks to liberate the poor is therefore an act of obedience to God's will. Spirituality thus involves both action and contemplation of God's word and is evidently related to discipleship which is the key to its close affinity to moral theology. The contribution of moral theology to spirituality is therefore seen as one of discernment of God's will. It can never be sufficiently stressed that the norms elaborated by and for christian communities must relate to the practice of God's will. In the BEC one can observe, in varying degrees, the concern to pray in such a way that takes into account both the situation of injustice in which people find themselves and their efforts to live the gospel coherently in this context. Prayer and action come together in an organic unity.

Undoubtedly the theological ethics of liberation have been emphasising issues of a social, economic and political nature. It must be stressed that these are human problems, they effect people in a very real way, and are especially decisive for the poor in a structurally unjust society. To emphasise these issues does not mean that other human concerns, such as personal problems or interpersonal relationships, are discarded or considered irrelevant. What is true it that, in the Latin-American context, the broader socio-political questions provide a backdrop for the personal and interpersonal issues, which can then be analysed more accurately.

Perhaps some examples can help to illustrate this point. Provoked abortion is inescapably a problem of human concern and has clear ethical implications. It can be studied as the problem of an individual person, but if this person is situated in a society which is itself abortive, where life is threatened and aborted, by hunger for example, then the analysis of the question must take this into account. Euthanasia is another case in point. It is undoubtedly a serious ethical question whether or not a human life should be prolonged, especially when one sees the sophisticated technology available in some countries. However, in countries like Brazil where forty million people (one third of the population) never see a doctor from the day they are born to the day they die, one can sense that euthanasia is an inbuilt factor of society. People are constantly allowed to die of hunger, misery and want of medical attention. This evidently implies that euthanasia cannot be treated just as an individual or isolated problem.

The theological ethics of liberation are elaborated in the perspective of the preferential option for the poor. It is true that the church has always been concerned with the poor. What has changed is the manner in which the ecclesial community views the poor: for example, the poor are people who should be magnanimously helped by the better off, or they are an inevitable factor in underdeveloped societies, or the poor are primarily the victims of a structurally unjust society, which is the view adopted by the theory of dependence, and is the sociological thesis adopted by the theology of liberation. Given this premise it is logical that the social, economic and political questions would predominate in the ethical debate, for these are the issues which are decisive, here and now, for survival and for life, and that in an urgent way for millions of poor people.

Perhaps this is a way of saying that charity must also be practised in macro terms, that is, it must penetrate the structures which determine people's lives. In the Latin-American context this means that it must penetrate the structures to the point of transforming them, making them just. It would be naive to imply that first the structures must be transformed and that following on this people will be transformed (converted). It would be equally naive to postulate the opposite. The two processes require one another. However, the Latin-American experience and reflection have shown that the structural question is of fundamental importance and a decisive element in the process of integral liberation. The documents of the conferences of Medellín and Puebla as well as numerous statements from different episcopal conferences in Latin America underline this point. But this is not just a concern of the Latin-American churches. There has been a growing sensitivity to social, economic, political and structural problems in the church's teaching, especially since Vatican II, and this has been influential for a renewed understanding of the situation of the poor. A study of *Gaudium et Spes* (1965), *Populorum Progressio* (1967), *Octogesima Adveniens* (1971), *Justice in the World* (Synod, 1971), *Evangelii Nuntiandi* (1975), *Redemptor Hominis* (1979), *Laborem Exercens* (1981), *International Debt: An Ethical Approach to the Problem* (1987), makes this clear. Latin-American society is conflictual and it is therefore imperative that the ethical debate concern itself with the causes of conflict. It is in the social, economic and political fields that some of the more fundamental causes are to be found.

In the BEC the Exodus event is one of the most frequently meditated biblical texts. The Exodus has both religious and political significance. The people liberated from slavery are called by God to form a covenant and to be his people, to give witness to his love. Thus, to be religious implies a political commitment because witness must be given in an historical setting. God's liberating action is not only an eschatological event, but also has an historical expression.[20] The meditation of the prophetic writings reinforces this idea.

While the broader socio-political questions are decisive and a suitable context for the analysis of other human problems, these also must be given due recognition and attention. God's offer of grace can be experienced at all levels of human existence and not just at the macro level.

Perspectives and challenges

It is not the objective of this final section to offer an evaluation of the theological ethics of liberation, but rather to indicate some perspectives that have been established and some challenges that must be faced.

Dialogue with the social sciences is a necessary part of the moralist's task. It is to the credit of Latin-American theologians that they do this in a systematic way. This does not mean that the dialogue is easy or without problems, for the moralist must be attentive to the internal logic of these sciences. These too are human undertakings and so have inherent limitations and ambiguities. A critical view of the social sciences is therefore necessary if one is to acquire a more profound understanding of society. In other words, there is no 'once and for all' analysis of reality. Contact with the human sciences may not have been as systematic but here too it is necessary to insist on the importance of a critical approach in an ongoing dialogue.

The theological ethics of liberation postulate 'liberate the poor' as its organisational principle. The theological arguments based on commitment to God's Kingdom and which justify this position have been widely discussed. Are there not other arguments also which are not specifically theological in nature? If not, the theological ethics of liberation may be really proposing some kind of theocracy

141

and proving themselves incapable of dialogue with the secular world. While it may be true that religious symbolism has played a big part in the elaboration of liberation ethics it is also true that much research has been done to establish the philosophical justification of 'liberate the poor', and in this regard the work of Dussel is important.[21] In other words, the theological ethics of liberation recognise the importance of human rationality for the ethical debate. It will always be a challenge to establish the correct articulation between 'faith' and 'reason'. The Latin-American experience of doing so in the context of liberation of the poor can open up possibilities for a new and more satisfactory theological-ethical synthesis.

Latin-American moralists seek to elaborate a moral theology which is relevant to its socio-political and ecclesial context. In other words, they refuse to be satisfied with just universal type norms and strive to establish a more specific normativity for and with the christian community. Thus, moral theology is attentive to social issues and is necessarily prophetic in a structurally unjust society. Its closeness to the poor and its pastoral concern are important factors in this regard. Understandably, indignation at the suffering of the poor is a characteristic common to many christians, including academic theologians, in Latin America. However, indignation and participation in the struggle for justice must complement and not substitute scientific rigour, which must always be pursued if the theological ethics of liberation are to retain credibility.

Latin-American moralists emphasise the community's role in elaborating moral theology. This must surely be seen in a positive light, especially when one recalls the thrust of *Lumen Gentium* and the many developments, both theological and pastoral, that have taken place since then, not least in the BEC in Brazil. However, one cannot ignore the challenge of establishing an ever clearer relationship between person and community, especially when it is postulated that the ecclesial community is the agent of the moral life. And of course it must be remembered that both person and community are situated in society and therefore one must be sensitive to the interactions between all three components.

In this context there is a specific question which has been the object of serious reflection in Latin-American theology, namely, sin. More specifically the issue of social/structural sin arises. How does this relate to individual/personal sin, presuming that it is not a matter of mere arithmetic? The theological ethics of liberation suggest that the threefold understanding of liberation makes possible a well-founded concept of sin and therefore facilitates the articulation of an adequate relationship between personal and social sin. This is evidently an area which calls for further reflection and is one of the bigger challenges resulting from the ecclesial community's insertion among the poor.

9. *Learning through Suffering: The Moral Meaning of Negative Experience*

ONE of the tasks of moral theology is the interpretation of moral experience. This paper is concerned with the interpretation of negative experience, and specifically with the experience of suffering. It seeks to answer two questions: how may suffering be understood within the christian tradition, and how does this understanding relate to the response to suffering?

There are four perspectives from which the experience of suffering is usually viewed in christian theology. The first is that of the relationship between suffering and God. Is suffering inflicted by God as punishment or retribution for sin? The second concerns the relationship between suffering and the sufferer. It is said that suffering in some way contributes to the formation of character, either as a discipline correcting faults or as positively nurturing virtues such as hope. Thirdly, in christian spirituality, suffering can be a sharing in the work of redemption, which is brought about through the suffering and death of the Redeemer. The christian suffers for the Lord and with him, in conformity to the crucified one. Fourthly, christian hope looks to an eschatological overcoming of suffering, a new heaven and new earth where suffering will be no more. The four perspectives could be called the retributive, the educative, the redemptive, and the eschatological.

While the second perspective, that of character formation, has the most obvious 'moral' significance, the others are also relevant to a vision of the moral life. If the christian is, in some way, called to be like God, the way in which God is understood to relate to suffering will shape the way in which the christian relates to it. If God causes suffering for some purpose, it would seem to be appropriate that christians might act to cause suffering for similar purposes. More specifically, if the christian is to be conformed to Christ in suffering, the way in which this conformity is understood will shape the response to suffering. Finally, if God's ultimate purposes include the overcoming of all suffering, then these should, in some way, form the purposes of the christian.[1]

The approach being taken here requires that we begin with a consideration of human experience. But that cannot mean that we set aside these perspectives. It is because we move from within this vision that we learn to focus on the experience of suffering as something of crucial importance. If Jesus suffered for us, if eschatological salvation includes being set free from suffering, then suffering claims a central place in our theological vision. But, in focusing upon it, we must try to grasp its human reality and not remain on the level of theological interpretation. Indeed, it is only in knowing what is being interpreted that we will be able to grasp the full meaning of the christian theological interpretations.

The experience of suffering

Suffering entails pain, but it is not the mere fact of some injury which is of primary significance. It is rather in the inner condition of the one who suffers, that the reality of suffering is present. Yet that inner condition is expressed in the physical, bodily signs of pain. It is these signs, evident in the faces and bodies of the suffering, which communicate the reality of the experience to the observer. Such communication is of a special kind since it resonates with the observer's own experience of the body and of pain.

All subsequent interpretations have an element of the conventional and need to be referred back to the initial bodily interpretation, if they are to retain their communicative force. This is, no doubt, the reason why the interpretations of more complex kinds of suffering retain a reference to physical pain. Thus, we commonly speak of the pain of loss and the pain of conscience. In the classic analysis of affliction given by Simone Weil, this condition is inseparable from physical suffering, even though it is distinct from it.[2]

It is because the experience of suffering has this physical connection with our own immediate experience, that it has such evocative power. The protest of the sufferer echoes the protest in our own bodily being. Pain is a primal human experience, and the confrontation with another's pain seems to open a fundamental path of communication with that other. In the protest expressed in the pre-verbal signs in the face of the suffering others, we grasp what ought not to be, and so also, in some way, what ought to be. What is normatively human comes to light, first of all, in its denial. And, again, this is why pain is the primary experience of negativity. Apart from the more subtle queries, there will always be one brute question provoked by suffering: why must this pain be?

Interpreting the experience: narrative

The immediate confrontation with pain and affliction stirs protest and provokes questions, but the experience is, at this point, mute and inarticulate. It needs words if its human significance is to be expressed. Human experience finds such a voice in narrative, in which it is intensified, crystallised and where its manifold contours are displayed.[3] Thus, in exploring the human meaning of suffering it will be appropriate to turn to narratives of suffering. It will be possible, of course, to consider some selected examples only.

One of the most compelling narratives articulating the experience of suffering, which I have been able to discover, is a story from *The Brothers Karamazov* by Dostoyevsky.[4] At the cost of losing much of the force of the original, I offer this abbreviated version. Mitya is travelling with his driver somewhere in the steppes. He sees a village not far off with the huts blackened and half of them burned down. As they drive in, peasant women draw up along the road. 'Why are they crying?' Mitya asks

146

as they dash gaily by. The driver answers, 'It's the babe crying.' 'But why is it crying?' Mitya asks. The driver replies, 'The babe's cold, its little clothes are frozen and don't warm it.' Mitya persists, foolishly, asking why this is so? The driver replies again that they are poor people and have been burned out. They are begging because they have no bread. 'No, no,' Mitya says, as if he still did not understand. He goes on into a series of questions: 'Tell me why it is that those poor mothers stand there? Why are people poor? Why is the babe poor? Why is the steppe barren? Why don't they sing songs of joy? Why are they so dark from black misery?' He felt that, although his questions were senseless and unreasonable, he had to ask them and in just such a way. He felt the passion of pity such as he never had before. He wanted to do something for them so that they would weep no more, so that no one would weep any more. 'I've had a good dream, gentlemen,' he says in a strange voice, with a new joy in his face. Mitya has this dream while he falls asleep at a court hearing where he is charged with killing his father. He awakens, and is eventually committed for trial. At this point, he feels the need to account for his own sufferings, and falls back on the notion of corrective suffering. As Mitya interprets it, he needs the check of suffering if he is to reshape his rather dissolute life. There are two interpretations of suffering here, set in tension, as it were, by the barrier of the dream. One reflects the experience of senseless and absurd suffering, for which an explanation is sought, but where the seeking becomes lost in the endless asking. Here the answer can only be groped for in the dream of a world without suffering. The other finds a meaning for suffering in its corrective function.

While this narrative provides an interpretation of the experience of suffering, it is the experience of the observer which is articulated. We do not know how the women by the road would speak, or what words, if any, they might find. Another narrative, of a contemporary experience of similar suffering, seeks to provide the alternative perspective, that of the sufferers themselves. In his novel, *One Day of Life*, Manlio Argueta has sought to find the words of other women, in El Salvador, who stand by wrecked homes with their hungry children. At the end of the day, one of the women describes her discovery of the word 'conscience'. One of the organised farm workers says to her, 'If I'm called on to shed blood, it doesn't matter because it is for the good of everyone else.' 'Conscience . . . is to sacrifice oneself for those who are exploited.' The woman says that she would never have known the meaning of that word if he had not explained it, 'because for me everything was part of nature. He who is, is. Everyone carries his own destiny. I used to believe in those things. If one is poor, well, that's life. What are we going to do if God didn't reward us with a better life?'[5]

It is tempting to suggest that there may be a kind of common structure beneath narratives of suffering. At least it can be suggested that there are several identifiable lines of questioning which such narratives evoke. There are at least three kinds of questions reflected in these narratives. The first concerns the factual, empirical causes of suffering. This is the kind of question to which Mitya's driver tries to respond, and which the woman in Argueta's novel has not previously asked. The second kind of question is the ethical; what should be done? Thus, Mitya experiences a sense of obligation to act so as to remove the causes of suffering. The woman grasps that conscience requires self-giving. The third kind of question concerns the significance of suffering and how it fits into a meaningful world. This is the sense of Mitya's repeatedly asking 'why?'. The woman had an answer—suffering is part of the natural order of things established by God—which she comes to see is wrong.

The quest for meaning has a religious dimension. Mitya's vision of a world without tears has an implicit religious character. For the woman, religion, up to the point of her 'conversion' still took the form of reassurance of a reward in the next life. It is clear that the ways in which the religious dimension is interpreted have direct bearing on the ethical response to suffering. Thus, if God rewards in the next life and, in the meantime, legitimates the existing, natural order of things, then the christian ought passively endure suffering. In Mitya's case, the dream entails both an inner transformation, a passion of pity, and a wanting to act so as to remove the suffering.

The analysis of these narratives suggests there is a basic structure in the interpretation of the experience of suffering which includes the locating of the causes of suffering, the ethical response, and the religious dimension. In so far as such narratives crystallise the human experience of suffering and articulate basic responses to it, they provide a frame within which we can explore the more abstract, theoretical interpretations provided by philosophy and theology.

Interpreting the experience: ethics and theology

One philosopher who has specifically addressed the kind of questions we have here is Stephen Toulmin. In his analysis of this narrative from Dostoyevsky, Toulmin situates the third kind of question, that is, the religious query, in the sphere of 'faith' or the 'irrational'. In his view, answers to such questions function so as to provide reassurance in the face of the unknown future.[6] According to Toulmin, such answers do not provide any ethical knowledge as such, but once the ethical decision is made, they help us to 'put our hearts into it'. Thus, this knowledge of faith provides reassurance, a sense that the world is not absurd or doomed, support so that one may continue to commit oneself to living in it, and motivation to act. This account dissociates the element of faith, that is, the vision of the world without tears, from the concrete form of the ethical response. Faith enables us to 'put our heart into it', but it does not inform us, in any way, what 'it', that is, the ethical response, should be. Against this it could be argued that the hope for a world without tears moves us to act concretely to bring about such a world. That is, the faith vision does provide ethically relevant knowledge concerning what ought be done. It is, admittedly, a peculiar kind of knowledge, and one of the tasks of this paper will be to clarify its nature, and elucidate its connection with the ethical response.

H Richard Niebuhr focused attention explicitly on the

second element, the ethical response to suffering. The response to suffering, he argued, has a crucial place in the ethical life:

> Suffering is the exhibition of the presence in existence of that which is not under our control, or of the intrusion into our self-legislating existence of an activity operating under another law than ours. . . . Yet it is in the response to suffering that many and perhaps all men, individually and in their groups, define themselves, take on character, develop their ethos.[7]

Niebuhr's argument involves a critique of particular models of the ethical life, which is not directly relevant here, but the point he makes concerning the fundamental role of suffering is important and deserves to be pursued further. The questions to be asked would be: what kind of self-definition, character and ethos might be expected to emerge from a christian interpretation of suffering?

Niebuhr also addresses the question of the religious dimension of suffering. In itself, suffering could be interpreted as destructive threat. But through Jesus Christ, his life, death, resurrection and reign in power, we are led to reinterpret life and death, and so also suffering. 'Insofar as that interpretation prevails against its negative we begin to understand all that happens to us and to which we react as occurring in . . . a universal teleology of resurrection rather than a universal teleology of entombment.'[8] Hence, responsibility ultimately affirms: 'God is acting in all actions upon you. So respond to all actions upon you as to his action.'

The following reflections are not proposed as an interpretation or correction of Niebuhr's position, but as an attempt to respond to the problem which has been raised. If this proposition is taken at face value, if God is acting in *all* actions upon us, he must also be acting in those actions which cause us to suffer. Would this mean that God has, at least on those occasions where persons are caused to suffer, temporarily set aside that purpose which faith assures us he has, namely, the overcoming of all suffering? Or could it mean that he is somehow using these sufferings as means to some further purpose, for example retribution and the vindication of the order of justice? Or might we say that God is indeed constantly pursuing his ultimate purposes, namely realising the good, which is what God positively wills, but the pursuing of such purposes in a finite and broken world also produces certain side-effects, including suffering, which God does not will but permits.[9]

Let us take, first of all, the suggestion that in those actions which cause suffering, the purposes of God are somehow set aside. This would not make theological sense, as it would imply, either that there are forces which are not subject to God, or that God is arbitrary. But it may be that the suggestion that God's purposes are somehow set aside in those actions which cause suffering hints at a truth. Could it be that such actions do not express the purposes of God, because they are simply not of God? This possibility needs to be examined further. In contemporary experience, it has been suggested, people interpret suffering as something caused by destructive or abusive power.[10] But Jesus has redefined power, in that what we see in him is not power in this sense, but total self-giving in apparent weakness. The abusive power which causes suffering is thus revealed as not of God, as not real power at all. This is not to suggest that the abusive power which causes suffering is a kind of evil deity in competition with God. Nor does it mean that suffering is not real and is an illusion. It is surely real enough. But the abusive power is not real in the ultimate sense, and the destruction it produces cannot be destructive of the real human self. Christians can thus look on the destructiveness of abusive power and not be terrified. Although this interpretation may seem to incline towards the thesis that christian faith merely supplies reassurance in the face of suffering, there is a valid point here. God is not active within those destructive actions on us which cause suffering, because this is not God's way of acting. We would only come to think that it is, if we make the mistake of transferring our notion of destructive power, from the realms of the finite world and human conflict, where it does apply, to the sphere of God's activity, where it does not. Granted that

151

God is the ultimate source of all power and activity, it does not follow that the ways in which power and activity manifest themselves in our world, are the ways in which God exercises his power and activity. God's ways are indeed not our ways. God's power is not abusive and destructive. From this several conclusions follow. Since this destructive power is not of God, it has no ultimate legitimation and may be challenged by christians. Those who make use of such power may in no way claim any religious sanction for it, since this is simply not the way God acts. The response to such imposed power clearly ought not be mere passive submission, since this would be submitting to a power which is alien to God. This would, of course, raise the question as to whether christians may ever make use of destructive power of any kind, for example in self-defence, war or revolution. If the christian does not oppose destructive power, that power may continue its swathe of devastation, imposing suffering and death on more and more innocents. Merely passive submission is not the christian response; the martyrs themselves were certainly not merely passive, but expressed their opposition to abusive power even in their dying. Further, given that the christian is called to reflect God's eschatological purpose of overcoming suffering, there is an imperative to oppose the agents of abusive suffering. That means that the christian is called to blunt the concrete, historical destructiveness of those who would impose suffering on others. This blunting may be carried out by active, non-violent resistance, or by that kind of forceful resistance which is proportioned to the destructive force of an aggressor. Such a use of force does not set the resister against God's way of acting.[11] But when the use of force goes beyond such proportion, it becomes an attack, an expression of that kind of destructive power which is not of God. The activist in Argueta's novel decides that shedding blood is acceptable, and does not matter, when the cause of the sufferers is at stake. Could a person who retains the christian faith consistently adopt such a position? It clearly does matter to a christian whether he is defending the sufferers from abusive power, or is himself becoming an agent of abusive power.

If one contests the agents of abusive destruction, only to become a similar agent of destruction oneself, one gives the victory to the alien powers which are not of God.

The second proposal must now be examined. Does God cause suffering for the purpose of retribution and the vindication of the order of justice? This interpretation takes its basis in a conception of justice, in which the law requires punishment for transgression. This thesis was, of course, contested in the Book of Job. The inherent fault in such a view is that it takes the model of a juridic order and applies it uncritically and univocally to the relationships between God and humanity. If this interpretation were correct, the appropriate response would be passive acceptance of suffering. If we hold to the juridic model of interpretation, then if we are suffering, we are being punished. If we are being punished we must be guilty. This is, however, precisely the view which Job will not accept. Within the juridic framework, the obverse would also hold; if we acknowledge our guilt and repent, we could expect God to be compelled to withdraw the punishment and restore us to favour. We could then, given this system, control our future by controlling God; his responses would be constrained by our responses. But, even granted that this could be so, it would imply a perverse notion of God and our relations to him. We could only really rely on him to care for our future if we could, in this sense, cause him to do so, or control him. But our hope is of a different kind, founded not on our powers of control but simply on God. It is a hope which cannot be adequately expressed in terms of causal language at all.

If we attempt such a causal account, then we have God causing evil (suffering) but then setting everything right at the end. Thus, God would be seen to cause evil and then engage in a subsequent repair job, or in some way to make compensation, or again to cause evil as a means to a further end (such as vindication of the juridic order). In any of these cases we have what is surely a distorted image of God. Edward Schillebeeckx is strongly critical of any interpretation according to which God wills or causes suffering for some purpose. God, he says, does not will suffering in any sense; suffering is not some kind of instrument in the divine plan.[13] Of particular significance in the present context, is that this critique arises, at least in part, from a perception of its ethical implications. If God is defined equally as the one who gives life, and the one who causes death, this cuts at the root of what Schillebeeckx calls 'the critical and productive force of religion'. Such a definition of God would imply that God is equally and in the same way, engaged in both those actions upon us which liberate from suffering and those which produce suffering. If we then assume that the christian ethic calls for imitating God, this would establish a distorting ambiguity at the very heart of the ethic; it would require and justify at the same time, action to liberate and action to destroy life.

The moral implications of rejecting this kind of interpretation of God's actions are clear. Those who engaged in violent acts, directly producing suffering and death, may not claim religious justification for what they do. Specifically, they cannot claim to be the agents of God's just retribution, because God does not vindicate justice in this fashion.

There remains, however, the 'permission' theory, according to which God directly wills good, but permits evil, including suffering. This notion has an obvious connection with the well-known principle of double-effect by which moral theologians have dealt with those cases where we seek to do good, but where this leads to evil effects. According to the principle such actions may be justified where the act itself is not evil, where we directly intend the good effect, but do not intend the foreseen evil effect, where the evil is not a means to the good, and where there is a proportionate reason. Could we invoke the principle, and apply it to God's mode of acting, to account for suffering in the world? Or is this yet another instance where categories which have validity in the human world are uncritically transposed onto God? One major difficulty here is that principles which bear on human conflicts in the practical order, are taken up to provide a metaphysical 'explanation' for suffering in the divine order. Does this 'explain' anything? Schillebeeckx thinks not. What we seem to have is not an explanation, but rather a restatement of the conviction that evil is evil, and has no ground for its existence in God, and that God wills only good. There is, however, some connection between the principle of the double effect and the religious understanding of how God acts. When this principle insists that we may not directly intend evil, or specifically suffering, it is requiring of us that, even in the midst of conflict in our broken world, we do not identify with those destructive forces which are not of God, but seek always to follow God's pattern of acting, which is directed to good, not evil.

The notion that God causes suffering cannot be sustained. How then are we to account for the connection between human suffering and human fault? If we reject the idea that God causes the former in retribution for the latter, what other explanation might be given? Suffering, or at least some kinds of suffering, are clearly the result of human fault; for example, much suffering from ill-health is caused by culpable neglect and much of the immense suffering brought by war results from culpable choices or omissions. But is suffering itself, in its total range, the result of human fault? If it is not, then we would have to say either that suffering is produced by powers beyond God's control, or that God himself causes it in some way. But christian faith would reject the idea that there are powers outside God's control. And the idea that God causes suffering, at least directly as a means to an end, must also be rejected. It would seem then, that suffering must flow from human agency in some way, and in such a sense be 'punishment' for human fault.

Paul Ricoeur has offered an account of the meaning of punishment which will be helpful at this point. Specifically, he has sought to determine the rational core of the law of punishment.[14] Punishment, he writes, implies suffering, the painful element of punishment, which belongs to the affective order and pertains to the realm of the body.[15] In what Ricoeur calls the myth of punishment, this pain is imposed on the sufferer by force for the expiation of the crime committed. The process of expiation involves the cancellation of the crime by the undergoing of punishment. But there are basic difficulties with this notion, since there is no apparent reason why the punishment should cancel the crime. The idea of punishment as penalty would make sense in the realm of law. In this sphere, free agents bind themselves to performances by contracts. If one refuses to fulfil part of the contract, the other may exact a penalty in 'punishment'. But this cannot be transposed onto God, or onto the relationship of the person to God. Moreover, the scriptural tradition provides other symbols which break down the myth of juridic order and transform it. These are the symbols of the conjugal relationship of God and the people and the 'wrath' of God. Sin, in the conjugal symbol, appears not as violation of right, but as separation of lovers. The wrath of God image may savour of retribution, but what it actually conveys is the tragic reality of separation from God. But God is engaged in overcoming separation, not in causing it. The logic of law and retribution thus gives way to the absurd or foolish logic of superabundance and gift which is realised above all in the gift conferred in the grace of Christ, in the folly of the Cross.

Following on from this, it could be said that the fundamental element is the separation of human persons from the God of love. From this separation, chosen by human agents, derives the brokenness of our world. This condition could be called 'punishment' for human fault, but it arises from the chosen separation, it is not imposed by external force. But this, of course, leaves unanswered the question of the suffering of the innocent. How are we to account for suffering in their case, where there can be no fault? But here we must ask whether, in determining our concrete, historical response to such suffering, we need or even should seek an abstract, metaphysical answer to this question. If God were thought to be causing such suffering, for some purpose, then it would be an intrusion on God's activities for a human person to seek to interfere by removing the suffering. But, as has been shown already, it is a mistake to think of God as causing suffering in this way. Once we understand that God does not cause suffering, that the forces which do cause it are not of God, the way is clear for human intervention. Further, when we understand that God is a God of love whose ultimate goal includes the abolition of suffering, then it is evident that this ought be the concrete, historical goal of christians.

The attempt to explain suffering in the categories of cause or law, in the senses described above, is essentially misguided. It is really a way of trying to make sense of it in an abstract, metaphysical sense. As Schillebeeckx points out, the historical root of such difficulties is to be found in the separation of suffering from the historical circumstances which brought it about, both in the case of Jesus himself and in that of other sufferers. Suffering thus detached became something in itself, a symbol, which theology attempted to systematise.[16] This it did in terms of the notions of cause and law, which as this inquiry has shown play a key role in many forms of distorted interpretations.

The practical response to suffering

Suffering cannot be given an abstract, metaphysical explanation, but it can take on meaning in the practical commitment of persons to overcome suffering. That is to say, it cannot be fitted into a metaphysical scheme, but it can be taken up into a practical project, and within that have a practical meaning. This brings us to a consideration of the educative role of suffering. What kind of practical project might this be? The notion of a practical project suggests external activity, but this would be an incomplete account of the response to which we are called. Herbert Fingarette writes, 'To suffer is to be compelled to endure, undergo, and experience the humbled will, rather than to be able to act and to accomplish one's will.'[17] Suffering then could apear as, '. . . the very holy medium through which God transmits his teaching'. What is involved here is a process of transformation in which the desire to dominate reality and control one's future is abandoned in recognition of one's finitude before God. It is a learning process, in which the person learns painfully that she or he cannot change things by acting, but must undergo. It is, in other words, the learning of patience. Further, as Fingarette shows, the interior humbling of the will is not humiliation. Existence in submission is not degradation. Nor is endurance in suffering mere misery. All these would apply only where the will remained untransformed in an attitude of dominative control and self-assertion.

Nevertheless, some questions remain as to whether this is a complete account. Such humbling would be meaningful, for example, in respect to the kind of suffering echoed in the words of Pascal: suffering as anxiety in the face of the experience of finitude and the threat of nothingness,[18] or suffering brought on by the inescapable cataclysms of nature. But that submission would not be appropriate in the case of calamities which could be averted, or where suffering is caused by malevolent human action. What then, within the christian vision, ought be the response to this kind of suffering?

The experience of suffering evokes a contrast experience in which the negation of human wholeness points to the positive value which is being violated.[19] From this experience emerges a particular kind of knowledge, namely the awareness of the possibility of overcoming the suffering or, in more concrete terms, the possibility of the world without tears of which Mitya dreams. This engenders an ethical demand for action to remove the causes of suffering. Or, in other words, there is a call to solidarity, to sharing the lot of the sufferers, such that one refuses to be reconciled to their condition of suffering. Such a false reconciliation is evidently intolerable in view of the possibility of the true reconciliation of all sufferers which now comes into view. Such a vision of possibilities might indeed be merely a dream, as it was for Mitya. But when the human dream is taken up in the faith vision of God's kingdom of freedom from suffering, it ceases to be merely such. God is now known to be working to achieve his eschatological purposes and to be active in overcoming suffering, an activity which is historically realised in the messianic mission of Jesus. Confronted with this vision, vague longings and tentative grasping at freedom become transformed into real hopes and concrete imperatives. The christian must, like God, be committed to the overcoming of suffering.

But in this commitment and active involvement another

modality of suffering is experienced. In seeking to over-come suffering we experience intensely our finitude and fallibility. We cannot with our human resources, even our most developed technology and planning or our most committed political engagement, overcome all suffering, and even our best plans are marred by our fallibility. The experience of suffering, and above all of death, critically challenges any merely human messianic pretensions.[20] Thus, we return again to the humbling of the will which remains an essential feature of the response to suffering. But this is a humbling, not a paralysis. The imperative to overcome suffering retains its force, and compels us to use our scientific and technical knowledge in this task. That means that we need to have the kind of knowledge the peasant driver sought to communicate to Mitya, for without it we remain locked in the world of dreams.

At the beginning of this paper, two narratives were proposed as interpretations of the experience of suffering. But they were both fictional. There are other narratives of suffering which are only too real and historical. These tell the stories of countless people, who suffered, and for whom there was no historical conquest of their suffering. In might seem that there is no moral significance in such narratives. They may be exemplary tales of human turpi-tude and heroism, but the sufferings of the past are clearly beyond the range of our present responsibility. We cannot do anything about the Holocaust, but we may well feel guilt from some sense of bonding with members of our faith tradition who fostered anti-semitism or in other, more direct ways, contributed to it. Indeed, we may experience a more general guilt in recalling the many stories where humans inflicted suffering on others. There is a clear ethical requirement to seek the causes of such events, locate any which still persist and, as far as possible, set ourselves to remove them so that such things may not occur again. But there is more involved than this. Narratives of suffering convey memories of exper-ienced suffering, which expand the contrast experience, intensifying the awareness of the negation of human wholeness and the urgency of its practical affirmation. The sufferings of those who were lost in the past do not remain

159

meaningless and absurd. We might say that they are, or could have been redemptive, in the sense that they atoned for human fault in some way. But then we would have to deal with the difficulties associated with the legal and metaphysical schemata discussed previously. But as recalled in historical memories, and so as intensifying our contrast experience, they enter into our practical consciousness and become the stimulus to conscience. We must not forget those sufferers of the past, lest their sufferings remain, historically and practically, pointless. Yet precisely in remembering what they lost, we are compelled to look to what can be gained today and in the future. Because we may not let those who suffered in the past slip from our sight, we cannot turn away from those who suffer today. Thus, we are committed to solidarity with all the suffering, in practical commitment to overcome their suffering.[21] Thus, we return to the basic christian perspectives with which we began. In following this commitment we are participating in the action of the redeemer who bore our sufferings, that we might be liberated from them, and who is bringing about the Kingdom where suffering will be no more.

What has been presented here is an account of learning from suffering, within the christian vision. The retributive, educative, redemptive and eschatological perspectives have been examined in terms of their presuppositions and moral implications. What is learned is that some of the ways in which the perspectives might be understood call for critical transformation. The true force of these perspectives needs to be regained, but the full significance of all is to be discovered in commitment to the suffering, in order that their suffering may be overcome.

10. *Alcoholism: A Course in Theology?*

IN 1961, when I was in my final year of Jesuit formation, I
heard one of our American priests speak on the subject
of alcoholism. During his stay in Ireland, he had attended
a meeting of Alcoholics Anonymous at the Country Shop
in Dublin's St Stephen's Green, where AA began its
European life in 1947.

Shortly afterwards, I paid a visit there myself and was
initiated into the world of alcoholism. It was here, too,
that I was first introduced to the writings on alcoholism of
Father Sean O'Riordan, Redemptorist priest and scholar
and, later, friend. His January 1952 *Furrow*[1] report, 'Round
the Reviews' was being distributed by the members as a
ten-page pamphlet, *Drink and Compulsion*. By 1961 the
pamphlet was already in its third printing, and it is still
being reprinted in the 1980s. In the Country Shop that
evening I learnt much about a pastoral problem and about
the communication of pastoral information.

When I started teaching moral theology in 1965 I
continued my own education about alcoholism, learning
most from AA meetings and members, but much also
from the growing literature—medical, legal, social, theological—both in Ireland and from abroad. I was also learning
from the individuals I tried to help with drinking problems. My difficulty then became: how was I to share with
students what I was acquiring? My response has been to
conduct a particular sort of course: Pastoral Theology and
Alcoholism, a course which over the decades has, naturally, changed and developed. The course is an educational
exercise. What I am doing in these pages is sharing ideas
about the pastoral theological education of mainly religious ordinands by me and by others involved in the

course, about alcoholism seen as one very small area within the vast field whose name is the pastoral life of the church.

Alcoholism as a part of pastoral *life*? The phrase is meant to be provocative. Whose life ? I am referring to the lives of the people who are the church, and I am thinking particularly of various units within the church in each country: of a diocese and a parish, a religious community and a school or a factory, a prayer group or a team of social activists. Alcoholism as part of this diocese, this school? Yes; most obviously through individuals who themselves are alcoholics, but through non-alcoholics also. I see the lives of both as pastoral lives: lives in which christians are actually shepherding each other, whether they know it or not, whether they are more or less failing or succeeding, by omissions and performances. That is a broad idea of pastoral life, and the corresponding idea of pastoral theology is equally broad.

The course I conduct is about one of life's problems, the alcoholic problem, the problem for alcoholics and for everyone around them. Part of our living is with alcohol: our own ideas and fears and ignorance and flights from understanding; our good use of alcohol and our bad use and our abstention, good and bad; our contact with others similarly involved.

These pages are about the course rather than about the alcoholic problem, and that is why we are enagaged here in pastoral theology of education, whereas I and the students engage in pastoral theology of alcoholism. The course, obviously, is an educational enterprise and it has a specific matter, an object being studied: problem drinking and alcoholism. It has stated aims, mentioned below. Its success or failure is to be measured by what happens inside its participants, not by any help they may have given, or failed to give, to others who are preventing or treating problem drinkers. My concern here, then, is to discuss, identify, criticise and justify what happens in one small exercise in pastoral theological education.

To some extent the method of the course is its message: increased ability to recognise and help problem drinkers in an ongoing process. It means becoming more sensible to alcohol in self and in others. It means becoming more understanding of alcohol as something which can quench thirst, alleviate hunger, increase weight, relieve pain, slow reactions, swallow fortunes, make millionaires, seal bargains, break homes, finance governments, bankrupt health services, inspire poets, puzzle psychiatrists. Alcohol can be used religiously, joyfully, courageously, wisely, fairly, moderately, or in ways that are foolish, escapist, stupid, hurtful, slavish, addictive; in ways that are excessive and even in ways that are murderous and suicidal. The product of growing in this understanding can be quickly indicated, but the process is more like distilling whiskey, which takes years to mature. Thus, the course is open-ended; whether students are taking their first or subsequent steps in this field, they are encouraged to view the process as one which should continue through the rest of their lives.

The course takes place at the Milltown Institute of Theology and Philosophy in Dublin and it is part of a three/four year theological programme. The students are usually ten to twenty religious clerics approaching ordination, with an occasional married woman or man, a religious sister or brother. So far, only Catholics have been students. Their ages are concentrated between twenty-five and thirty-five, with exceptional persons in their forties or older. Some already have considerable experience with problem drinking, their own or others'; some have a degree of knowledge from books, seminars, videos, television; others have had no education at all on the matter and have been unaware of what relevance their experience contained. The course runs for ten weeks and is scheduled at two periods per week.

My aim in the course is to help all involved to increase their ability both to recognise problem drinkers and to provide non-specialist help—the sort of help reasonably expected of anyone with a pastoral role, clerical or not, male or female. The aim is thus conceived in order to provide a unified focus for the different tasks involved in the course such as reading, attendance at AA meetings, watching a video, visiting relevant organisations, monitoring personal drinking or media coverage, listening to lectures and participating in class discussions.

Reading

In addition to the thirty pages of course notes which I supply, some basic texts are required.[2] The first is John C Ford's 'Alcoholism' in the *New Catholic Encyclopedia*. The second, the sixteen Fact Sheets which now form part of a kit for second-level school programmes, *Living and Choosing, an approach to alcohol education*. The third required text is *one* of the following: Max Glatt, *Alcoholism*; or, Royal College of Psychiatrists, London, *Alcohol and Alcoholism*; or, James S Royce SJ, *Alcohol Problem and Alcoholism*.

Alcohol and Alcoholism, being the shortest of these three, tends to be the favourite, and it is an excellent survey of the state of alcoholism studies for any member of the public interested in the practical question of what is to be done about the problem. The other two are also excellent and the job of choosing between the three is part of the educational task. A score of other books is on display during the course; a little browsing by each student usually leads to the appropriate conviction that a wealth of wisdom has been distilled on this subject and that it is easier to learn with the help of the experts than to rely simply on one's own experiences and insights.

Alcoholics Anonymous

Perhaps the students' most fruitful task during the course is the three visits to the Open AA meeting. These ensure firsthand acquaintance with six to nine people who have been in serious trouble on account of alcohol, whether physical, mental, moral, religious, financial. They also meet people who are now living without alcohol, one day at a time, in, to a greater or lesser extent, contented sobriety.

The stories at Open AA meetings reveal the different types of alcoholic drinking and the problems which are painfully the same. It is never easy to distinguish the characteristics of alcoholic drinking from those of other-wise problem-drinking; from a study of technical litera-ture, a minority of people do grasp the distinctions; the majority of us will never be able to formulate or appreciate all the technical distinctions, but face-to-face meetings with people whose lives have embodied the distinctions can enable us to recognise an alcoholic, not when we meet one, or hear about a particular drinking incident in a person's life, but when we elicit and ponder the full story of a drinker. 'Narrative theology' is the title of one of the many fashionable forms of theology in recent decades: christians in AA seem to have been doing this before it was properly named.

Personally, what encourages me most of all when faced with a drinking alcoholic is hope. Real, live, non-drinking alcoholics renew and strengthen my hope, my conviction that people *are able*, through a power greater than them-selves, to do all the very difficult things required on the road to sobriety, and on the ongoing road of 'contented sobriety', as AA so wisely calls it. Whether they know it or not, my faith tells me that the road they are on is The Way, who is Jesus. From listening to their stories, I know that protracted effort is needed by an alcoholic, even if he or she is one of the few who was able to stop suddenly, never to start again, at the first attempt. I know, too, that concerned neighbours who try to help an alcoholic are faced with a task which stretches over years. For anyone in any sort of pastoral ministry, these thoughts induce a calculating if not a contented sobriety.

Some years ago, Radharc, the Irish religious film-makers, produced *Dying for a Drink*, a forty-minute video, which has been shown several times on television.[3] A common task for the class during the course is to watch this and discuss it, a task made much more profitable when use is made of the eight-page study guide sold with the video. It tells the stories of three people, Joe, Alice and Ita, who come from different age groups and social backgrounds but have one thing in common: from being ordinary drinkers they became, almost without realising it, abusers of alcohol. The strength of the video is the educational significance of its every detail. It is so crammed with messages that one needs to view it several times before one registers all it has to communicate. Serious viewers realise this and thus invite repeated showing.

Organisations

There are many different organisations relevant to alcohol problems. Students are required to choose a few and to visit them—perhaps a library, a hospital, a prison, a brewery, AA's General Service Office, the Irish National Council on Alcoholism, the Pioneer Total Abstinence Association. Each visit increases their knowledge about alcohol, about related problems and the range of people concerned with these problems. My hope as a teacher is that subsequent class-sharing will convince the students that the general pastor's most basic role is to be a cooperator; too often there are rugged individualists who regard their own ministry as that of the one Messiah. The class is meant to discover the multitude and variety of the relevant organisations in the field of alcohol problems and to appreciate the many ways such organisations can be helpful. But it is also my hope that this class experience will lead each student to the more general conviction that other pastoral problems such as unemployment, strikes, family violence, which may present first-time tasks for the student, are already old chores for many other people who have built up much wisdom and established valuable helping networks and concerned patterns of care.

It would be easy for me to decide on two or three of the 'best' projects and to arrange with an organisation to receive a visit from the whole class, or to send someone to talk to the class. I do not do that. Instead I choose to provide the class with an exercise in self-organisation, an exercise which varies significantly from student to student and from year to year. Some students perform many fruitful projects while others fit in very few. I see my role as helping the whole class to recognise what has happened and to offer explanations for the variety. The ultimate aim in this exercise is to appreciate the difference between good intentions and actual performance, to notice that one can have had insights without having made decisions, and that decisions require time for their execution, and that time has to be shared with other courses as well as with the rest of living, of getting and spending, praying and playing. Without self-organisation no one will ever even discover other organisations, much less become skilled in cooperating with them.

The course is about alcohol problems, but it is a course in pastoral theology: in the systematic knowledge of how christians do and can and should care for each other in matters related to alcohol problems. Hence, appreciative knowledge of the role of self-organisation and other-organisation is one of its fundamental objectives; the sort of objective which any pastoral course can have, the sort of knowledge required in every area of pastoral life. The class has the chance to learn through failure. The already gifted self-organisers can learn to interact with those who attempt fewer projects or who don't make a success of them. It is obviously an enormous advantage for any pastor to be able to cooperate effectively with people less *and* more gifted than herself, himself, whether more or less intelligent, industrious, holy.

The students' own behaviour

One of the tasks I suggest to students is to monitor their own behaviour in relation to alcohol, whether they are regular drinkers, occasional drinkers, or abstainers. Some years there is open class discussion about this; every year students are invited to talk about this with me in private at one of the personal interviews which form part of the course. Monitoring their own behaviour is a required part of the course; but discussion, public or private, is totally an option of the students.

It will be noticed that here we have a change in the way theology is done. Just as scientists have discounted the myth of the detached observer, so teachers and students of moral and pastoral theology have come to realise that both teacher and student are changing too if they are really learning anything about human, and christian, behaviour.

In the Catholic tradition of the earlier part of this century, seminarian students of theology learnt the right words about God and about everything in relation to God. Words had meanings. Minds grasped meaning. The student used his head to penetrate the meaning so that he was not stuck with a particular set of words, Hebrew or Greek, Latin or Irish or English, technical or popular. It was hard work and heady work. Achievement was mastery of true teachings, competence in saying sound doctrine. Students were familiar with Denzinger's collection of official teachings which recorded the ultimate sanction: 'If anyone says . . . let him be anathema.' And examination marks, the immediate sanction, were not determined by being charitable or prudent or prayerful or sober, by the degree of one's faith or hope. The task was to bring intellectual skills to bear in order to have the right words about being charitable, prudent or sober.

Nowadays theology has changed. It is still an intellectual exercise, but there is much more recognition of the fact that feelings are important and that they influence what is learnt, what can be learnt—for example, about alcohol. If Judas was present at Cana, I wonder did he feel that a great business opportunity was being wasted? The person fearful of alcohol easily learns about the destructive ways it is used. The person coerced into a youthful 'pledge', to abstain completely from alcoholic beverages either for life or until the age of, say, twenty-one, does not easily learn about the advantages of a free commitment to abstain. Persons at ease with their own moderate drinking may feel that alcohol cannot be destructive and that all problem drinkers have only themselves to blame. By examining their own feelings and monitoring their own behaviour, students gain a better grasp of the complex unity of the human person, the interplay of individual and social forces, the developing relationship of body, mind and soul in each of us.

Right and wrong

Pastoral workers are always at least implicitly guided in their work by convictions about right and wrong behaviour.

In pastoral theology, such convictions need to have been consciously articulated and justified. Hence, in my course there is some direct treatment of the moral questions raised by alcohol. 'Three behaviours with alcoholic beverages pose ethical issues: drinking, drunkenness and alcoholism' says the world-renowned alcoholism scholar, Mark Keller in his article in *The Encyclopedia of Bioethics*.[4] Throughout the course the three issues tend to recur in various texts, in reflections on successive experiences, and in class discussion. In these pages there can be no attempt to synopsise Keller's excellent article, but his triple division will be used to organise some moral points differently presented throughout the course.

Issue one: Is drinking alcoholic beverages wrong in itself? There are christians—among them Irish Catholics—who still think it is, and whose practice is guided by this judgment. But which of us admits to being a manichee? Yet, are we not 'whole in earnest' in our joking about the demon rum and in our cursing of the bottle? And when we face the Cana story of water turned into wine can we not cling to our condemnation of all drinking by lapsing into christological heresies? We could avoid the conclusion that God approves of some human drinking by denying the divinity of Jesus, or the humanity, or the unity of both in him. We might not reach such outright denials, but do we not sometimes recognise in others a bias in this direction, and even glimpse the same tendency in ourselves?

Issue two: Is getting drunk wrong? If so, what precisely is wrong in it? The question uses the term 'drunk' in its popular meaning, the morally normative and negative sense which repentant christians have used for centuries. Not much discussion is required to realise that losing consciousness does not constitute the moral evil. Anaesthesis by alcohol is getting drunk in the physiological sense where the term has no moral meaning. If one locates the moral evil in 'excessive' drinking the new term will shed no light until one indicates ways in which drinking involves 'too much'. If one says that drinking is excessive when it is unreasonable, or irresponsible, or unloving, one has introduced three terms which can be very fruitfully used for basic categories of morally bad human behaviour. They indicate what is common in all sins, whether these be listed as the deadly sins (pride, covetousness) or as violations of the Ten Commandments (murder, adultery), or in any other way. But whatever way the list is made it does not magically distinguish justified from unjustified killing, or losing consciousness.

So one tries to state ways in which drinking is excessive—morally. How much is too much, morally? In these pages, elaborate answers cannot be discussed, but some basic positions can be indicated:

(a) Any amount of alcohol is too much for an alcoholic.

(b) A little amount is often too much for anyone using the roads, whether they are a driver, cyclist or pedestrian; it slows reactions, depresses; it can endanger life, limb, property.

(c) A little amount taken by the tired or the hungry can lessen their sobriety, their self-possession, their ability to control themselves and their activities in the ways in which their sober selves not only demand but are able to achieve.

(d) For those whose drinking is regular and frequent, the 'too much' can in some cases be measured in time: a reasonable amount of time is not left for sleep, for family, for work, for God.

(e) For other drinkers the 'too much' can be measured in money when an unfair amount of their wealth and income is left for food, housing, clothing, recreation, religion, for self, family, world. Obviously, the person who spends too much money on drink tends to be the same as the one spending too much time and offending against sobriety, but that merely indicates that excessive drinking tends to be a complex, multi-dimensional excess.

(f) There are those who drink for wrong reasons, among which escapism may be the commonest; for such people, it could be said that any amount is too much, though the defect is in the motivation rather than in *what* they are doing; they tend to be seeking an unreal world and to be drinking as a way of lying to themselves, about themselves and others and the whole world; one of the tragic results is that they often continue this over months and years until they have moved from psychological to physical dependence on alcohol.

Issue three: Is alcoholic drinking ethically different from getting drunk? If not, it is still a complex psychological, medical, social and pastoral problem. And healing the sick is an evangelical example and task, one of the traditional corporal works of mercy. But if alcoholic drinking is a distinct ethical problem—as almost all the experts now hold—the question of its definition arises.

Problem drinkers have infinite scope for their escapist manoeuvres in debating the many learned definitions of alcoholism. To avoid that trap in these pages, a helpful description may be more appropriate than a definition. John C Ford, SJ was already quoted in 1952 in Sean O'Riordan's *Furrow* article on alcoholism. In 1967 the *New Catholic Encyclopedia* employed Ford to write its article on alcoholism. As recently as November 1986, the *Homiletic and Pastoral Review* carried an article by Ford where the same description is repeated: 'a triple sickness—a sickness of the body, a sickness of the mind, and also a sickness of the soul'.[5] It is a condition in persons, usually in those who have been given to grave excess in the use of alcoholic beverages over a long period of time. Long excess, dependency (what used to be termed 'addiction') and life problems linked to drinking, are the common traits of the majority of alcoholics.

During the course, many moral points about alcoholism are discussed. Some of these are considered here in replying to five 'responsibility' questions. This method will help to emphasise that there are both degrees of responsibility and different things for which a drinker can be responsible.

1. Are Alcoholics to blame for acquiring the condition?

I have met many alcoholics, but none who in my opinion are responsible for *being* alcoholics, for having the condition. A small minority seem to have had the condition from birth: from their first drink, whether at the age of thirteen or thirty or sixty, they could drink only in the way that alcoholics do; one cannot be responsible for one's genetic constitution. The vast majority were not born alcoholics but acquired the condition over a period of years. Very few saw alcoholism as a condition at all, or as something anyone could acquire. Even if they did have a vague and general understanding of the condition, they did not see themselves as acquiring it, and even less did they want to do so. The moral pre-requisites for being responsible for having/acquiring the condition were simply not present. Their concerned and informed neighbours might have continually cried: 'you must see what you are doing to yourself', and resentful victims of their drinking continue to cry aloud: 'they must have known what they were doing'. But the alcoholic didn't see and didn't know. The christian neighbour who finds such a fact hard to swallow may have a faith with too little room for the mystery of sin, original as well as actual.

2. What about the alcoholic's responsibility for the way she or he drinks, for compulsively taking a drink or for drinking excessively even after deliberately taking a drink?

Those types of drinking behaviour are precisely the expressions of the condition called alcoholism; the alcoholic cannot be responsible for those expressions *until* s/he has come to recognise the condition in which s/he is, has come to accept that the condition means an inability to drink normally. Neighbours, again, may find it painfully obvious that an alcoholic will take too much if he goes to the pub, but the condition itself is partly a blindness in the alcoholic and an inability to see that he is somehow different. No one likes to see himself as unable to do what others can do. So, responsibility for alcoholic drinking does not occur until after acceptance of the condition of being an alcoholic. In the language of AA, one must first 'hit bottom'; in christian terms, one must undergo internal conversion.

3. Are alcoholics to blame for what they do while 'under the influence?'

Many drinking alcoholics are frequently burdened with desperate feelings of responsibility for the things they have done while drinking. They have battered their spouses, crashed cars, robbed, lied, injured their employers, their colleagues, their clients, hurt their parents and their children. They weep bitter tears over their long list of wrongs. It would be a mistake to think that none of them was ever responsible in any degree for any such wrongs, but, in my experience anyway, problem drinkers of all sorts and alcoholics in particular tend to exaggerate *afterwards* their responsibility for the bad things done while drinking. Just as they are almost never responsible for becoming alcoholics, so they are *little* responsible for the things done 'under the influence'; and the reason is that they do not beforehand see that they will be thus 'under the influence'. Each time—incredibly to the uninformed observer—the alcoholic believes that s/he will take just the one or two drinks and then stop; they can see that bad consequences follow from taking too much, but they cannot see that on this occasion they will take too much.

Another aspect of this excessive self-blame for the consequences of drinking is that, rather than face the basic problem, the alcoholic applies a displacement mechanism and concentrates instead on resolving to avoid all the rows, dishonesty, ill-health and other bad consequences. The basic problem is the type of drinking within the capacity of an alcoholic; to put the matter even more basically, the problem is not the behaviour of the alcoholic but the sort of person he is, a person with this condition, this sickness or disease.

4. Is there anything for which alcoholics are responsible?

Usually the alcoholic is responsible neither for having or acquiring the condition, nor for much of the disordered type of drinking, nor for the things done 'under the influence'. This view leads to an emphasis on the one thing for which the alcoholic is capable of taking responsibility:

dealing with the condition he or she has. The meaning of 'dealing with' has already emerged. It is a process, not a single act. It is the process of understanding (adequately, which need not mean technically) what alcoholism is, of understanding what it would mean to say: 'I am an alcoholic', of deciding to admit to being an alcoholic, of deciding to abstain from all alcohol, one day at a time, with the help of a Power greater than self; of being convinced that this is the absolutely first step necessary on The Way to Life, no matter what other steps are also needed, and no matter what deep personal problems may have triggered the alcoholism.

Dealing with alcoholism will always involve a personal process of that sort. For members of Alcoholics Anonymous, the process is divided into their Twelve Steps which demand consistent and ever-renewed commitment: an admission to 'being powerless over alcohol', a turning over to God of 'our will and our lives', confessing to God and to another human being 'the exact nature of our wrongs', willingness 'to make amends', 'prayer', carrying 'the message to others'. It would be easy enough, surely, to identify the same process, differently expressed, in non-AA alcoholics who reach lives of contented sobriety. Certainly that holds for Matt Talbot, who turned from drink to God in 1884.[6] His expressions of penitence were different, and his message to others was by example rather than by words; but the whole process was basically the same.

5. What about the 'converted' alcoholic's responsibility for starting to drink again?

My estimate is that this sort of alcoholic will often be responsible *for the cause* of the renewed drinking but not responsible for the actual drinking. The cause is likely to be the omission of some elements of the programme which until then had enabled the weeks and months of abstaining.

In this section on responsibilities, the present pages say nothing about the many persons and groups who *have* responsibilities, nor about the many alcohol-related things for which we all share responsibility: public attitudes to drink, familial and school education, legislation, the way alcohol is produced, promoted and sold, as well as the ways it is actually consumed, in society nowadays, by the variously distinct groups of people who are not (yet) alcoholics. One would need to address almost all of those issues and others if one were to articulate a comprehensive view on the prevention of alcoholism. But this section has been limited to a consideration of individual responsibilities with regard to alcoholism itself. In my opinion, it makes perfect sense to call alcoholism a disease. That is a negative term; it leaves room for all the distinctions just outlined, even if estimates differ as to the proportion of people falling into the various degrees of the not-responsible side of each distinction.

Helping problem drinkers: treatment and prevention

What precise help can be offered to problem drinkers? By whom? In what way is any of that part of any christian's pastoral life and of my own particular pastoral role? In the course, such vast questions are briefly considered under the headings of treatment and prevention.

We need to recall that we are asking what treatment can be offered by pastors, whether these be spouses or parents, neighbours or teachers, religious or priests, when confronted with a person thought to have a problem with alcohol or even with someone clearly recognised to be an alcoholic. As pastors we are not specialists: in detoxification, in behaviour therapy, in chemotherapy, in any of the myriad forms of psychotherapy, individual or group; we are not in the police force nor an employment agency; our role is not defined as housing the homeless, feeding the hungry, lending to the penniless, nor even as recruiting members for Alcoholics Anonymous or the Pioneer Total Abstinence Association. Yet, it is seldom that a problem drinker is helped without the intervention of several such specialists. Thus, I view the general pastoral role as requiring first-hand knowledge as to what specialist help is available, here and now. The 'here' is the very local district where the problem drinker is; knowledge of all the services available in some central agency is of no help in moving the person from where s/he actually is. And the 'now' has to be really up-to-date to be effective.

Frequently the pastor is confronted, not with the persons recognised as having a problem with alcohol, but with their concerned 'partners': the spouse or parent or child, the colleague at work, the next-door neighbour. This presents the pastor with a radically different task, which is hard enough to recognise and even harder to perform. It is so easy to accept the caller's presentation of the problem and to enlarge on the many things which the drinker needs to do, to be, to become. But here the pastor's job is different; it is to deal with the needs of the concerned partner, the persons actually present. What are *they* to do? What are their feelings? What have they been doing, and leaving undone? What illusions have they, what resentments, what misunderstandings, what strengths, what resources? In their actual situation what in fact can they do? Typically they present the other person as their problem and the pastor's first objective has to be to help them accept themselves as problem people with needs which they *can* meet because they have been willing enough to seek help, even though they may have mistakenly assumed that the help should be directed completely towards the drinker.

The inter-personal pastoral role is the first to come to mind when we think about helping problem drinkers. But wise pastors devote as much time and energy to more remote ways of helping. These are often felt to be rather impersonal. But if there is no water available now, it is not impersonal to employ water diviners and to sink wells so that next year's caller can be offered a cup of water. Is it not tragic when the immediately possible is the horizon of our pastoral enterprises? That reduces pastoral care to emergency services. Of course these will always be needed; and some pastors will rightly devote all their energies to these opportunities for face-to-face caring. It is only tragic if all of us do that.

In the present context of discussing treatment, we need to identify, to appreciate, to perform the non-immediate tasks in this pastoral field. No adequate list could be offered, but a few examples will illustrate the point. To ensure that one's own locality has active groups of AA and Al Anon, the support group for families and others closely involved, is a long term and continuous task. To ensure that the medical services in the district—public and private, nurses and doctors—are informed about alcohol problems and willing to help professionally: that is an enormous task which could involve contributing to curriculum revision in medical schools, to refresher courses for civil servants, to reform of the tax system, to changing the priorities of politicians and legislators. In these ways, one could be just as actively involved in providing treatment for problem drinkers as the pastor who is more directly caring for people.

In Dublin, to use the example best known to me, there have been excellent developments over the past thirty years; some of them local, others national. When Sean O'Riordan first wrote on alcoholism in *The Furrow*, the Irish National Council on Alcoholism did not exist; the St John of God Brothers had long been treating alcoholics but they had not then established the specialised Pampuri unit in their hospital in Stillorgan; the Alcohol Project Group had not begun at Eblana in Dun Laoghaire, nor the Counselling Service at Stanhope Steet, nor the Rutland Centre, nor the Alcoholic Rehabilitation Centre, which was established by the Irish trade union movement in 1980. When Jonathan Swift died in 1745 he left around £11,000 'To build a House for Fools and Mad'; since its two hundredth birthday St Patrick's Hospital has developed magnificently in buildings as well as in methods of residential and outpatient treatment of alcoholics and its example has been followed by other private and public hospitals. To have created such centres, and to maintain them, is to perform a task of pastoral treatment; unfortunately, the need for even more such creations is almost as big as ever. Perhaps the most encouraging development has been the establishment of an Alcoholism Policy and Programme in a number of Irish organisations. The Electricity Supply Board led the way in 1976, and other businesses have followed the good example. Dioceses and religious provinces have been urged to do the same.[7] In Britain, the Social Welfare Committee of the Bishops' Conference of England and Wales produced a report through its working party entitled 'The Catholic Approach to Alcohol Abuse'.[8]

Positive people, including pastors, dislike being preventors. Perhaps two of the reasons for this are worth pondering. Successful prevention is negative. The prevented do not become victims of avarice or AIDS or alcoholism. The prevention is unreasonable unless something bad is being prevented. Positive people are perhaps too reluctant to commit themselves to plain judgments about bad things; of course they do not go round saying that cancer is harmless; they simply avoid thinking about it. We must commit ourselves to the position that alcoholism is, while not a sin, something that is bad and disordered, a disease, and to the identification of what is bad in it. Then our negative preventing will be both easier and more reasonable.

A second reason for disliking preventive roles may be more powerful: we shy away from coercion and we tend to associate prevention with coercion. Thus, the medical professions try to minimise the 'preventive detention' of the insane; the legal professions are rarely happy with an internment system aimed at forestalling crime, whereas they can tolerate at least the principle of coercion after crimes have occurred.

We may overcome our reluctance to be negative through prevention if we reflect on the huge and varied horrors associated with alcoholism which are clearly worth preventing, if possible. So what is possible, reasonably possible? Is any coercion part of the reasonably possible, the lovingly possible? Who should do what coercing of whom? Let us approach the question from a different angle. The power of the law over us all is fundamentally in the reasonableness of its guidance and demands, not in the pain of its penalties, not in its coercive sanctions. The fact that our use of the road springs from our own free decisions does not exclude the fact that these decisions have been influenced—and continue to be—by factors external to us: by education, at home, at school, throughout life by the many agencies continually addressing us; by public opinion, by legal prescriptions, by the threat of legal sanctions. While we know that there are coercive laws about pedestrian crossings and about lights on bicycles and alcohol in drivers, we may be rarely conscious of them, yet their influence on occasions may have saved us when we were tempted to act in an irresponsible way.

I am labouring a very general point, because I fear we too often neglect it in our pastoral practice: we are social and incarnate beings and only as such can we behave reasonably, responsibly, lovingly. Whether we like it or not, we are influenced by those around us; in fact, as christians, we know that each of us is a member of one body, that 'God did not create man for life in isolation, but for the formation of social unity. . . . '[9] Thus, too, we are educators by the way we live. In our uncertainties, as in our respect for the freedom of others, we cannot avoid some share in the role of being legislators for others.

We are, however, often afraid of misleading or of manipulating others, especially those who are weaker in age or in power or in status. Our fears can be helpful when they lead us to weigh factors that we would otherwise overlook. But the fears can be harmful if they lead us to conclude that it is possible for us to be neutral: to leave our children without influence on, for example, their views on the existence of God or their convictions about addictive drugs or their behaviour with alcohol. We may say 'We'll let them decide for themselves when they grow up.' But they will do that anyway, and they ought to. What we probably mean is that we do not want to influence them, one way or another, and that is to want the impossible. No one decides without influence from others. And if we decide to say nothing, our silence will communicate something; probably that we do not care for them; perhaps that we are afraid of the topic, or that we realise our own behaviour fails to match our own standards; whatever we do, we'll be influencing others.

179

Conclusion

In these pages I have been discussing a course in theology. Topics like education and alcoholism are the focus for courses in many different disciplines such as medicine, law, psychology, sociology, history, literature as well as philosophy and theology. Each discipline deals with the same matter, but from a different viewpoint.

I conceive this theological course as an exercise in faith by teacher and students: we are seeking, first, a deeper understanding of God's work in the world, of how the Father, by the power of the Spirit, through the incarnation, death and resurrection of the Son, draws each person and all peoples to himself—in particular how God draws to himself both drinker and abstainer, both alcoholic and pastor. But we are also seeking to develop our capacities for co-operating with God's work in the world—in particular his work in each of us as we face and admit and try to resolve the problems of alcohol in ourselves and in our neighbours. Throughout the course I make many brief remarks which remind students that the course is theological. In these pages such remarks would have been either brief and obscure or long and distracting; in the course itself they are, I believe, quite effective, because they are spread over many weeks, they are addressed to people immersed in other theological courses and pastoral experiences, and when necessary they are made the centre of further individual or group study and discussion. I already mentioned that over the decades the course has changed, and I expect it will go on changing. My hope is that it will always be experienced as theological and as part of the process of growth into the fullness of Christ.

11. *Structural Sin: A New Category in Moral Theology?*

THIS paper sets out to analyse the concept of 'structural sin' from two points of view. Firstly, it examines the recent origins of this theologico-moral category in theological reflection and in declarations of the ecclesiastical magisterium, and secondly it attempts a personal systematic presentation of the subject.

In this way I hope to make a contribution to the clarification and development of some insights in moral theology which have emerged in the church since Vatican II, intuitions shared by those Catholic moral theologians who initiated and oriented the renewal of Catholic moral theology in the second half of the present century. Among these moralists should be reckoned Father Sean O'Riordan who, in addition to making other special contributions in the field of moral and pastoral theology, has highlighted the social and communitarian dimension of christian moral life.[1]

Recent origins in the concept of social sin

In recent centuries there has been a strongly individualistic tone in western moral thinking in both christian and non-christian circles. For a great variety of reasons moral life and ethical discussion underwent a process of individualisation. The discovery of the notion of individual freedom, the emergence of liberal ideologies and the predominance of forms of social life marked by the capitalist ideal are other factors which help explain the widespread and profound process of the individualisation of moral conscience.

Nor was Catholic moral theology in this period immune from the same markedly individualistic tone, especially that destined for the use of confessors. Vatican II alludes to this situation when it urges the church to advance beyond a merely individualistic ethic: 'Profound and rapid changes make it particularly urgent that no one, ignoring the trend of events or drugged by laziness, content himself with a merely individualistic ethic' (*Gaudium et Spes* no 30).

This concept of morality played a decisive role in the way in which the reality of sin was formulated in theory and lived out in practice. Both the living reality and the concept of culpability were presented mainly in individualistic terms, both at the theoretical and at the practical level.[2]

In opposition to this a marked emphasis on deprivatising moral thinking has become widespread in recent decades. This movement should be seen as part of a wider trend which, in the whole of human and christian life, has shifted the accent from the individualistic (existentialist, privatised) interpretation of human and christian existence to a deprivatised (public, political) one.

The theme of sin, once a privileged point from which to observe the individualistic orientation of moral theology, is now a decisive aspect of a deprivatised morality. There are numerous signs of a new ethical sensitivity towards moral evil which indicate a shift in the understanding of human and christian culpability from the closed framework of individualisation towards the more open horizons of socialisation, or social structures. In this new climate a type of theologico-moral reflection has emerged which uses renewed categories of thought to incorporate the social and communitarian dimension of sin. Even though these new perspectives do not all use the term structural sin, they nevertheless open up horizons which in one way or another contextualise this new category of theologico-moral thought. I will indicate as I go along the theologico-moral perspectives which have made a decisive contribution to our understanding of social and moral culpability.

Vatican II: the ecclesial dimension of sin and its dehumanising character

Taking its point of departure from the newer developments in ecclesiology which had preceded its work, Vatican II gave a decisive communitarian expression to the notion and reality of sin.[3] The Council recognises the presence of sinners within the bosom of the church, declaring her to be at once holy yet in need of purification (*Lumen Gentium* no 8). In vigorous terms, it notes how sin 'wounds the Church' (ibid no 11).

Likewise, the Council insisted on the 'dehumanising' character of sin. The Pastoral Constitution, *Gaudium et Spes* no 13, sets forth the consequences of sin for the human person in these terms: sin creates within the person a tendency towards evil and engulfs him in many evils; it turns him away from his ultimate end, it disrupts his inner harmony, creating division and struggle in his heart; it is stronger than the person and enslaves him, diminishing and blocking the path to fulfilment. The Council states that sin has disastrous consequences for society also, and devotes a long paragraph of *Gaudium et Spes* (no 37) to pointing up the 'deformation of human activity by sin'.

The biblico-theological category of 'the sin of the world'

Stress on the biblico-theological category of 'the sin of the world' has played an important part in making moral theology aware of the social and communitarian aspect of culpability. This category highlights in a particular way the situation of sin in which humanity finds itself owing to the solidarity which exists between all the sins of history.

Everyone is born into a world where 'besides the solidarity of salvation there is also present a solidarity of condemnation. Both are found in the same field, like darnel in wheat fields. Man lives in a world of sin, that is, in a family, in a culture, in a society where the solidarity of condemnation is strong and powerful, even if in varying proportions.'[4]

Piet Schoonenberg interprets this solidarity in sin in terms of the concept of situation, or more precisely, being situated.[5] As persons we are rational beings. The freedom of one person has an influence on the freedom of others. This influence can even have a delayed effect in space or time. Today's sin can not only degrade others by its seductive power: it can have a similar influence on posterity.

This solidarity is something more than the sum of individual sins without any intrinsic relationship between them. But neither is it simply a question of the guilt of one person passing on to someone else, for this would run clean contrary to the spirit of personal responsibility. Rather, over and above the sins of individual persons, there must be a bond of connection which unites the sins of one person with those of others.

All the influences which pass from one free person to another free person—influences that respect the freedom of the latter while making an appeal to it—can be summed up in the concept and term of situation. My free action always places the other in a situation which incites him to good or evil, which offers him a support or deprives him of it, which presents him with values and norms or deprives him of these. The situation is the bond which unites one free decision with another in such a way that history can be defined as the interchange of decisions and situations.

However, what is of concern here is not the situation but the fact that the person is situated. What is ultimately of concern, as a component of the sin of the world, is not the link between personal sins but the fact that the person himself is influenced. The sin of the world, like the sinful history of a community, is a reality within the person himself. The fact of being situated in sin is what must be added to individual sins if one is to speak rightly of the sin of the world.

The political interpretation of sin

According to the presuppositions of what is known as 'political theology' sin must be conceived fundamentally in terms of social mediation. In face of the temptation to individualism which springs from existentialist-type theories, political theology sees its goal as the recovery of the social dimension of personal decisions. With such presuppositions in mind, it would not be wrong to speak of 'sin interpreted politically'.[6] According to Dorothee Soelle the crucial difference between the various concepts of sin is to be found in whether they accept or reject this 'political' interpretation of culpability.

Traditionally, our understanding of sin has been dominated by an apolitical interpretation which has led to an individualistic understanding of culpability. However, the greater sinfulness resides in the real contradictions of society. The privatisation of conscience, on the other hand, leads to an absence of effort in transforming unjust situations, and to a feeling of impotence in face of moral evil. If the starting point is an apolitical understanding of sin, it will be impossible either to formulate a critique of society or to bring about a change in unjust structures. As political theology sees it, 'the sinner is the one who collaborates with structurally-established injustice, most often anonymously so.'[7] The religious dimension of sin and responsibility can be retained within this vision provided the relationship with God is interpreted in terms of its human mediation.

The theology of liberation

Both theologians and the episcopal magisterium of Latin America have given particular prominence to the category of structural sin. Here I focus on the theology of liberation, holding over the consideration of the Latin-American episcopal magisterium for my next point.

The theology of liberation emphasises the importance of christian salvation understood and brought to fruition as integral liberation. It can be said that this understanding of salvation is one of the pillars on which the theological thrust of the theology of liberation rests. Salvation/liberation is the positive aspect of a reality which, unfortunately, also has a negative side, namely non-salvation. The theme of sin receives full attention within the framework of liberation theology: 'The Latin-American theology of

185

liberation, unlike other currents of theology, regards sin as a central and urgent priority.'[8]

Although liberation theology in no way overlooks the personal dimension of sin, both in reference to God or in relation to the neighbour, it places the accent mainly on the social and structural aspect of culpability. If salvation is understood as integral liberation, it would be difficult to think of any sin which did not have dimensions of solidarity. As liberation theology sees it, sin is the root and source of every oppression, injustice and discrimination and is fundamentally incarnate in every class of injustice, servitude and oppression.

The theology of liberation offers useful theological frameworks for regarding sin from the perspective of historical solidarity. Christianity understood as the gospel of integral liberation finds its starting point precisely in the theological insight that there is a 'mystery of iniquity' at work in human history. From the contrast between the painful experience of slavery and the proclamation of the gospel of liberation in the Risen Christ there arises the imperative need to denounce sin in all its forms and in particular social and structural sin.

Liberation theology's contributions on the subjects of structural sin are of great value, particularly since they are expressed in lively and stimulating terms. Latin-American theologians prepared the ground for, supported and developed the positions taken up by the episcopal magisterium (Medellín and Puebla) on the structural and social dimension of sin. Studies such as these offer abundant material for the construction of the theologico-moral category of structural sin.

From among the contributions that might be cited, I chose an early one from EF Pironio which outlines a number of aspects of the situation of sin:

> Situations which depend on the unjust attitudes, more or less conscious, of other people. Unjust attitudes which give rise to a state of oppression and dependency. Excessive accumulation of material goods, which God has created for the service of all, with consequent misery for the majority in the form of

hunger, nakedness, sickness, unemployment, home-lessness. The cornering of decision-making power by a few, and the consequent lack of participation by the majority. Subhuman living conditions which make access to the benefits of civilisation and culture impossible for many. The self-interest of a few which holds back unjustly the integral development of the many.

All of this constitutes an oppressive state of dependency, at the level of peoples, classes or individuals, and prevents the full exercise of freedom. Economic, social, political or cultural dependency, which prevents an individual or a people from ever realising themselves in their own originality.

Here sin consists in the injustice of those who by reason of selfishness, evasion or lack of sensitivity, create or culpably maintain structures which oppress human dignity. They create a state of 'institutionalised violence' which easily provokes 'the explosive temptations of despair' (Paul VI). All these things destroy, block or disfigure the image of God in the human person. They attack God (and this is what sin is) in attacking his handiwork. They make personal freedom difficult and are a threat to peace.[9]

Gustavo Gutièrrez approaches the reality of sin from the vantage-point of the integral salvation brought by Christ the liberator.[10] In this perspective sin appears as 'a social, historical fact, an absence of brotherhood and love in relationships among men, and by consequence an interior personal rupture'. Such an approach reveals in the clearest way 'the collective dimensions of sin'.

For Gutièrrez sin 'is evident in oppressive structures, in the exploitation of man by man, in the domination and slavery of peoples, races and social classes'. In this way, the radical iniquity of sin is exposed. 'Sin shows itself as fundamental alienation, as the root of a situation of injustice and exploitation.' The partial alienations of concrete sinful situations are evidence of the radical alienation of human history, an alienation which cries out for the radical liberation that Christ brings. 'Only by participating

187

in the historical process of liberation will it be possible to show the fundamental alienation present in every partial alienation.'

Latin-American Bishops at Medellín and Puebla

At the 1968 Medellín Conference the historical reality of Latin America was interpreted as a 'situation of sin'. In various passages the documents refer to the social dimension of sin, rising above the biased tendency to give an individualistic or spiritualistic interpretation of culpability. Sin becomes crystallised in 'unjust structures', in 'a situation of injustice', in 'institutionalised violence'. For this reason conversion, besides being a personal transformation demands also a change in social structures. These are some of the more significant texts of the Medellín Documents:

> Lack of solidarity leads, at the personal and social level, to the commission of real sins, the crystallisation of which become evident in the unjust structures which characterise the situation in Latin America (I.1).
> When we speak of a situation of injustice we refer to those realities which embody a situation of sin (II.1).
> In many areas, Latin America is faced with a situation of injustice which can be described as institutionalised violence (II.2).

Even if these Medellín texts 'were not quite the first of their kind, they are the best known for their prophetic power and dynamic effect. Moreover, in spite of the fears and misgivings which these texts aroused in certain quarters in whose interest it was to minimise themes such as these, the Latin-American episcopate continued to use, and to deepen and sharpen, the notion of social sin as a necessary and appropriate one for Latin America. A complete study still remains to be done of the use and significance of the expression "situation of sin", both in theological reflection and in the magisterium of Latin America.'

The meeting of the Latin-American Episcopal Conference held at Puebla in 1979 provided the setting for the statement of John Paul II on the 'situation of sin'. In his homily at the sanctuary of Our Lady of Zapopan in Mexico he declared: 'She [the Virgin Mary] enables us to rise above the multiple 'structures of sin' in which our personal, familial and social life is caught up.' The Puebla conference, building on this directive of John Paul II and going forward in the spirit of Medellín, produced a document which contains important references to the social and structural dimension of sin. One meets expressions such as 'situation of social sin', 'personal and social sin', 'structures of sin in personal and social life', 'systems marked by sin'. These and similar expressions are a landmark in the theological interpretation of social and structural injustice. 'It is not surprising, on the basis of texts like these from the episcopal magisterium of Latin America since Puebla, that the theme of social sin or the structural dimension of sin has been acquiring full citizenship in the world of moral theology.'[11]

Recent statements of the ecclesiastical magisterium

A full understanding of the *status quaestionis* of the social and structural nature of sin in moral theology must take account of recent doctrinal orientations from the church's magisterium on the subject. I refer in particular to the direct and explicit orientations which are contained in three significant statements:

There is an abundance of references to the theme in the preparatory documents, in the synodal proceedings and in the concluding statements of the Synod of Bishops, 1983. It was not directly referred to in the preparatory document, the *Lineamenta*, but in the second document, the *Instrumentum Laboris*, there was one explicit reference which indicated Puebla no 28 as its direct source:

The inclination to evil which has been present since original sin and which is enhanced by actual sins, exercises an influence on social structures themselves which in a certain manner are marked by human sin. There is a question of an objective situation of a social,

189

political, economic and cultural character which is contrary to the Gospel. The human person must bear the responsibility for this since it has its origin in human free-will, either of individuals or of a group. In this sense one can rightly speak of social sin, which some call 'structural sin'.[12]

Allusions to the theme in the course of the Synod were frequent. The official relator, Cardinal Martini, for example, referred to no 281 of *Puebla* and to the text cited in the *Documentum Laboris* (22). In the closing address John Paul II referred to 'structural sin', giving it an 'analogous significance'. 'One can and one must speak in an analogous sense of social sin or of "structural sin" since sin, properly speaking, is the act of a person.'[13] The expression 'structural sin' does not, however, appear in the Post-Synodal Apostolic Exhortation *Reconciliatio et Paenitentia* though it does treat of social sin extensively and vigorously (par 16). The Exhortation has two main concerns: on the one hand, to underline clearly the 'personal' character of sin over against Marxist or determinist theories and on the other, to spell out clearly the 'social repercussions' of sin. While it warmly upholds each of these assertions separately it does not appear to achieve a clear formulation of the synthesis between them.

In the concluding part of its treatment of sin as the 'source of division and oppression', the Instruction *Christian Freedom and Liberation* refers to the 'creation of structures of exploitation and servitude' by sin:

> Having made himself his own centre, sinful man seeks to assert himself to satisfy his desire for power and pleasure, scorning other people whom he unjustly despoils and treats as objects or instruments. In this way he makes his own contribution to the creation of those very structures of exploitation and servitude which he claims to condemn (no 42).

Proposal for a systematic presentation

The theological perspectives noted above offer valuable insights in moving towards a systematic presentation of the notion and significance of 'structural sin' in moral theology. Notwithstanding the studies of the term that have already appeared,[14] a systematic presentation of it is still lacking.

In this second part of my paper I propose to analyse the key-point of the systematic exposition of structural culpability: in what measure can we speak of 'structural sin' as a theologico-moral category? In order to answer this question it is necessary to indicate, as a point of departure, the proper 'location' of sin as well as the typological forms in which its social dimension is manifested. Proceeding from there we can grasp the accuracy of the category of theologico-moral culpability as applied to 'structural sin'.

The personal world: the proper 'location' of culpability

Sin springs from the person and refers back to the person. 'Sin is always to be found in the interior of the person, who in virtue of his human freedom, is capable of rejecting love and replacing it with injustice. That is to say, he is capable of rejecting God. Fundamentally, it is always the human person who sins.'[15]

John Paul II forcefully underlines the personal condition of every sin: 'Sin, in the proper sense, is always a *personal act*, since it is an act of freedom on the part of an individual person, and not properly of a group or community' (*Reconciliatio et Paenitentia* no 16). Consequently the element of personal responsibility cannot be diluted by attributing the origin of moral evil 'not to the moral conscience of a person' but to 'some vague entity or anonymous collectivity such as the situation, the system, society, structures or institutions' (ibid).

It would be incorrect, therefore, to speak of structural sin without referring it back to the person. If this bond with the personal world is broken, then structural sin does not belong within the category of culpability which is one that demands personal responsibility. On the contrary, it would be a concrete expression of faith in historic determinism or materialistic structuralism.

The culpability of structures consists in 'the accumulation and concentration of many *personal sins* ... of

191

those who cause or support evil or who exploit it; of those who could do something to eliminate or at least limit certain social evils but who fail to do so out of laziness, fear of the conspiracy of silence, through secret complicity or indifference . . . who side-step the effort and sacrifice required [to change the world] producing specious reasons of a higher order. The real responsibility, then, lies with individuals' (*Reconciliatio et Paenitentia*, no 16).

In the light of what has been said above, we can understand John Paul's affirmation that the term 'structural sin' has an 'analogous significance'. Properly speaking, only that can be considered sin which proceeds from personal responsibility. The evil of structures constitutes authentic sin in so far as it participates in personal responsibility. There is no opposition between 'personal' and 'structural'. Personal is the opposite of deterministic. Structure, although it does not totally encompass the area of personal responsibility, is an important aspect of it in which it comes to concrete expression.

The typological forms of personal culpability in terms of their social dimension

Human culpability is a complex reality which is made concrete and manifests itself in many ways. To capture this rich complexity, moral theology has introduced many distinctions into its analysis of the concept of sin. Here I limit myself to the framework of typological forms within which culpability, in terms of its social dimension, becomes a reality. In terms of the greater or less reality of its social dimension, sin can be classified according to the typological forms set out in the following schema.

Sin in its social dimension:

— at the *subjective* level can be either individual or collective;

— at the *objective* level can be intra-individual (disvalues of the individual person), inter-individual (disvalues of the relationship between persons), social (social disvalues) or structural (disvalues of a given structure of living).

With this schema in mind, the social dimension of sin can be described in five successive categories going from less to greater intensity: 1. the social repercussions of every sin; 2. collective sin; 3. inter-individual sin; 4. social sin; 5. structural sin.

The social repercussions of every sin, both individual and intra-individual

Every sin has social repercussions at both the objective and subjective levels. These repercussions occur through the influences which such sinful actions exercise on the collective conscience, in so far as this is deformed in its criteria, in its false prejudices etc. In a certain measure we all share in the culpability of other people—scandal and cooperation being two particular forms of such participation.

When the social and ecclesial dimension of sin, both one's own and that of others, is viewed at the subjective level, there emerges a view of moral responsibility which integrates the individual aspect of sin with the communitarian aspect of it. There exists a solidarity of all persons in the moral evil done by each one of them. This sharing of responsibility in regard to the social and ecclesial dimension of every sin is something that the christian conscience today is fully aware of.

In *Reconciliatio et Paenitentia* no 16, the social and ecclesial repercussions of sin are given clear expressions:

> To speak of social sin means in the first place to recognise that, by virtue of human solidarity which is mysterious and intangible as it is real and concrete, each individual's sin in some way affects others. This is the other aspect of that solidarity which in the religious is developed in the profound and magnificent mystery of the *Communion of Saints*, thanks to which it has been possible to say that 'every soul that rises above itself raises the world'. To this *law of ascent* there unfortunately corresponds the *law of descent*. Consequently one can speak of a *communion of sin*, whereby a soul that lowers itself through sin drags down with itself the Church and, in some way, the whole world.

193

Collective sin

The objective expression of collective sin can be inter-individual, social or structural. Collective responsibility means responsibility as exercised and lived out in a human group. There is collective sin when the sin is attributable not to the personal action of an individual but to the responsibility of a group. It is to this form of sin that Vatican II refers when it affirms: 'When the order of values is overturned and bad is mixed with good, individuals and groups pay heed solely to their own interests and forget those of others' (*Gaudium et Spes* no 37). Collective sin is not simply the sum or juxtaposition of individual sins. It is an evil entity in itself, a dynamic unity founded on a convergence of forces and wills towards a common moral disvalue.

The following positive definition of collective sin can be accepted:

> It is a conjunction of the related sins of the members of a community, that is to say, a coming together of personal acts referred to a common evil instead of being referred to a common good. The disorder of collective sin springs from the disharmony of the action accomplished in common with the just law of the community and, consequently, with the eternal law from which every just law derives. In the full and formal sense of the word, collective sin is organised sin — the sin, for example of a legislative assembly or of an electoral body in its entirety. Collective sin is in this case a sin in the formal sense of the word since it is a responsible human act, just like every personal sin. However, it furthermore embodies a relationship to collective evil. It is what we might call a *relational sin* which constitutes a *certain order in disorder*.[16]

Inter-individual sin and social sin

Here subjective responsibility can be both individual and collective. These two forms of sin exist when human culpability is concretely expressed in disvalues which belong in the world of human relationships. Inter-individual sin focuses more on the interhuman relationship as such, while social sin adds to the interhuman relationship the factor of social mediation. John Paul II considers both these forms of sin under the heading of 'social sin' in the second meaning he gives to the term 'social' in *Reconciliatio et Paenitentia* no 16:

> Some sins by their very nature constitute a direct attack on one's neighbour or, more exactly, in the language of the Gospel, against one's brother and sister. They are an offence against God because they are offences against the neighbour. These sins are usually called social sins; and this is the second meaning of the term. In this sense, social sin is sin against the love of neighbour, which, in the law of Christ, is all the more serious in that it involves the second Commandment which is 'like unto the first'.

Structural sin

Structural culpability is that which comes into being in the area of human structures. Structural sin can also be called 'a situation of sin'. Structural sin should not be thought of as a projection of subjective responsibility on to structures. The reason is obvious: 'A situation—and likewise an institution, a structure, a society itself—is not in itself the subject of moral acts' (*Reconciliatio et Paenitentia* no 16). Neither should it be understood as an affirmation of historical determinism or as a mere succession of material conditions (Marxist structuralism). On the contrary, structural culpability is a concrete objective expression of personal wickedness. It flows from personal responsibility while at the same time having its location in human structures.

In order to examine the concept of structural sin more exactly, a precise definition of what is meant by structure is necessary. The Congregation for the Doctrine of the Faith defines structures as:

> the combination of institutions and practical devices which people find already existing or which they create, on the national and international level, and

195

which orientate or organise economic, social and political life. While being necessary in themselves, they often tend to become fixed and crystallised as mechanisms relatively independent of the human will, thereby paralysing or distorting social development and generating injustice. However, they always depend on human responsibility, which can alter them, and not on an alleged historical determinism.[17]

This idea of structure is arrived at by analysing human reality as a synthesis of intimacy and openness—what Ortega y Gasset called 'the I and my circumstance' or 'absorption in self and otherness'. Circumstance or otherness constitutes the 'incline' of the human person, which in turn becomes the 'social environment'. The social environment has been analysed from different perspectives as the reality which configures the person. The person is defined necessarily in terms of his social or intersubjective dimension.

The social environment is neither purely determined nor purely undetermined. On the one hand, it is shaped by human freedom, while on the other, it eludes free human intervention. It shares the *chiaroscuro* quality which is so characteristic of human reality.[18] Translating this insight into ethical terms, we can see how some aspects of the social environment, although in themselves they do not reach the perfection thought possible and desirable, cannot be considered as sins but rather as technical imperfections. That is to say, they are imperfections which fall within the finite and progressive structure proper to human reality.

There are however other aspects of the social environment—the greater number of them in fact—in which justice is not realised because of the interposition of human freedom. In cases such as these, we are dealing with a social environment which has a sinful character.

This sinful social environment embodies itself concretely in sinful social structures—political, economic, cultural, judicial, religious structures, etc. Objective culpability thus finds here a concrete verification, namely structural sin. Although sin is always in the interior of the person, from there it passes into human activities, institutions and things, into the structures created by man. Creation itself—the work of God—can be subjected to futility and slavery 'by the will of him who subjected it' (Rom 8:20). Thence arise situations which, while subjectively free from the immediate responsibility of many people, nonetheless result objectively in situations of sin. They constitute a disorder, they manifest it or even cause it to come into being.[19]

This theologico-moral orientation was recognised in the Puebla Document when it affirmed that sin is a permanent obstacle to growth in love and communion 'both within the hearts of human beings and within the various structures which they have created and on which their sin has left its indelible imprint'.

In determining personal responsibility for structural injustices it is necessary to take account of the fact that the structures of society are limited, and in ways that cannot be ascribed to human freedom. They form part of the finiteness inherent in human beings and in human history. Nonetheless there are also structural aspects of our society which are unjust because they do depend on free human action. These are situations of sin or institutionalised injustice. No one can escape responsibility for these structural injustices in society. We cannot escape, by means of the pharisaical and hypocritical mechanisms of subtle distinctions (like the distinction between 'formal' and 'material' cooperation), into an ethic of 'puritan justification'.

The extent of participation in structural injustices is measured by the criterion of action and passion, that is, by the extent to which each person shapes the unjust social situation and allows himself to be shaped by it. Here we must take up again something that we have already said earlier: every sin—individual and structural—is in the interior of the person. The personal and structural dimensions once again combine to give the exact configuration of sin.

One particular criterion of discernment should be borne in mind by any theology which would set out to criticise social reality:

> We cannot make a consistent critique of society as long as we are unable to make clear how we ourselves as 'important' individuals are immersed in the general structures — that is to say, how we profit from them, cooperate with them and transmit to others the deep structural norms which we ourselves consider obvious — the norms, for example, of production, of consumption, of state supremacy — even though privately and in words we reject them. A critique of society which does not take account of these interiorising processes, which does not discover and bring to light the capitalism that lives within us, nay the concentration camp guard living within us, but instead sets up enemies by means of alienating projections — such a critique is, to my mind, an evil political propaganda and not a political interpretation of the Gospel.[20]

Moral theology needs to continue to deepen its reflections on the reality of structural sin. In particular, it must integrate personal responsibility with social and structural situations. Its task must be to lead christian reflection and praxis back into the channels of solidarity in responsibility and responsibility in solidarity.

In this connection it is natural to ask a question about the importance of structural sin in the framework of the typological forms of culpability. Elsewhere I have written about and analysed the possibility of considering structural sin as the 'first analogue' of the forms of culpability. In the light of what I have said here, I would add for clarity's sake that this type of analogy refers to the forms in which culpability is objectified (intra-individual sin, inter-individual sin, structural sin). All these are in turn analogous to personal culpability which is the principal source and proper field of sin in the strict sense.

12. *The Functions and Disfunctions of the Idea of Sin*

THE event of Jesus Christ was 'for us' and 'for our sins'. Exactly how? What is the value of applying the notion of sin and of the removal of sin, to the reality that Jesus is for us? The notion enters into the discussion about Jesus very early in the christian tradition: it represents a dimension of the Jesus mystery that can hardly be expressed in any other way.

And yet, there seems to be something amiss with the theory of sin. I say this, despite obvious advances in that theory in recent decades. We have moved from a focus on the act of sin, to the attitude of the sinner, to the sinner as a personal agent, to the arena or environment of his action; we have stressed his act of subjective formal sinning rather than an objective assessment of moral values: and still, there seems something amiss with our 'sin theory'.

Let me introduce my questioning of it with a reflection from pastoral, confessional practice. It is my growing conviction that people's 'practice' in sinning is different from—and probably better than—our theological 'sin theory'. How many 'real' sins do confessors hear in the sacrament of reconciliation? And if there are real sins, how 'sinning' are they? Can people move as readily as our theory has often suggested from sin to grace to sin to grace to sin again? My growing conviction is that there is a basic goodness in ordinary people. They are often morally ignorant, emotionally weak, and sometimes they do 'sin'—but they do it in their own way, with far less malice and awfulness than our theory attributes to the word 'sin', even though they are conditioned to speak about what they have done according to our rhetoric. I am not simply suggesting that subjectively, there may be limited factors in the performance of sin (eg that all 'serious' sins may well not be 'mortal' for them); I am probing into the validity of how we apply the very idea of 'sin' to what ordinary people do when they sin.

Basically, there is a language, a rhetoric, of sin: a way of speaking into which we fall when we have to discuss sin, that seems special to that situation. It is an overstated language, a language of extremes, absolutes, and ultimates in the order of offence, malice and mortality. It is an emotive language, a language of fear, guilt, and desire — desire confessed in the sinful act, and desire re-emerging in the attempt to repair it.

This language is not just stamped with exaggeration: it is truly a 'language of its own', depicting and creating a system of relations that is unique, a 'world' of its own. We seem to use this language only when it is a question of what we call sin and its reparation. What exactly is the 'situation' we are attempting to describe? It is one of striving for too much; failing; blaming one's self for not making it; trying to get the damage repaired; starting to strive again. Even people who are not notably obsessive in other things, can get 'caught' by the fascination of this 'system', so that they can't reach out to others and enjoy the realness of life around them. The problematic of sin — of the attempt to be sinless, and the recognition of being sinful — becomes the focus of attention.

This special language-system of sin is not deliberately meant or consciously intended. It appears to come most of all from the unconscious — in each individual, and more so, in the commonality of human cultures themselves. That the unconscious exists, and is the source of our language when we say more than we know, and other things than we think we are saying, has long been recognised. It is particularly true in the case of sin-language.

My proposal is to examine the influence of the unconscious on sin-language and so to see where sin-language in some ways distorts the basic meaning of the Jesus event, although in other ways it has a unique power to convey it.

I want to take up some of the archetypes of the unconscious and see how they lead us to say many things about sin and its removal. This archetypal analysis will not, I hope, be finally reductive. When it is done, there ought to remain, not a consignment of sin to the realm of the useless, but a new and real sense of sin and of what Christ has done by dying for our sins.

Two archetypes: Narcissus and Adam

The two archetypes that will be used here are Narcissus the seeker, and Adam the paradise-seeker. Both the Greek myth and the biblical (Hebrew) myth can be looked at together: they evince some common element in the human unconscious itself. I will first describe the story in the myths, then look at the dynamics of the unconscious that they reveal.

First, the stories. Narcissus is young, lovable, untried, untested. He is told that he will live to a ripe old age if he never knows himself. He does not know himself. He goes in search of himself. He is also told that one day he will love, but that he will love himself, and so not know what it is to love another, and to have his love requited by another. Forgetful of real others, he comes to a garden with a pool, and in the pool he sees and loves a face—his own, yet separate from him. Seeking to get to it, he dies. And so does the image of the boy that he loves. In the underworld, he is still gazing into his pool, and on his grave blossoms the narcissus flower, with its yellow centre.

This story repeats itself many times in other classic stories. It is the story of Snow White, of the Wizard of Oz, of Eros and Psyche, of the Hymn of the Pearl. It is always the story of someone fascinated with seeking after their own image, their own perfection. It is something that comes from the unconscious: it is not to be confused with legitimate, proportionate goal-seeking, or genuine idealism (which are of the conscious order of the ego). The story reveals how deep and powerful is the movement of the unconscious into fascination with the lure of an impossible quest.

It may not be immediately evident how this archetypal pattern of the unconscious relates to sin-language. It can be spelt out better if we first tell the kindred story of Adam, seeking his paradise, from the biblical accounts.

Paradise is presented as a place or state of totality: in it, Adam (man) is all that he wants to be, and has all that he wants to have. He is innocent, can do all that he wants, lives in perfect undisturbed partnership with Eve, and is the author with her of the life they impart to their children. Together, they are two in one flesh; living together, they are lords of all living things; together, they author life. Intimacy and vitality are there, in a totality called paradise. Within man, there is a deep, profound desire for this paradise: he wants it, and he wants it fully, and without alloy. It is not good enough for him to have it, shall we say, by 'participation'. If he is to have a 'real' paradise, he must have it by appropriation, so that he himself is the all-authoring source of his own good. Then, and by then alone, he would be in utter possession of the totality he desires: and his desire would be identified with his very self.

There is of course an internal contradiction in this very notion of paradise. It means 'to be as God' when you are really not God. It engenders a superlative desire, the temptation of a fantasy that cannot fulfil. That is why it interdicts itself in the very act of its desiring.

The interdict, the 'no' to the desire for such a paradise, defines the transgression of Adam, his fall. It is not so much the disobedience of a particular and extrinsic precept as it is the inherent falseness of his own paradisal aspiration. The guiltiness is contained within it, and its symbolic consequences are that he can no longer be creative without sweat in his work, or procreative without the pain in the childbearing. There is ambiguity in his sexual intimacy: the drivenness of the desire, and the domination/submission of the other, make it less than his paradisal dream of closeness. Death hovers like a shadow over the vitality that he knows: it is no longer 'fully' life. And with it all, there is the sense of having offended the one who is really the only aboriginal author of all life.

The first fall, or failure in paradise, engenders in Adam

a perpetual cycle of attempts to repair the damage he has done and to reconstitute the paradise he has lost. Paradisal desire does not die with the fall. Unconsciously, man is drawn into a fascination with the lure of an impossible paradise, and into deeper and deeper dimensions of the experience of the intrinsic guilt of that desire. So many stories of conversion, and so much literature of spirituality bear witness to the continuing reality of the paradise myth.

The Narcissus myth and the paradise myth are two aspects of one thing. They are ways of getting in touch with some of the dynamics of the unconscious as they affect the life of everyman at every time.

So, secondly, let us look at those dynamics, especially as they help to interpret the sin-language. At the core of both our stories, in the symbolic patterns that they unveil to us, lies a myth—the myth of development. We learn it from our forebears, create it for ourselves and leave it behind for our posterity. It is the untested, unconscious belief that we are the centre of a process that can only go forward, that evolution is not simply a description of (some stages of) our past, but a prescription for all stages of our future. It is the myth of 'success for me'. 'I' in that sense become the centre: the wonder-child, the enthroned king of all processes, a sort of canonised Infant of Prague! *Tout, et toute suite*! All for me, and all for me now! That is why the totality motifs abound. We would want to know no sin, no sexual problem, no aging, no dying, no ignorance, no impotence, no finitude. We are trapped in a megalomania that will become our undoing.

The contingencies of life soon work upon us that very undoing. Our limits, our destiny, the unresponsiveness of others, even our sensitivity to the needs of others, creates wounds in the heart of our aspirations. We are left with a seeming 'nothing' instead of the desired 'all': the 'all or nothing' syndrome has shown us its darkest result. Our desires themselves, at the very point at which they are paradisal, suffer a narcissistic wound.

From the point of view of sin-language, the most interesting of the dynamics we are discussing occurs exactly here, in the way that man attempts to cope with this failure. His pattern can be called that of nostalgic projection. Failed as he feels himself now to be, he looks both back and forward: back, to dream of his origins, in a paradise that is now conjectured to have been real then; and forward, to dream of his ends, in an omega point that is assumed to be the final paradise. Beginnings and ends meet. Protology and eschatology are ultimately the same thing. An ideal picture of man, the perfect Adam is born, and it is paradisal. In between, the real, limited, wounded human being is the one who dreams it all.

In all this, what this real, limited, wounded human being has been doing, is setting up a theatre for a play. A play that will be both drama and liturgy — a dramaturgy. How shall he act in it? What is the script? In the action, 'everyman-at-everytime' finds an object that pleases him. He 'cathects' on that object: that is, he invests it with a very large quota of affect, he surcharges it with importance for himself, he occupies it. Through this cathexis he makes it absolute. He clings to it, and will not let it go, as though it, in its own small way, were a substitute for the paradise that was once and that will one day be again. This act is what our theory usually calls his 'sin'. It has immediate and profoundly disordering consequences: for the self, for the sense of the world, for the link with God.

The self senses a certain inferiority in the very act of so cathecting. I am not thinking of an inferiority complex. It is rather an intrinsic dimension of the very act of cathecting. There is an existential false consciousness in it, a sense of lived-with guilt in the attempt to claim something in this compelling way. As though the unconscious somehow knew that its desire to reconstitute a moment of its lost paradise and indulge in an instant of self-redemption was not only doomed to failure but also branded with an internal wrongness: the law of paradise is that there can be no paradise! There is profound conflict here: between the desire for a paradise and the guiltiness about the desire for paradise. At root it is double-binding: man is guilty for losing his paradise, and guilty for re-attempting his paradise! This is close to the peculiar wrongfootedness with which he approaches any expression of his position: it is why he enters into a new way of using language about his 'sin'.

The world (the environment, or the arena in which he is) also feels wrong. It seems inadequate to his attempts to grasp his satisfaction; it seems too shallow for that; it is a disappointing, insufficient world. It too can be accused of being internally branded with the disorderedness of the first 'fall'.

The link with God has many dimensions here. Most likely the deepest response of the unconscious is a sense of stain, of sully or impurity, which makes the presence of the All-Pure hard to bear. Closely linked with it is a feeling of broken relationship, of violated rightness with God, of being in his debt, of having offended him (justicially). Both stain and debt combine into a gestalt of personal offence to God. The still-alive narcissism of the person tends to enlarge it into a radical, mortal, death-dealing to all positive relationship, and inherently paradise-defeating. The depressive wretchedness of guilt lies here. It is inevitable that this entire disorderedness, coming from the cathexis, displays itself most in the twin areas of intimacy (sexuality) and fertility (life-processes).

'Everyman at everytime', then, is caught in a compulsive bind with God. He wants to be a partner with him, and finds himself a stranger to him. He ends up being a struggler—partner/stranger, stranger/partner at the same time. And God seems to be the same to him. It appears to be an unresolvable situation. The grandiose-but-wounded self is split from the idealised-but-offended God. This is a state of 'sin'.

It is time, at the end of the entire analysis of this sorry human situation to ask, what then really is sin? And what would a redemption, or a radical removal of sin, really be?

Finding a new paradigm for sin

My suggestion is that, in our prevailing theory of sin, the basic paradigm of sin has been taken to be cathexis made on an inordinate object by 'everyman at everytime'. In other words, the primary analogate of sin has been taken to be the personal sinful act committed by man. My suggestion is further that this may be an error. Positively, the basic paradigm or primary analogate of sin would seem to be the fundamental and unconscious quest for a paradise, of which the act of cathexis has been shown to be only a secondary expression and particular manifestation. This paradisal desire is deeper than both the sinful cathecting act, and the sinful disordered environment in which we now live. It is the narcissistic demand for a paradise, for an apocalypse now, that is our radical sinfulness and that creates the arena, the theatre, and the script of the drama that we act out with God in our particular sinning.

Radical redemption from sin would then be the de-paradisation of desire. It would be a fundamental 'decathexis', not simply from the particular object on which we had cathected, but from the entire language-system of 'paradisiality' that infects our desire. It would be, in the words of TS Eliot, 'the purification of the motive in the ground of our beseeching'.

What would this leave us? With an awareness of our own limited reality and history as places in which our life can be possible, that is, livable in a peace that is real, without the over-reaching that destroys us. This would be a presence in our world, and an intimacy with others, that is real, but neither paradisal nor dramatic. It would be living in an ordinary garden without a pool to look into or a tree of life to desire — without a mirror to distract us from reality or a supposed language of perfect expression to attract us. It would be historical, not fantastic, reality.

God would be that quiet, unspoken dimension with ordinariness who makes possible our Shalom, the root of our peace, not the rival with whom we compete to be the author of all peace. He is a gentle presence, who takes pleasure in being with us as we are, and who infectiously makes us take pleasure in being with him where he is — with us. He 'homes' into us, and makes us at home with him. His allness and our realness (or littleness) no longer compete, they belong. The problem could be expressed as 'all or nothing'. The solution is 'all in nothing', someone and someone. It is perfectly natural for contingent things to be contingent, for finite things to be finite. God is a 'yes' to all that, not so much spoken as breathed towards us, in such a way that it cannot solicit the desire-dynamics for paradise. The life of the redeemed is the discovery of that redeeming blessing of the divine presence in every place in which it has not yet been tasted. Our relation with God is a 'yes' to his 'yes'; we meet in such a way that totalising tendencies are not aroused in the other partner, that the tendency to elevate and then attempt to destroy the other does not arise, that the discovery together of a new and positive frail beauty of life is possible.

In this approach, neither the negative pole of the discussion (our sin), nor the positive one (our redeemed state), come through with the absoluteness of the usual presentations. The former does not have the malice or the awfulness that is rightly attributable to the unconscious paradisiality of desire; the latter does not have the finality-perfection of total removal of the problem. Rather, we are healed from our own real sins, to our own real finite-world.

St Augustine may well have grasped all of this in his formula for sin: *'uti fruendis, frui utendis'*. The simplicity of real limited life, which we are intended to enjoy simply, we turn into material that we can use and manipulate for our own fantastic paradisial purposes: that is sin. The contentment we envisage for ourselves, but never quite arrive at, in the results of our own striving and achieving, that too is sin. Only when we move from the *cupiditas* (desire) to the *caritas* of a benign and redeeming God (peace), are we really redeemed.

St Thomas put it differently: he said that in every act of sin there is an *'inconsideratio regulae'*, an inattentiveness to rule of right reason. The rightness of reason consists in its knowing alignment with the law of peace in finitude. To live in that rightness, is blessedness: that is the finality of our being. But it is not a goal that we construct or achieve for ourselves.

It is true that we do not really come to know what sin is until we have decathected from it. We do not glimpse the paradisiality of our desire until it is de-paradised. The awareness of sin is largely hindsight. Discernment is a reflection after the event, on what was really going on when we did not know. The release of such an awareness seems part and parcel of the healing of sin.

In this hindsight, what does sin turn out to be? Is it no more than a fantasy which is branded as such after the event of its healing? In some ways yes, but in bigger ways no. Yes, it is a fantasy, and known to be such after the healing, if we think of the impression that so much of our sin-language gives, that each sin of ours (in our sinful world) is so utterly and radically awful. But no, it is not a fantasy, and after its healing it is known in all its frightening realness, if we think of the huge over-drive in the unconscious of the whole human race to reach, have, and to be its own paradise. Then we can truly look at the enormity of sin itself, and see its expressions today in the almost cosmic social evil it engenders rather than in our particular *peccata*. I am not suggesting that they are not wrong, or even that in a derived sense they are not 'sins'. I am merely saying that the derived sense is not the primary one, and that the rhetoric that goes with the primary one is not legitimately linked to the secondary. That leaves the primary analogate in all its own realness.

Sin-language, seen from this angle, turns out to be a hybrid. It is the at-least-partial use of the mythic language of the unconscious to describe a realistic non-mythic personal situation, personal sin. Its extension to the notion of a world of sin in the situational or environmental sense is an attempt to validate the use of such mythic language, but it rests and falls on the false identification between the environment and the unconscious. Sin as we do it is much less than we make it out to be in this sin-language; but it is also very much more than the sins we do.

I am suggesting then that we ought in all conscience refrain from the manipulative use of the ambiguity in our sin-language in our pastoral rhetoric. It is very possible to preach on the awfulness of the sins that ordinary people do in such a way as to induce a traumatic anguish of conscience or a shocked horror at the incapacity of grasping it, or the desire for some inexplicable absolute release from the absoluteness of it all, beyond the realistic proportions of sin in real people. It is said at times that today's people have lost the sense of sin. If they have lost the exaggerated sense of mythic sin as if it were their very own, it may not be a bad idea. Perhaps it could be the first step to a recovery of an authentic sense of the different, much more limited, and thereby more real sense of what they have done in their own finite consciences. My pastoral hunch is that very many ordinary people, in their basic common sense, have actually done this at the roots of their experience, while remaining faithful to the language-systems they have been taught, and not knowing any other one. My quarrel would not be with their perception, but with the language as language. And with some of the preaching.

Jesus and the language of sin

After this analysis, it is time to return to the context of our question. The event of Jesus Christ was 'for us' and 'for our sins'. What is the theological value of applying the notion of sin and of its removal, to the reality that Jesus is for us?

My conviction is that Jesus approached the field of sin concretely. His starting point is not sin in general, nor is it the particular *peccata* of individuals. It is the situational wrongness of the creation and oppression of rejects from a socio-cultural-religious system, by the human highlighting of an élite as the core beneficiaries of that system. In the cultural language of the day, the 'central' temple people called the rejects sinners; the real sin was in the system. The critique sustained by Jesus against this sin-situation was not really limited to its current form in Israel; it embraced all such situations. It was implicitly universal. But there is a point at which Jesus' encounter with such 'sin' becomes transcendently larger, and that is the point at which the system becomes powerful enough to reject his challenge, and even to induce disillusionment in the anawim and cowardice in his disciples. The sin-power of the system is then much larger in its presentation than the contingent and concrete expression it then took. It is too big—even assuming the proportions of absoluteness. It is evidence almost of the unconscious root of evil itself. *Hamartia*: it is almost personalised.

What Jesus has done against sin is, then, more simply going about with forgiving reassurance to the despised 'sinners': he has encountered the sin that the system reveals. His encounter with it, in the fidelity of the passion and cross, is a successful encounter, because it has touched the fidelity of the Father, and poured out with him life upon the poor. This life means that the poor can and shall live, free from any impression that the undoubted power of the unconscious in its radical sinfulness is absolute. By the passion and resurrection it has been definitely relativised, and submitted to the supremacy of the final given love and life of God in Jesus.

Paul Philibert, in a valuable study has summarised his nuanced view of sin as follows:

> There is no escaping the great mystery of sin in the world of human life, but sin never negates the love God has for sinful persons and can mysteriously function as the tutor of God's freedom and mercy. Sin is present in the lives of every person, either through the sinfulness of the social environment or the sinfulness of personal weakness and vindictiveness. Sin is one pole of the christian mystery which moves between human need and divine forgiveness. 'A spiritual portrait of the christian as seen in recent church teaching' (Philibert 1980, 264).[*]

I would say that sin is indeed present in each person's life, and there is indeed no negating it, but that it is radically present in the radical communal unconscious, and expresses itself, to some degree, either in the sinfulness of social environments, or the sinfulness of personal deeds. I would agree that it never negates God's love for sinful persons, but I would want to say much more. In the event of Jesus Christ, God's fidelity-love, as poured out definitively on his own poor, has negated the absoluteness even of the radical sin-unconsciousness, and has all the more provided an entitlement for all persons to live consciously

[*] See works consulted, Notes, p.312

free of the *ultimate radicality* of that power over them. They can still sin, indeed, but it is in their own smaller way, real as that still is. But they cannot be touched by an alleged absoluteness of an awful evil, nor can they commit exactly that. I believe it is time to drop a rhetoric alleging a virtual equality between a radical-sin-at-the-unconscious-level, spoken of as though it were translatable to the conscious level of imputable action, and the presence of grace to the person. A 'good or bad, take your pick' rhetoric often comes through like that. To speak like that is to compound what seems to be an error in logic in the correct alignment of language systems, with an error in theology, in under-estimating the mystery of Jesus. 'Thanks be to God, who has given us the victory in Christ Jesus our Lord.' 'The Spirit of life in Christ Jesus has delivered us from the law of sin and death.'

In this way, the categories of sin and its removal, are of profound value as tools of interpretation of the Jesus event. They—rightly understood—show the fullness of liberative redemption that has taken place in Jesus. They suggest, in conveying a sense of the limitation of the entire sin-field, what marvellous freedom is indeed made available to us in Christ. They point the way, in this freedom, to a much more realistic, and less religiously inhibited, look at the authentic human wrongs people are doing to one another, and at the possibility of humanly putting them right again in the confidence of redemptive grace.

13. *The Fate of the Moral Manual since Saint Alphonsus*

WHEN analysing literature as voluminous and technical as the moral manuals since the death of St
Alphonsus the initial temptation is to deal in generalities.
One could simply accept the broadly agreed divisions: an
attitude vacillating between suspicion of and opposition to
Alphonsus' method that is tempered with his canonisa-
tion in 1839, a gradual rallying round the moral views of
Alphonsus that reaches a symbolic climax when he is
declared *Doctor Ecclesiae* in 1871, a period of controversy
centering on the precise status and exact interpretation of
Alphonsus' views that begins with the controversy surrounding the publication of the *Vindiciae Alphonsianae*
(1873) and ends only with the turn of the century, and
finally the acceptance of Alphonsus as the preferred
ecclesiastical authority in casuistic moral theology compar-
able, in an analagous sense, with the authority of St
Thomas in dogmatic theology.

There is truth in those broad divisions, with the reservations one normally has about too general notions. It would
be possible, methodologically, to chart the systematisation
of the Alphonsian moral method by applying those
broadly accepted divisions to particular manuals of various schools, eg Redemptorist, Jesuit, Dominican, and thus
discover what was transformed, abandoned or rejected in
the Alphonsian method. This paper approaches these
questions in a more limited way. Because of the great
number and often intimidating length of these manuals it
seemed advisable to opt for some principles of control in
the material to be examined.

The twenty or so manuals referred to in some depth in

this article represent publications from most of the decades between 1800 and 1960: that is, the period when the manuals were very definitely 'in possession' after the bitter systems' controversies of the 1700s and before the dramatic and virtually universal collapse of the manual in the 1960s. Within the kaleidoscope of interesting questions treated by the manuals, one is particularly considered here: *de habituatis et recidivis*. Why? The major methodological concern of the manuals was the preparation of future confessors for the juridically correct administration of the sacrament of penance: on the basis of that fact it is fair to make the further assumption that the manual treatment of *habituati et recidivi* (perhaps numerically the majority of penitents?) would give a reasonable indication of the overall method of the manual writer, and thus show in what way the teaching of Alphonsus was transformed, abandoned or rejected. The perspective from which the questions of this article are asked is, therefore, limited. There is, also, an inevitable subjective bias and arbitrariness of selection in choosing both the manuals themselves and the main questions from them which are studied here. Within those limits, a chronological assessment of some major moral manuals from the optic of their treatment of the *habituati et recidivi* is, I believe, a plausible way of looking at the development of the moral manual since Alphonsus.

Saint Alphonsus

The *Theologia Moralis* went through nine editions in the saint's lifetime, the first in 1748, the last in 1785. In the century after his death there were, at least, sixty-six editions, the majority being in France and Italy.[1] With the edition of Leonard Gaudé in 1905 a standard critical version was established, and it is to this that reference is made here.[2] Alphonsus treats the question of the *consuetudinarii* and *recidivi* in volume 3 of *Theologia Moralis*. The treatment bears the marks of pastoral realism and prudential balancing of opinions which were later seen to be a characteristically alphonsian approach.

With regard to the *consuetudinarius*, (one confessing a

bad habit for the first time), the presumption is given to the penitent in that coming to the sacrament is, in itself, a good sign and absolution is to be given unless sorrow is absolutely lacking. In giving his opinion on the *recidivus*, (one who relapses into the same sin after confession of the sin), Alphonsus, characteristically, searches for the middle ground that avoids dangerous extremes. Not for him the lax view that will allow absolution as often as one confesses, nor the strict view that demands total emendation before any absolution. The laxist view is rejected on the grounds that such a practice would not give the basis of a prudent assessment for the priest-confessor to have moral certainty in his judgment; the strict view is rejected because it implies that doubt or suspicion is equivalent to certainty in forming a judgment on the penitent's dispositions. The middle position espoused by Alphonsus states that absolution is to be refused to the *recidivus* unless there are extraordinary signs of sorrow.

These extraordinary signs are then listed: tears/weeping, a lessening in the number of sins, notable efforts at emendation such as fasting or almsgiving, evidence of a search for new means of moral improvement, spontaneous confession, special motivation such as the fear of some impending disaster, confession of sins previously and culpably omitted, prior restitution or the signs of a new awareness of guilt. It is evident that there is a flexibility of applying the apparently rigid principle 'no absolution for the *recidivus*' within these extraordinary signs of repentance. And Alphonsus urges the confessor to have great confidence in applying the principle within these circumstances.

Between the positions of giving and refusing absolution Alphonsus next discusses the possibility of deferring absolution. Absolution is to be deferred when the confessor is morally certain of the wrong disposition of the penitent. What is required is moral, not absolute, certainty: that is, the certainty of a prudent and probable judgment. Moral certainty is sufficient to proceed with since absolution should be deferred only when there is clearly positive doubt about a total lack of sorrow. Delaying absolution is less a question of the juridical requirements of confession than of acting in the interests of the penitent's spiritual health. Absolution is not to be deferred if there is a danger of more harm than good being done.

Alphonsus rejects the stern rigidity of absolutist principles for the milder view of pastoral sensitivity to the circumstances of the case, particularly if there is question of a penitent reverting to the same sin more through the intrinsic causes of human weakness than through voluntary and extrinsic causes. The reason is, again, a pastoral one: in the sins of human weakness the grace of God is always more helpful than a harsh moralism. Alphonsus acknowledges that, at times, absolution should be deferred: he is, however, at pains to stress that this should never be done in a way that deprives the penitent of God's grace if there is a prudent possibility of the penitent responding to this. In a *cri de coeur* the pastorally-minded Alphonsus acknowledges that deferral of absolution may often lead the penitent to despair and to a neglect of the sacraments. Legally speaking, the confessor may be within his rights in deferring absolution; ordinarily speaking, however, the properly disposed penitent who shows some extraordinary sign of sorrow should be absolved at once.

This cursory summary of Alphonsus' views on the *consuetudinarii et recidivi* highlights some important points from his total manual system:

1. The selection of the mediate position between the Scylla of laxism and the Charybdis of rigorism marks the characteristically alphonsian search to avoid extremes of theological expression.

2. Alphonsus' abiding concern is the spiritual welfare of people. This spiritual welfare is to be based on sound common sense; the loose views of the laxists lack a firm foundation for moral growth while the stern views of the rigorists lead only to despair. The former view lacks a sense of christian realism, the latter a sense of christian hope.

3. Alphonsus had great trust in the power of God's grace, more so than he had in any moral self-righteousness.

As long as there is a prudent possibility of good will on the penitent's part, the grace of the sacrament should be given.

4. Moral principles are to be clearly articulated, but they are to be applied prudentially in view of the prevailing circumstances. That is why Alphonsus upholds the legal requirements of the priest as judge on the one hand, while on the other, through his comments on the extraordinary signs of sorrow, he goes to great lengths to find ways of understanding the human condition, especially in terms of the weakness of human nature.

5. The concern of Alphonsus is to uphold the sovereign goodness of God along with a patient understanding of how humans grow in a painful and often sporadic way. He will defer absolution — but only if it is unavoidable. The reason is that he does not wish to deprive any properly disposed penitent of grace, nor to make a bad situation worse by inducing despair.

6. He writes, as is customary for him, more to clarify a problem for ordinary people than to achieve stylistic elegance of expression. He presents the views of other theologians in a fairminded way in order to reach his own reasoned opinion of prudent and pastoral judgments.

The treatment of the *consuetudinarii et recidivi* is a useful example of the overall spirit of Alphonsus' moral system. How later theologians treat the same question will show, in however limited a way, what ideas of his were later transformed, abandoned or rejected.

The struggle for acceptance, 1800–1850

The authors chosen to represent the first half of the nineteenth century include some re-publications from the eighteenth century as well as representatives of the new writing in Europe and North America. The juxtaposition of the older and established authors, which were still widely used, with the modern moral writing of the early nineteenth century will indicate how Alphonsus influenced the development of the manual through the treatment of the question of the *habituati et recidivi*.

Published in the previous century the work of Paul

216

Gabriel Antoine[3] was still very popular in the 1800s. Over sixty editions of his work appeared after 1726. It carried a recommendation from Pope Benedict XIV and an *'approbatio multiplex'* from Italian and French sources, which prefaces the first volume, indicates that he was an established authority.

Characteristic of his general approach, Antoine first decides on those to whom absolution is to be refused because of defect of matter or of disposition. Ten categories are given, all in a rigorist tone: little room is left for a prudent interpretation of circumstances. The concern is with the legal requirements of the confessor rather than with understanding a problem from the penitent's viewpoint. Even if the penitent does not know what is binding in law he cannot be absolved; the penitent's own word is not to be trusted. Quoting Suarez, Antoine gives the primary consideration to the role of the priest as judge and the need for material integrity, with scarcely a mention of other roles and needs. The presumption is against giving absolution, thus making it difficult to positively conceive the circumstances when absolution can be given.

When he comes to the possibility of deferring absolution the same harshness prevails. The emphasis is on external appearances, not on internal grace; no flexibility is given to understand, for instance, the psychological pressures on young people. One senses that the main concern is with the confessor as controller of the confessional tribunal; the penitent's own testimony is untrustworthy and evidence of good works seems more important than the converting grace of the sacrament. The overall tone is of the great difficulty in granting absolution: even when it is a question of a *per accidens* occasion of sin, absolution is ordinarily to be deferred, and when the lesser threat of deferral fails the confessor is to force the penitent towards repentance with the greater threat of total refusal. There is a begrudging attitude even towards those who are contrite and rightly disposed; the overall tone reflects a restrictive access to the grace of the sacrament and such a concern with the judicial role of the priest that the other aspects of the confessor's sacramental position, eg healer, teacher, are virtually obscured. Antoine represents those harsh moralists whose narrow concern for the externals of orthodoxy contributed to despair among ordinary people and, in time, to the great pastoral problem of the neglect of the sacraments. In Antoine, the perspective on the *habituati et recidivi* is predominantly that of a priori judicial requirements rather than the actual and pressing needs of people. There is no evidence, in this revised edition of Antoine, that the thinking of Alphonsus has influenced the treatment of the question.

Born near Antwerp in 1690, Peter Dens, died at Malines in 1775; he is, thus, broadly a contemporary of Alphonsus. He taught at the Benedictine Abbey of Afrighen and later at the seminary in Malines, of which he was President from 1735–1755. In his zeal for the moral and scientific training of the clergy, and in his simple piety and love of the poor, he is quite like Alphonsus. The work mentioned here[4] was first published after his death and remained popular well into the 1800s. We can take it that the work is substantially his, though an uneven style and presentation suggested posthumous editors. This, combined with a didactic question-and-answer style, do not make it easy to read now; on the other hand, the casuistic treatment of practical questions no doubt contributed to its popularity as a work of reference for the busy priest of those days. What the book lacks in consistency and coherence of presentation is compensated for by the wide base of its learning and the practical bent in the application of principles.[5]

Before treating the question *de consuetudinariis et recidivis* Dens examines the qualities of the confessor. These include virtue, wisdom and prudence which are to be exercised through the offices of the confessor as father, teacher, doctor and judge. Great care is to be taken in analysing the dispositions of the penitent, and Dens tries to avoid the extremes of rigid and lax abuses in his general principles regarding the refusal and deferral of absolution. Though clear in articulating the principles, he avoids rigidity of application. Though I could find no evidence of Dens being familiar with the works of Alphonsus, the treatment of these questions is fairly similar to that of

Alphonsus in the *Theologia Moralis* and the *Praxis Confessarii*.

In the actual treatment *de consuetudinariis et recidivis* Dens is a benign anti-probabilist. He takes the main questions in turn—refusing absolution, giving absolution, deferring absolution—and treats them in a casuistic way. That means that he is strict in the formulation of the principles, but shows pastoral sensitivity in the application: this is particularly notable in his analysis of the possibility of granting absolution. His starting points are often restrictive, but in practice he is more flexible within the limitations of his casuistry. In this he is unlike Antoine who is restrictive in both the articulation and application of principles. Dens, at least, shows an awareness of the pastoral care of tortured individuals.

Because Dens' work is written in a catechetical question-and-answer style it is hard to evaluate as a manual of moral theology. Overall, the cryptic legal tone dominates, giving the impression that the questions are asked less from a theological than a canonico-legal point of view. He avoids the harshness of an Antoine: yet he fails to integrate the theological emphases of an Alphonsus.[6]

Constantine Roncaglia (1677–1734), an Italian moralist from Lucca, was a prolific writer on moral, dogmatic and scriptural questions: his moral theology was known and respected by Alphonsus, and it was republished well into the 1800s.[7] The treatment of the question of the *habituati et recidivi* is prefaced by an extended exposition of the priest as minister of the sacrament of penance: the tone is very legalistic, with the main emphasis falling on the obligations of the confessor. He is strict with regard to the articulation of principles: this is evident when he discusses people in a proximate voluntary occasion of sin. Such people are judged to be in a continual state of actual sin: the consideration, for instance, that the occasion, though voluntary, may be necessitated by other unavoidable circumstances does not substantially lessen Roncaglia's harsh expression of the principle. The same strictness applies to the habit of sin due to internal human weakness: absolution is to be denied to these. Firstly, as judge, the priest is forced to doubt the disposition of such people: secondly, as doctor, the priest must at least defer absolution until there is positive evidence of emendation. The impression is given of the priest as a strict controller of people's lives, with little emphasis on the present, actual needs of penitents themselves; the penitent will always be judged on the basis of the past, with little attention being given to the possibility of all sin being taken away by the grace of God.

A milder approach is evident when he deals with actual confessional practice. Though he, like Antoine, quotes Bellarmine on the dangers of too easily giving absolution, he adverts to the harm that is done by those of an overly rigid view as well. He professes, in practice, to follow a middle view: it is this, perhaps, that enabled Alphonsus to recommend Roncaglia as a moralist.

There is no evidence that the later editors of Roncaglia incorporated any specific points from Alphonsus. Though there are certain similarities with Alphonsus, as noted above, overall Roncaglia appears more harsh than Alphonsus, at least to the extent that there is a more rigorist articulation of the principles. The rules to be followed in practice, though milder, lack that sense of pastoral awareness of the actual human problems which permeates the writing of Alphonsus.

As the other authors to be considered all wrote at least fifty years after the death of Alphonsus, an interim comment is appropriate. The beginning of the nineteenth century shows a variety of views on the question of the *habituati et recidivi*: the views of Alphonsus are in contrast, to varying degrees, with the other popular moralists of the time. There is a clear choice facing the moral theologian after 1830: does one follow the views of Alphonsus, or the more rigorist views of the likes of Antoine, Dens and Roncaglia?

The Irishman, Francis Patrick Kenrick is a good example of the new generation of nineteenth century authors who would have been familiar with the writings of both the rigorists and of Alphonsus. Born in Dublin in 1797, Kenrick studied at the Propaganda College in Rome before his ministry in America where he was, firstly, Professor of Theology at Bardstown, Kentucky, and in turn, Co-adjutor Bishop of Philadelphia, Bishop of Philadelphia and Archbishop of Baltimore (1850) until his death in 1863. His moral theology was widely used, not least because it was clearly the work of a pastor engaged with the problems of his own day.[8]

Kenrick's fundamental principle in discussing the *habituati et recidivi* is that the properly disposed penitent has a right to absolution even though the confessor, as physician of the soul may at times defer it. His statement contrasts with the rigorists who so hedge this right as to make it virtually meaningless. The emphasis is on the state of the conscience of the penitent at the time of confession, a view very close to that of Alphonsus whom he quotes on the matter. The confessor's duty is to concentrate on the essential rather than the peripheral. Kenrick's overall analysis of the occasions of sin is also close to that of Alphonsus; he tries, understandably, to translate the views of the saint, culturally conditioned by the Kingdom of Naples in the mid-eighteenth century, to the differing conditions of mid-nineteenth century America. For instance; the fact that a particular maid may be an occasion of sin for a male employer does not necessarily mean that she has to be dismissed, since the problem may not be the maid but the man's lust. It is this which must be remedied and dismissing one maid, though she be the present object of the lust, leaves the basic problem untouched. Kenrick's concern is with the spiritual growth of people above all else. A further example is his rejection of Alphonsus' views on betrothed couples going to each other's house, something which Alphonsus thought would almost inevitably lead to sin. Kenrick thinks that Alphonsus' harsher views were necessary because of the depraved morals of the Italians, and suggests that a milder view might be possible for the Americans who are, presumably, to be more trusted in these matters! In general, Kenrick's moral doctrine on sexual matters is milder than that of Alphonsus. Kenrick writes as a practical pastor with the care of souls, rather than as a scientific theologian. Though, clearly, he does not wish to see people sinning, he shows a tolerance of the human condition and he tries to avoid making life more complicated than is necessary.

Consuetudinarii should be absolved if they show some signs of sorrow, but absolution is not to be given indiscriminately. In the case of the *recidivi* the decision to absolve or to defer absolution is to be based on the penitent's conscience and the possibilities for future growth. Less indulgence is to be shown to the latter than to the former, but this implies that some indulgence be shown. Kenrick envisages deferral until such time as the confessor is morally certain of the penitent's good disposition, since the confessor is both judge and doctor: deferral is recommended only if it helps the penitent's spiritual growth. This is close to Alphonsus' teaching, a point further evidenced by the quotations from St Thomas and the Roman Ritual on the power of grace over that of good works and on the benefits of frequent communion. Kenrick is aware that although, legally speaking, one may consider deferring absolution, there may be spiritual dangers in so doing: a person left without sacramental grace may be worse off than before. Prudence is to be exercised: sometimes the case is clearcut (total lack of sorrow, no sense of faith, no minimal purpose of amendment) but the confessor must avoid rash judgments. For instance, lack of external signs of sorrow is not necessarily lack of sorrow.

In the Preface, Kenrick had acknowledged Alphonsus as one of his chief sources, and this is borne out in the treatment of the *habituati et recidivi*. Kenrick was writing before it was commonplace, indeed fashionable, to acknowledge the importance of Alphonsus, and in this his pioneering insight is to be acknowledged. In large measure Kenrick simply repeats Alphonsus' doctrine though in matters of a practical import he was not afraid to state his own view. In combining a loyalty to the central alphonsian principles with a liberty to vary their application to a new culture, he shows a sense of judgment that was not always matched by later writers.

Review of the authors of the first half of the nineteenth century ends, appropriately, with Thomas Gousset. Born in 1792, he taught for thirteen years at the seminary of Besançon and was progressively Bishop of Perigueux, Archbishop of Rheims and Cardinal (1850) until his death in 1866. The symbolic appropriateness of Gousset is that, having been educated on the principles of rigorism, he made a chance discovery of the works of Alphonsus in 1829 and he took a vow the following year to consecrate himself to the defence and spreading of the views of Alphonsus. Gousset came to appreciate the errors of the rigorists and found, in Alphonsus, the theological expression of those principles of practical moral wisdom which he wished to follow. His moral theology had thirteen editions in his lifetime and was a major influence in establishing Alphonsus as an accepted author for the pastoral solution of moral problems.[9]

Gousset distinguishes between those with the habit of sin and the recidivists *pour la direction*: that is, for him it is not simply a legal distinction but more a matter of spiritual discernment. His teaching on those with the habit of sin, following Alphonsus and the Roman Ritual which he quotes, is that, generally speaking, absolution is not to be deferred or refused. His approach is thoroughly pastoral. A habit of sin is not, in itself, a presumption of bad will since it may be the result of human weakness rather than moral depravity. Even though the confessor may feel that the penitent will sin again, absolution should be given if there is a prudent probability of good dispositions. Gousset combines an understanding of human weakness with a great belief in the power of God's grace that allows him to act in favour of the present good conscience of the individual. Of course, Gousset acknowledges that prudence may at times dictate a deferral of absolution: but this is to be done rarely, and only in favour of the penitent's spiritual health. Interestingly, at this point Gousset refers to confession as *'le sacrement de la réconciliation'*, thus anticipating by over a century the currently preferred nomenclature.

With regard to recidivists, the same awareness of the sensitive application of basic principles is evident. Just one of the extraordinary signs suffices, each case is to be treated on its own merits, full reversal of a habit is not easily achieved. Though he does not use the precise term, what he is concerned with in the case of recidivists is the establishment of whether there is a basic option for sin. Otherwise, one can consider the possibility of absolution: for example, if there is a diminution in the number of sins. He repeatedly distances himself from the harsh views of the rigorists which he sees as not properly understanding the nature of human weakness or the strengthening power of God's grace: rigidity is not necessarily a gospel virtue. Gousset is very understanding of the problems of young people, and of the fact that conversion is often a gradual process. One must uphold moral principles, but equally one must avoid counsels of desperation: as far as is morally prudent and spiritually beneficial one must act in favour of the freedom of an individual's present good conscience.

The same alphonsian spirit of prudent judgments comes through in his treatment of the occasions of sin. His analysis of the principles governing occasions of sin—proximate and remote, necessary and voluntary—is standard. What is noticeable in him is the way the principles are applied: distinctions are necessary; there are always exceptions to the rule; one must take local customs into account.[10] Gousset avoids the rigoristic restatement of principles by emphasising that judgments are relative to particular cases, and must be in favour of the spiritual health of the individual.[11] Gousset is a classic exponent of the alphonsian spirit: knowledge of the principles must be combined with a knowledge of the human heart and individual circumstances. Prudence is that virtue by which one combines and preserves both, in favour of the individual's good conscience empowered by God's grace in the sacrament.

By the middle of the nineteenth century it can be said that the moral theology of Alphonsus was established as a solid pastoral guide for confessors. As yet, not much of Alphonsus' system was transformed, abandoned or rejected. The reason is that the arguments centred on the general acceptability of Alphonsus rather than on the particularised examination of his views. The theological disputes of the time were more limited (though not, for that, less important) in their focus; was Alphonsus a solid guide for moral practice? At the beginning of the century the rigorist heirs of Arnauld, Pascal and the anti-Probabilists were in the ascendant, particularly so in France. The delay of absolution was the norm rather than the exception, and this was justified on the basis of a rigid theory of the role of the confessor-as-judge. The undermining of the dominance of this view, which owed not a little to the jansenistic theories of grace and predestination, came from the pastoral experience of those priests who saw that such a restrictive view of the sacrament led to despair, a decline in the practice of the faith and, ultimately, the decline of faith itself. Their arguments were, at first, more the reflective instinct of pastoral insight than the result of the sustained argument of scholarly theology. That is where the importance of the alphonsian manual lies in the early nineteenth century. He was seen by people like Kenrick and Gousset as an authoritative expression of what their own pastoral instincts were telling them.

The acceptability of Alphonsus was, of course, helped by the interventions from Rome in 1803 and 1831.[12] These were seen as official approval of what was already beginning to happen pastorally and, later, theologically. But it is here, precisely, that the seeds of future problems were being sown. The focus of attention too easily shifted from the intrinsic merits of Alphonsus' theological method to the extrinsic acceptability of his position as an ecclesiastical authority. One can understand Kenrick and Gousset using Alphonsus in a somewhat extrinsic sense, though as was shown, not even they took Alphonsus 'literally': they were, after all, trying to refute the rigorists and they needed all the help they could get, even if it was based on authority. The difficulties will arise later when it is only the extrinsic authority of Alphonsus that seems to matter.

By 1850 there was a widespread acceptance of the moral manual of Alphonsus, at least in contrast to the position at the turn of the century.[13] That this later proved to be more the use of Alphonsus as an extrinsic authority than a promotion of the study of Alphonsus in the original text and spirit is not to be attributed directly to the pre-1850 moral theologians. They were trying to establish the acceptability of Alphonsus in opposition to the rigorists: the development of the manual in the early nineteenth century is the story of that gradual acceptability.[14]

Transformation and fossilisation, 1850–1900

To assess the influence of Alphonsus on the moral manuals in the second half of the nineteenth century the same, admittedly limited, method used for the first half of the century is followed here. Publications from each decade will be taken, again focusing on the question of the *habituati et recidivi*.

Peter Scavini (1791–1869) was Professor of Theology at the seminary of Novara, and he presents his moral theology as a faithful reproduction of Alphonsus.[15] This acknowledgement of Alphonsus, now becoming commonplace, is a reflection of the growing acceptability of Alphonsus, a position that was to be copperfastened with his being declared a Doctor of the Church in 1871.

The *consuetudinarius* is defined as 'the one who is in a proximate and intrinsic occasion of sin' and is, generally speaking, to be absolved: notable, however, is Scavini's belief that, with sexual sins, a harsher definition of what constitutes a habit is proposed. The recidivist is not to be absolved unless extraordinary signs of sorrow are shown. This rule is to be taken as generally true but there are exceptions in the line of the extraordinary signs of sorrow which he accepts when they are solid and well based. He acknowledges the power of God's grace conferred in the sacrament.

Scavini's moral theology is straightforward, even perfunctory. It is not original, and lacks personal insights. He repeats the traditional teaching of Alphonsus, but in a very cursory way that, perhaps, does damage to the spirit of Alphonsus. The theological content of Alphonsus is replaced by dry formulae; the nuances of Alphonsus' arguments are lost, with the result that Scavini appears more rigid than the master he professes to follow. Those who would have known Alphonsus only through Scavini would have had a truncated vision of the saint's original insight.

John Peter Gury (1801–1866) taught moral theology at Vals in France from 1833 until his death, apart from a one-year professorship at the Collegio Romano which was abruptly terminated by the revolutionary disturbances of 1848. A follower of Bussenbaum, Alphonsus and Gousset, he had, firstly, urged the Abbé Neyraguet to publish the alphonsian *Compendium Theologiae Moralis*, before publishing his own in 1850. It was to be extraordinarily successful: on the basis of forty-three editions between 1850 and 1890, James Healy estimates that there were 200,000 copies printed in that time.[16] The success of the work is due to a combination of factors; the clear presentation, the evident scholarship and, not least, the fact that it was written by a theologian who was very active pastorally, evidenced by the fact that he died while conducting a parish mission.[17]

In explaining the differences between the *consuetudinarius* and the *recidivus* Gury, characteristically, gives an extended historical footnote to explain the possible different nuances. One with a habit of sin can be absolved even before improvement actually takes place: Gury rejects the rigorist view as unrealistic, on the basis that everyone is constantly affected by sin. The possibility of occasional refusal is granted. Extraordinary signs of sorrow may be grounds for the absolution of the recidivist though not always. Even with the ordinary signs of sorrow absolution is possible if delay is dangerous and immediate absolution may be beneficial. He is at pains to show that his interpretation of Alphonsus is the correct one, thereby showing the beginnings of future controversies on the exact meaning of alphonsian texts. In doubt, one must defer absolution but there is always need for mercy and patience: Gury tries to establish a benign application of the accepted principles. The method of Gury's exposition — short enunciation of principles together with long historical footnotes — was to cause controversy later among those who questioned his historical interpretations. Overall, Gury is at pains to administer the sacrament in a benign way, showing God's mercy and proving that the good of the penitent is always greater than any particular rule. His common sense approach is transparent: good examples are his treatment of those who refuse to go to frequent confession and his way of listing the extraordinary signs of sorrow.[18] The work of Gury represents a further stage in the evolutionary influence of Alphonsus on the moral manual. It is no longer a question of giving an apologia for the defence of Alphonsus; such is clearly no longer necessary. What is now in the forefront is the disputed interpretation of alphonsian texts: Gury (and his adversaries, later) will claim that they have the correct interpretation of the matter. The hidden agenda of many of these controversies was the older question of the probabilist and equi-probabilist opinions. By raising these questions, however indirectly, Gury and others were to take the focus away from the alphonsian spirit to the more literal questions of correct interpretation.

The work of Ernest Müller,[19] though never as popular as Scavini or Gury, has its own merits. He treats, firstly the occasions of sin according to three principles: those in remote occasions are not to be denied absolution; those in necessary proximate occasions are not to be denied absolution if they use the normal remedies; those in voluntary proximate occasions are to be denied absolution. Most of his examples are sexual ones, thus representing the growing identification of moral questions with one area of life: his language is more legal than theological, again indicative of the further identification of moral theology with canonical terminology.

His factual definitions of *habituati* and *recidivi* are the by now common ones. His basic principles are that those with a habit of sin are usually to be absolved though occasionally, if prudence demands, one may defer, and recidivists are not to be regularly absolved though occasionally, if prudence demands, one may absolve. Having enunciated the principles he counsels consideration of particular circumstances: in doubt one may consider a conditional absolution, as the power of God's grace and mercy are never to be underestimated. He finishes with a *casus* on masturbation, which he solves in a sensitive way.

A casuist, Müller tries to apply the principles in favour of the individual. His method is: firstly give the factual definition of terms, secondly give the moral principles, and then deal with individual cases. It is a classic presentation of casuistry. Though he quotes Alphonsus, one can note in him a certain transformation and rejection of the alphonsian method. Gone is the overall theological basis and the sense of christian discernment: in their places are legal formulae and a deductive, though benign, application of the principles to the case. The question is not the acceptability of Alphonsus (which is presumed) nor the precise interpretation of disputed texts (in which Müller shows no apparent interest). The method of Alphonsus is here transformed into neat categories and definitions, denuded of a sense of theological depth and spiritual insight which one finds in the original alphonsian texts. The transformation has occurred, largely, because the focus of the manual is now more clearly the didactic purpose of the moral classroom. This dictates a definite approach, and many of the nuances of the original alphonsian synthesis are lost.

The Dutch Redemptorist, Anthony Konings (1821–84), had a varied career as teacher, prefect of students and Provincial in Holland before his transfer to America in 1870 to teach in the Redemptorist seminary at Illchester, Maryland. It is interesting that, like Alphonsus, he was in his fifties when he wrote his moral theology[20] which he intended to be a less bulky work than the older manuals, and more adapted to the particular problems of North America. A didactic work intended for the ordinary student, his moral theology does, however, show the experience of one familiar with practical pastoral problems.

A factual and commonplace definition of the *consuetudinarius* and *recidivus* is followed by an elaboration of four principles governing confessional practice. Because a habit is not per se a sign of bad disposition, such people are to be absolved on a regular basis, though the possibility of deferral can at times be considered. A recidivist who is only materially such is to be granted absolution; but the disposition of the recidivist who is formally such is questionable, and absolution is to be usually refused, unless some extraordinary sign of sorrow is given. The fourth principle is concerned with the deferral of absolution which the confessor uses in his role as physician of the soul if such is the prudent judgment on the penitent's spiritual health. He finishes with some practical examples (people who are of a frivolous disposition, or who are weak-hearted); kindness is to be shown to all.

In Konings a transformation of the alphonsian manual can be noted similar to that already seen in Scavini. Technically, Konings follows Alphonsus but, somehow, it is more a material repetition than otherwise. Lacking is the alphonsian feel for the prudential moral judgment and the emphasis on the power of grace. It is as if discipline is brought to Alphonsus' thought in order to make moral theology more easily memorised by the student. All is neatly worked into principles, explanations and examples. Though Konings is clearly reliant on Alphonsus, he lacks the flexibility of the alphonsian position; he seems more anxious about the duties of the confessor (who should, of course, be prudent and kind) than about explaining the forgiving power of God's grace. The transformation that is occurring in a manual like Konings is one dictated by the didactic focus of the manual as an accessible textbook. It is not that Konings is, as such, unfaithful to Alphonsus; indeed he did much to explain the alphonsian theory of equi-probabilism. In reducing Alphonsus to a compendium-style presentation, however, the theological perspective and spiritual discernment of Alphonsus are lost in the principles and examples which, however neat, miss the inner spirit of Alphonsus' broader vision. The external forms of some of Alphonsus' teachings are still there, but the inner vitality is missing.

The final author chosen to represent the second half of the nineteenth century is the little-known Anthony Haine.[21] Precise definitions of the *consuetudinarius* and *recidivus* are given; the definitions are more legal than strictly theological. In treating the *consuetudinarius* he, again, uses legal terminology full of intricate distinctions. His practical conclusions are benign: but his arguments are extrinsic, authority based, and legal. He is concerned with what is legally possible, and though he may come to some of the same conclusions as Alphonsus, his way of reaching them is very different. The same general remarks are true of his treatment of the *recidivus* who is, again, defined in a legalistic way though, in practice, Haine wishes to be benign.

We are at a further stage of the transformation of the alphonsian manual here. Legal precisions have replaced nuanced theological arguments; extrinsic authority has taken the place of the intrinsic merits of an argument; the nominal duties of confessors take precedence over other considerations. Haine, no doubt, reflects the mood of the times. Neo-scholastic formulae are now commonplace in the theological textbooks, and fear of the anti-modernist watchdogs had driven most theologians to the calm, but stagnant, waters of authoritarian harbours. There is not a conscious transformation of Alphonsus evident in an author like Haine: but, in fact, the tenor of Haine is so different from Alphonsus that one is hard put to see a continuity of spirit between the manuals both of them wrote.

Why did this transformation of the alphonsian manual take place? To try to answer this question one must, firstly, be aware of the nature of the change and the general historical influences that were at work throughout the nineteenth century. The nature of the transformation is more easily stated. Looking at the later nineteenth century manuals, the outward presentation of an issue like the *habituati et recidivi* has not changed substantially. What has happened is that, materially, the presentation becomes more ordered (in terms of 'definitions', 'laws' 'principles' and 'cases') and the primary emphasis of Alphonsus on the prudent application of principles within the primacy of grace becomes less pronounced, with the result that the later manuals appear more rigid. Historical reasons contributed to this. At the turn of the century, the struggle was for the acceptance of Alphonsus as a legitimate moral theologian, as shown in Gousset and Kenrick. With the growing ecclesiastical approval of Alphonsus within a church that was becoming more centralised, an ironic change takes place in that Alphonsus, once under suspicion for over-liberal views, is an establishment theologian by the latter part of the century, as noted in people like Konings. The focus now becomes: what is the proper interpretation of Alphonsus, and in what sense is he to be seen as probabilist or equi-probabilist? That becomes clear in a manual like Gury's. The more distant they are from Alphonsus, the less theologians seem to rely on his primary text; the debates that dominate are what particular schools believe that Alphonsus said. It is in this limited sense that the prudential moral spirit and dominance of God's grace and mercy, so evident in Alphonsus, becomes less pronounced, even though, in a material sense, the manuals increasingly seem to be 'alphonsian'.

Three areas of misunderstanding, unrelated in themselves but interconnected in their cumulative influence, contributed to the process by which Alphonsus' teaching was, in part, transformed, abandoned or rejected: 1. misunderstandings, on the part of Catholic theologians, as to the precise authority of Alphonsus in moral theology; 2. misunderstandings, on the part of Protestant theologians, as to the theological method of Alphonsus, and 3. misunderstandings, between moral theologians, as to the sense of Alphonsus' equi-probabilism. I will comment briefly on each of these in turn.

The three major Roman statements on the authority of Alphonsus already referred to (those of the Sacred Congregation of Rites 1803, the Sacred Penitentiary 1831 and the official declaration as *Doctor Ecclesiae* in 1870) need to be carefully parsed. Positively, these statements show that Alphonsus' moral theology is in accordance with Catholic teaching, can be safely followed, and is a practical guide for christian living. Given the opposition to Alphonsus on the part of many rigorists and the lingering suspicion that, being tainted with probabilism, Alphonsus was a laxist, these statements, undoubtedly, represent official approval of Alphonsus. That said, one needs to be careful in analysing this approval. Alphonsus is free from error, that is, at the time he wrote and according to knowledge then available about matters of faith and morals in church teaching; he can be safely followed, but he is not the only moral theologian who merits respect; he is a sure guide for pastoral practice, but that does not mean he has a preeminence in all areas of theology. It is my impression that not all Catholic theologians of the nineteenth century subscribed to these caveats in the interpretation of

Alphonsus. On the one hand, the defenders of Alphonsus took an ahistorical view of his growing church approval that led, in time, to the fossilisation of alphonsian thought: on the other hand, the opponents of Alphonsus too easily dismissed his importance simply because he had not the speculative genius of an Aquinas or was not in tune with the new insights of the positive and psychological advances of the late nineteenth century. The approval of Alphonsus is a nuanced one, relating to the practical genius of his moral theology in the context of the eighteenth century confusion in that science, and it is limited in the scope of its intentions. To approve of Alphonsus is not to disapprove of Aquinas: to value the insights of the patristic era is not to undervalue Alphonsus who was writing at a different time and for a different purpose.[22] The passions aroused by the theological debates of the nineteenth century did not, unfortunately, allow for such eirenic assessments.

Accustomed, as we now are, to an ecumenical tone in our theological discussion we can forget the debates of a former age when Catholic and Protestant theologians attacked each other with a virulence akin to the tribalism of a 'holy war'. Alphonsus was a major victim of Protestant misunderstanding in mainland Europe, Britain and America during the nineteenth century.

The pamphlets of Grassman, Hermann, Harneck, Von Hoensbroech and the German Evangelical Alliance may now cause more amusement than annoyance, but their influence was substantial in the nineteenth century popular Protestant press. Alphonsus was, in particular, seen as dangerous: 'Whatever remained of St Augustine's thinking in the nineteenth century had been thrown aside by Liguori. Casuistic morals, together with the doctrine of attrition, have forced all dogmatic teaching into the background. It has been torn to shreds by probabilism and papalism. It is at the present time a legal system either rigid or elastic as circumstances demand.'[23] This is one of the milder quotations that I could use, but one can infer from its tone that Alphonsus was, in Protestant eyes, a symbol of the unbiblical and deceptive morality of Rome. Alphonsus' cause was not, admittedly, helped by some of his defenders who were as vehemently anti-Protestant as the attackers were anti-Catholic. Not all Catholics defended Alphonsus in a literalist sense,[24] but for many Protestants on mainland Europe Alphonsus was seen as an exponent of all that was evil in the modern Roman Church.

An extraordinary book by RP Blakeney[25] is typical of a certain type of fundamentalist Protestant reaction to Alphonsus in Britain. Some quotations give the flavour of the book: 'No attempt has been made to rebut the charges of immorality which are brought against the Saint's moral theology. The conclusion may fairly be drawn that the attempt is regarded as hopeless'; 'We the undersigned beg to state that the Latin not translated in this volume, especially that on the Confessional, is unfit for Protestant eyes or ears and must therefore be left in the original'; 'Thus the moral theology of Liguori has received in the most marked manner the imprimatur of Rome. That Church, by her authority, has proclaimed with one consent that his works are worthy of the highest praise and that they contain not one word worthy of censure . . . the principles of Liguori are the principles of Rome'; 'Oh, how different is the morality of the Bible! The religion of Jesus will make no compromise with sin, nor will it, under any circumstances, or for the accomplishment of any good, recognise and adopt the principle of doing evil that good may come.'[26] Blakeney's work has the appearances of scholarship, comprising eighteen chapters that purport to analyse the text of Alphonsus. In fact, the point of Alphonsus' method is altogether missed: that is, the enunciation of principles and their application to particular circumstances with a view to the good pastoral administration of the sacrament of confession. What, for a standard Catholic moralist, is the interpretation and application of principles taking the human situation into account, appears to the fundamentalist Protestant, like Blakeney, as anti-gospel equivocation.

In America it was possible, in the nineteenth century, for Protestants and Catholics to live and die without ever meeting each other. In that atmosphere, total misunderstanding was possible, and for the poorly educated

Protestant Alphonsus represented the worst of the 'harlot Rome': 'To American Protestants, Liguori stood for the threat that Catholic immorality could overwhelm American virtue.'[27]

Distant from the theological perspective of today, also, are the quarrels over the interpretation of probabilism and equi-probabilism and the precise role of Alphonsus in these debates. But in the late nineteenth century this was still a very live issue, as is instanced by the publication of *Vindiciae Ballerinianae* and the *Vindiciae Alphonsianae* in 1873. These works generated immediate and widespread controversy.[28]

This is not the place to argue the merits of either of these voluminous tomes, as I only wish to comment on them in the context of the development of the manual. It is clear, from the *Vindiciae Alphonsianae*, that the status of Alphonsus was a very sensitive issue for the Redemptorists of the time, and there is a hint of wounded pride that the founder of their congregation could be in any way maligned. Much of both *Vindiciae* now seems like an arid debate, far removed from the realities of the time. It seems strange to have leading moral theologians quibbling over the niceties of probabilism when the major issues of the day were political upheaval, the industrial revolution and growing religious indifference. The *Vindiciae* debate cemented the tendency towards the use of Alphonsus as an external authority in moral matters: what was at stake, particularly in the *Vindiciae Alphonsianae*, was the need to uphold the authority of Alphonsus against any other authority that did not have Alphonsus' ecclesiastical standing. The Redemptorist authors of the *Vindiciae Alphonsianae*, aware that probabilism was equated with laxism in many minds, wanted to preserve the authority of Alphonsus from being tainted with a laxist brush. This positive aim was, however, advanced more by arguments of extrinsic authority than intrinsic merit.

Some conclusions, based on the manuals analysed, can now be made as to how the alphonsian moral system was transformed, rejected or abandoned by the end of the nineteenth century. Alphonsus was open-minded in the terms of his own day, and his moral theology was part of a wider theological and spiritual vision. Because of the misunderstandings just mentioned, the text of Alphonsus was, increasingly, used in a defensive way as the century progressed. Anxious to prove Alphonsus' orthodoxy, his defenders used extrinsic arguments to avoid any expression of ambiguity in the alphonsian interpretations. Conscious of Protestant objections, Alphonsus' defenders were all the more anxious to protect his position as a Roman Catholic theologian: and within the narrow confines of the moral schools, the defenders of Alphonsus tried to protect their master from the contamination of dubious, especially probabilist, authors. Taken together, these meant that, by the end of the nineteenth century, Alphonsus was interpreted in a more rigid sense than his own text implies. The theological context and inner spirit of Alphonsus' own moral theology were obscured, at least, by the effort to condense his thought into compendia of statements, laws and principles.

What were the concerns of these late nineteenth century manualists? They wished to be seen as supporting Alphonsus' views; they were anxious to incorporate relevant Roman legislation and citations of approval in Alphonsus' favour and they wished to provide textbooks that were concise and easily studied with a view to the sacramental administration of confession. In themselves, all these are obviously laudable concerns. In practice, however, they obscured the purpose of the alphonsian manual. Support for the alphonsian view is not as easy as stating that one writes '*secundum doctrinam S Alphonsi*' or even as easy as quoting him: interpretation of Alphonsus demands a knowledge of the original texts and an evaluation of their historical setting, qualities not immediately obvious in the later manuals. Incorporating new Roman decrees can, too easily, become a litany of references grafted on to a basic text in a way that the focus of the original text is obscured by the addition of many details. A compendium is attractive in that its brief formulae are easily learned: the summary of a complex theological problem (like the *habituati et recidivi*), without reference to the underlying psychological and theological problems, can, over time, become quite ambiguous.

By the late nineteenth century the moral manuals had become introverted: their agenda was set a priori, and they were little interested in the new scientific knowledge, or the new social and economic problems. It is not that they are unaware of these, but the presumption is that, within themselves, they have the principles to solve any new problems. A further stage of isolation occurs with the tightening control of the moral schools by the respective religious orders: many opinions appear to be 'commonly accepted', possibly because only authors of a certain view were studied.

It is a major irony of the nineteenth century development of the moral manual that Alphonsus, in his own time the seeker of the pastorally viable middle way according to intrinsically meritorious arguments, became, after his own time, an establishment theologian quoted as an extrinsic authority to head off any further arguments. The problem, looked at from this safe distance, was that there was little knowledge of the primary alphonsian texts and little appreciation of their historical context.

Decline of the manual tradition, 1900–1960

As in the previous sections, editions of manuals for each decade of this period were taken to chart the systematisation of the alphonsian manual. My comments will be brief, as there is little of note in these manuals in that they represent, for the greater part, a consolidation of the changes that have already taken place in the late nineteenth century, rather than any notable evolution in their own right.

Thomas Slater's manual[29] is broadly within the then accepted interpretation of Alphonsus; he seeks the middle view and tries to uphold the good faith of the penitent's conscience. By placing the question of the habitual and recidivist sinner within the discussion of the roles of the priest as physician and counsellor he is able to take a more realistically pastoral view than some of the more rigid manuals. The manual of Jerome Noldin[30] is representative of the probabilist tradition. The particular emphasis is on the obligation of the confessor more than the power of grace operative in the penitent.[31] His method is careful and legalistic though, within the tight formulation of principles, he tries to apply them in a benign way. Overall, the impression is of a manualist more concerned with exactitude of legal formulation than with the liberating power of God's grace. Reading Joseph Aertnys and Cornelius Damen[32] one is aware of their Redemptorist loyalty to Alphonsus: a learned work and up-to-date with Roman legislation, it is more in conformity with the material words of Alphonsus than with the inner spirit. The emphasis is, too often, on negative fear rather than on the positive power of love. Louis Wouters,[33] also a Redemptorist, is more of a casuist than Aertnys-Damen: the emphasis is on extrinsic authority and upholding the views of one particular school of moral theology.[34]

Representative of the main alternate moral school, the Jesuit, Edward Genicot and his nephew Joseph Salsmans, produced a manual still being published in the 1940s.[35] It is in the tradition of Gury and Ballerini, though written in a more popular vein. There is not much difference in the practical conclusions that Aertnys-Damen or Genicot-Salsmans come to, but their way of argument represents two differing strands in the tradition, an indication that the internal tensions of the nineteenth century moral debates still lingered on. Our final manual by Heribert Jone and Urban Adelman[36] shows the poverty of theological vision and moral prudence to which the manual had descended by the middle of the twentieth century. Questions are seen from the narrow perspective of the confessor's legal duties, rather than from that of the conscience of the penitent.[37] The possibility of sin is everywhere seen, rather than the opportunities for love.[38] Good works seem more important than the power of grace. A cryptic legal tone takes the place of the theological and moral categories evident in Alphonsus. The transformation of Alphonsus is now so marked that, even if one cannot say that Jone-Adelman reject Alphonsus' views explicitly, in practice these views are abandoned.

The transformation of the alphonsian manual to the point where Alphonsus' views were neglected, as in the question of the *habituati et recidivi*, left the manuals incapable of incorporating the new psychological and theological insights that were being articulated in the 1940s and 1950s: for instance, the psychological factors involved in defining sin; the primacy of love in defining the christian moral life; the distinctions between venial, grave and mortal sin; the degree of freedom and knowledge necessary for sin in the moral sense; and the replacing of a juridical model of confession by one that sees it as a sacrament of joyful reconciliation.[39] All of these insights could have helped the manuals in their treatment of the *habituati et recidivi*. Because of the transformation of the manual in the late nineteenth century, a transformation that became fossilised in the twentieth century, such new insights were seen as incompatible with the manual system, as it had become. Had the manuals remained more in the spirit of Alphonsus, these would have been seen as organic developments, and some of the practical advantages of the manuals could have been saved. Instead, they wrote their own death-sentence by, in practice, abandoning some of the alphonsian views.

14. *Sign of Contradiction or Sign of Hope? The Mariology of Saint Alphonsus Today*

THE best-selling publication of all times on our Lady is St Alphonsus of Liguori's *The Glories of Mary*.[1] Between 1750 and 1950, no less than 750 editions appeared. No doctor of the church has been so popular a writer, both in the extent and the depth of his influence. A people's missioner, he was also a people's writer. In the age of baroque, his simple and direct style was a marvel for his time. His Marian teaching was trustworthy and effective and contained a heartwarming message of hope. The book is alive with the faith of an ardent advocate, witnessing to the presence and influence in his own life of the mother of mercy.

But the book is also a sign of contradiction which belongs to the later stage of the counter-reformation period. The reformers of the sixteenth century, in their attack on the cult of the saints, had gradually focused on Marian devotion as the supreme example of their complaint. They argued that it was not based on scripture, that it gave too much honour to a creature, and that it conflicted with the unique mediation of Christ the Lord. Instead of contesting this charge, Catholic writers developed an enthusiastic theology of the privileges of Mary which was not well based in scripture or tradition, and in consequence slipped the bonds of control. In *The Glories of Mary* for instance, Alphonsus defends the view that Mary had the use of reason from the first moment of her life.[2] By and large, however, the book avoids extremes and is a decisive work which brings to an end the early stage of counter-reformation enthusiasm, and expresses a Marian theology faithful to the best pre-reformation tradition.[3]

The Glories of Mary was also a sign of contradiction to the Jansenist movement in eighteenth century Italy. The two reformations, Protestant and Catholic, had tried to purify christianity but often at the expense of earthly and human values. People who lived 'in the world' had to choose between God and the world as if the world were not God's world. In this unhealthy climate of rejection, there was a strong sense of sin and guilt with an obsessive need for liberation. The rigid Jansenist ethic, together with its theology of a fearsome God of justice, restricted easy access to the full life of the church.[4] Unlike France, Italy was fortunate in producing a traditional but new kind of leader in Alphonsus, who helped stem the tide of Jansenism and build up the spiritual resources of church life to face the age of revolutions ahead.[5]

Alphonsus was a man of tradition rather than of the enlightenment, and his book is a further sign of contradiction in the age of reason, when the great philosophers of the time tried to test and control all life, even the life of faith, by critical reason. Inevitably, a gap had grown between the enlightened few and the illiterate many, whose religion was often primitive and superstitious. Muratori, a pioneer in the church of critical scholarship, sought to adjust popular piety to theology and liturgy. Alphonsus, however, felt that Muratori 'whom I have always venerated' took too negative a view of popular forms of devotion to Mary, and it was this feeling that led him to write *The Glories of Mary*.[6]

The book divides into two sections: 1. A commentary on the 'Hail, Holy Queen' (Salve Regina). 2. Sermons for the feasts of Mary; The virtues of Mary; Practices of devotion. For Alphonsus, the principal devotion to Mary was imitation of her virtues, which is why he treats of these before discussing practices of devotion. Overall, his book is about the pastoral meaning of Mary, especially as mother of mercy and refuge of sinners.

Every chapter of the commentary on the 'Salve Regina' develops a theme based on the phrases of the prayer. The writer is concerned not so much with his own faith as the faith of the christian centuries. His pages become a pulpit from which the great voices of the past witness to the church's faith in Mary. The force of his argument lies in these witnesses to the living tradition of the church. He shows how all ages have called Mary blessed and have seen in her intercession a gracious and effective provision of God's loving kindness to his people. What unifies the book, with its many quotations, is the living faith of Alphonsus; what the quotations proclaim, he lived in his ardent Marian spirit.

Towards the end of every chapter, Alphonsus uses a story to illustrate the theme in terms of concrete experience. To a modern reader, some of these stories sound far-fetched, for example, about pacts with the devil, and show little critical sense of history as it is understood today. He was a man of his own time, more accepting of the marvellous than the modern age, yet he insists that he chose only stories that were taken by his contemporaries to be well founded.

Every story leads to a prayer, which is natural with Alphonsus, who was a praying man and all his books praying books, written out of and leading to prayer. Prayer for him was a way of life; his words are in deep harmony with the throbbing movement of his heart-surrender to God. In all his teaching, he wanted doctrine to come alive, which it did primarily through prayer.

A deeper ecumenical issue

Even in today's ecumenical climate, *The Glories of Mary*, with its main theme of the power of Mary's intercession in christian life, continues to be a stumbling block to other christians. Within the church too, in theological and pastoral circles rather than at the popular level, the scruples evoked in Catholic hearts by the reformation still exist, causing fear that Marian devotion may take from the absolute primacy of Christ in the faith and cult of the church.[7] Hesitations about Our Lady, however, frequently accentuated larger and more basic differences between Catholic and Protestant theologies. The

Protestant emphasis on God alone, Christ alone, grace alone, faith alone, excludes creatures from any role in the work of salvation. The real issue for the ecumenical debate lies in the precise relationship between God and human beings. For the reformers, human nature is totally corrupted by sin, though now forgiven and justified. By contrast, Catholics hold that human nature is not totally vitiated by sin; God's grace brings about an inner change which enables the believer to cooperate freely in the new life. True, God alone is holy and makes holy; it is, however, his gracious will—respecting and indeed creating our freedom—not to make us holy without our consent, which, of course remains his gift.

This is clearly the scenario presented in Luke's gospel of the Annunciation. What comes first in the story is God's initiative of free grace, his favouring of Mary and invitation to active cooperation with his plan. Mary's reply is the model response to God for every disciple, servant and true relative of the Lord: an obedient listening-to, and doing, of God's will. God's grace is not a substitute for freedom, nor is freedom a substitute for grace; what happens is a mystery of faith, cooperation, communion between grace and graced freedom. The permanent pattern and law of God's incarnation in human life is here: God redeems us all the more by gracing us freely to cooperate with his love. Though Karl Barth accuses Catholic mariology of by-passing Mary of Nazareth, he still speaks of her as exemplary for all christians by her servant response to the Lord.[8] 'Mary's consent is indeed the happy beginning of a new creation, of a Church without spot or wrinkle', as Paul VI said in *Marialis Cultus*.[9] She is the specific sign and guarantee of the Lord's humanity and she continues to be such throughout his life and through his redeeming death and resurrection, and on into the life of his Church. Notice how Luke's gospel takes care to give a consistent picture of Mary from the Annunciation through to the coming of the Spirit, where she is present among the disciples. In John's gospel, at the hour of Jesus' going to the Father, she is given the role of spiritual mother to the beloved disciple and to the new eschatological family of the Lord.

243

The logic of the Incarnation is that God redeems us through the humanity of Christ. The Incarnation is for ever, and its logic continues in and through the church which is the body of the risen Lord, prolonging his humanity in time and place. Christ the Lord lives on in the church, which through the apostolic ministry of word and sacrament manifests and exercises his unique mediation in all her life. Earthly and sinful though the church is, she is holy in her essence, betrothed to the Lord and sharing his Spirit. She is a new environment and creation.

This fundamental conviction of the holiness of the church is expressed in the role given to Mary, the mother of the Lord. In her the church has a sign of final victory over sin and death; what all christians hope for is already a reality in Mary, the first member of the church. The doctrines of the immaculate conception and the assumption throw new light on the mystery of salvation which continues to be made flesh in God's people. It seems to be a pattern in God's ways to realise in germ at the beginning of his works, in one person, the ideal of perfection which all will reach at the end. In contrast with the 'high' ecclesiology of Catholicism, that of the churches of the reform is 'low', stressing rather the weak sinfulness of the human community, ever in need of repentance.

Mary's conscious and committed role at the beginning of salvation continues with her entry into glory. The doctrine of the communion of saints is about the interdependence among all those, past and present, who enjoy the life of the Spirit by baptism into the community of Jesus. Christian life is a holy communion of prayer and mutual help. Communion with God is considered in terms of human mediation, because of the pattern revealed in the human life of the Lord and in the apostolic preaching. The living Lord alone is mediator of life for the church in all its members, including Mary. But the life and love he mediates are self-communicating; to share in the life is to be called to communicate it to others. Therefore, everyone in the holy fellowship is of spiritual importance to every other. This means that every christian is called to be a co-mediator and co-redeemer in total dependence on Christ. This no more takes from Christ's unique mediation than the priesthood of the faithful takes from the unique priesthood of Christ, which is its foundation. No more than the goodness of christians takes from God's goodness, who alone is good. In the communion of saints is our Lady, first of the Lord's disciples and his closest relative, mother not only in faith but in the flesh as well. She is the virgin to whom we pray that we may be made worthy of the promises of Christ. She is the first and most loved Christ-lover. In being loved and honoured, she brings the communion of saints to life for us, opening up a vast world of mutual giving and receiving.

Marian theology today sees Mary as all relative to the Lord in the mystery of the church; and the church has grown to see Mary in her own true face. 'Celebrating the mysteries of Christ, the church gazes at Mary and in her joyfully contemplates, as in a faultless image, that which she herself wholly desires and hopes to be.'[10]

Mary, then, is image, type, icon of the church, so what is said in describing her refers not only to her as a unique, historical person, but it also has a symbolic quality in the context of the church as a whole, of which she is a living member.[11] Mary points beyond herself to the greater mystery of the whole Christ which enfolds both her and us. To look on Mary of Nazareth, to surrender in faith to her inner secret of graced discipleship, is to come to a heart-knowing of her, and of how truly to respond to the Lord. To praise her as blessed and holy is really to say something deep about ourselves: that we are redeemed by a gracious God and called to the same discipleship. To honour her as full of grace, highly favoured, is to honour in ourselves too the gift of grace. As Karl Rahner said: 'It is possible to say when involved in Marian devotions: we are engaged in a christian understanding of the human situation. It is God's word concerning us we are concerned with—a blessed and holy understanding of our life.'[12]

The Glories of Mary was written long before the recovery of the church dimension in Marian theology. In preaching on Mary today, she must be set firmly within the life of the church. It is worth noting, however, that the recent theology of mediation emphasises the motherly function of Mary.[13] This harmonises well with the central message of St Alphonsus, which is still relevant today: Mary, the mother of mercy, is a living and active presence in christian life at every stage of the christian journey, from conversion to glory.

Modern enlightenment

Part and parcel of modern culture is the approach to life which starts with concrete human experience. For this we are indebted to the philosophers of the last century—the 'masters of suspicion'—who reacted against the rationalism of the eighteenth century. Now we benefit from a new enlightenment which is the fruit of the scientific exploration of the world of human experience. A hallmark of this thinking is the awareness of the historical aspect of all human realities. Historians, for instance, question the extent to which the Europe of the eighteenth century became dechristianised; that depends on the extent to which it had been really christian. The phenomenon of religion has been under scrutiny so that we are better able to discern in Marian devotion how much is from the Spirit and how much is due to cultural influences and to folk religion. It is possible to see more clearly the gap between the universal teaching of the church and the way it is received and lived by differing cultures and sensibilities.

Already in scripture there is evidence of a pluralism in theologies and spiritualities. The roots of differing attitudes to Marian doctrine and devotion may be discussed here. The Protestant attitude seems to be influenced by the silence of Paul about Mary and his emphasis on the self-emptying of Jesus. The gospel of John harmonises well with orthodox devotion to Mary as *Theotokos* or 'God-bearer' and with the rich Marian symbolism of their liturgy. Catholic theology is shaped by the spiritual and dyamic personality of Mary as described by Luke. Similar differences are manifest in later centuries: Newman wisely comments about *The Glories of Mary* that St Alphonsus wrote for Neapolitans whom he knew but 'we did not know'.[14]

Critics find echoes in Marian devotion of primitive mother goddesses, who played an important part in ancient religion. The mother goddess myths say something about the earth as source of life and fertility, a nurturing mother to humankind but at times destructive. The mother goddess was often named as virgin too, in symbols of purity. There is a new interest in such myths today, due perhaps to our greater sense of embodiment in our environment. It may be also that this technological and bureaucratic civilisation of ours, so ready to violate the good earth, begets in us a deep insecurity and sense of vulnerability; we find ourselves to be again 'children afraid of the night'.[15] Certainly, the mother goddess symbol is not adequately explained as merely a reflection of the place of women in society, nor as a mere projection of the human need for tenderness and affection, nor indeed as an archetype of the feminine in everyone. It also has something to say about the mystery of God, which is the mysterious source of all motherhood, femininity and humanity.

The theme of the divine motherhood of God is powerfully expressed in the text of Isaiah: 'A mother may forget her child but I will never forget you' (Is 49:15), and it has been kept alive down the ages in east and west. In Catholic life, Mary, the mother of God, is a vivid symbolic reminder that the ultimate mystery of God contains and surpasses both femininity and masculinity. She is an icon of innerness, caring, receptivity and tender mercy. God himself, of course, is infinitely all of these things more than Mary, who is a mere creature, but it is a comfort to our humanity to have in the mother of mercy a human symbol of this aspect of the divine mercy.

The symbol, however, must not take the place of the reality. The mother of God must not replace God the mother.[16] The point is made, for instance, that the cult of Mary grew as the use of feminine images of God declined. It is as if the images of Mary were needed to compensate for the tenderness not emphasised in God, and for the lack of stress on the humanity of Christ. There is no doubt that Marian piety has at times tended to see Mary not as symbol so much as substitute for the mercy of God and of his Christ, which she is meant to reflect and on which she totally depends. She has been used both as a defence against the rigours of God's justice and a sedative for religious anxieties. This is a caricature of true devotion to Mary. *The Glories of Mary*, by contrast, emphasises how precisely Mary's motherhood of mercy reveals God's merciful design; it is through her that the tenderness of his mercy is seen more clearly.

Myths, symbols and images are essential in the effort to grapple with the mystery dimension of life. They involve a deep exercise of the human imagination, and they reflect too the likeness to God hidden in the depth of the human spirit. Instead of undermining doctrines, they supplement them and help us to understand who we really are.[17] They may, of course, prove harmful if absolutised. What is distinctive about christian myths is that they are based on historic fact and are therefore to be tested by the critical standard of the word of God, alive in the ritual and preaching of the church. That is why cultural images of Mary need to be evangelised and compared to the historic Mary of Nazareth.

Some religions seem to omit or suppress all feminine symbolism: Judaism, Islam, forms of Protestantism. Mary was the chief icon to go in the iconoclasm of the Reformation. She continues to be for Catholics a special focus for inconicity or image-making. Behind all making and breaking of icons is a basic insight that the God we seek is both unseen and seen at the same time. The challenge of icons is to hear truly what they are saying and not to identify them with the mystery they convey.[18]

Marian devotion, like any other form of religion, may take strange shapes and be used for strange purposes. It may be used politically against other churches or as a conservative force against the scientific mentality and new religious trends. It has been alleged that devotion to Mary, Queen of Poland serves to bind the nation 'by a chivalrous bond to the eternal feminine embodied in a feudal queen'.[19] The mother-son focus in Catholic mariology may have in it an element of compensation for a celibate clergy. In today's nuclear world, an apocalyptic mariology appears to expect Armageddon and creates a friend-foe hostility, with communists as the foe and Mary as conqueror treading the dragon underfoot. Moltmann comments that not all the dragons in our world are red![20] Marian devotion obviously can be a melting pot of the most diverse needs and desires, which is why, like all attitudes, it needs to be regularly evangelised.

A critical factor for Marian theology in the socio-cultural changes of the present time is the role of women. Not to be seen as sexual object, nor as housebound, nor merely as mother, woman takes her place in modern society as free, equal, independent in decision and responsibility. For Paul VI, Mary is a mirror for the expectations of modern woman in her active and responsible cooperation in the supreme 'event of world importance', the mystery of the Incarnation, where Mary is present as a woman of strong faith and decisive action, quick to respond to the prompting of the Spirit and to human need, who proclaims, too, that God vindicates the humble and the oppressed.[21]

The Second Vatican Council aimed to make worship true and spiritual as opposed to an external practice which in spite of good faith can often border on superstition. Yet, popular piety has been little influenced by the Council, as witnessed by the weakening of Sunday practice by contrast with the flourishing of Marian shrines and pilgrimages. The frontiers between religion, devotion and superstition are not easy to fix. In the eyes of non-believers, every religious action may seem superstitious. Yet, for many people, the only practical way to relate to the object of faith is through a personalised devotion. In fact, there seems to be some link between the collapse of external devotions and the waning of faith. Without understanding what practices mean to the devotee, they should not be labelled as superstitious. Pascal describes a practice as superstitious when it offers salvation 'regardless of how one has conducted one's life'. He comments that 'devotions to the Virgin are a powerful means of salvation when they are motivated from the start by faith and charity'.[22] The superstitious pilgrim, like the pagan of old, tries to control God by formulas and techniques; whereas the essence of true religion is to commit oneself to God and not just for gain, indeed, against personal satisfaction if required. A notice found behind a candle-stand at the ancient French shrine of Rocamadour suggests the spirit to aim at: 'What would my light be without your prayer?'[23]

A devout reader

Cardinal Dechamps of Malines once told a friend of his who used *The Glories of Mary* as a spiritual thermometer: 'When I am not faithful to grace, it enlightens me and sustains my confidence; when I grow negligent, it is too much for me.' This is a useful incident to introduce the problem of communication: how to read a spiritual best-seller which is also two hundred years old. A 'devout author' really needs a 'devout reader', lest the reader 'hearing might not hear or understand'.[24] St Augustine expressed it: 'Give me a lover and he will understand.' Speaking of *The Glories of Mary* Newman warns against being surprised at finding the extraordinary in the writings of a saint because they function at a different level: 'The spiritual man judges all things and he himself is judged by no one.' Burning thoughts and feelings are as open to criticism as they are beyond it: 'in a particular person they may be becoming and beautiful; formalised into meditations they may be as repulsive as love letters in a police report.'[25]

Certainly, critical reason is not always the best approach. It is interesting that, while resisting the age of reason, the church was contaminated by it to the extent that Catholic writers tended to make reason the source and test of religious knowledge, as if one could, as Barth said 'pocket God at the end of a syllogism'. But christian faith is not an ideology to be passed on by reasonable instruction; it is a way of life communicated. What comes first in the journey to faith is religious experience which affects senses, feelings and imagination. The importance of intuitive and affective knowing has been recovered today, with the symbols, myths and ritual through which it is expressed. The meaning of word and ritual is apprehended and felt by participating in the personal experience which underlies them. 'We need to open our hearts so that our minds be renewed' (cf Rom 12:12).[26]

This is not to undervalue reason as critical intelligence nor to minimise the role of judgment in theology. While language about religious experience is descriptive, yet it implies a theology and it is necessary to care about the orthodoxy and adequacy of that theology. Reflection ought to be done prayerfully in the Spirit, not a prayer that is merely emotional but a prayer with heart, soul and mind (1 Cor 14,15). It is a matter of finding a balance between thought and feeling, between what is intelligible and what is mystery.

The knowing of God is the heart-knowledge of faith, which is a gift of the Spirit. What specially nourishes that knowledge is prayerful listening to the word of God which is the training ground for all devout reading. It is the skill of the disciple and relative of the Lord, and it is a Marian skill. The full process demands listening, reflecting in the heart, responding with the heart, becoming absorbed by the word. Moreover, the words of scripture are performative; they need to be acted on to be truly savoured. It is necessary to live at their pitch. To really hear the words of eucharistic consecration, a sacrificial spirit is called for.[27] Such a high form of knowing is not for the worldly-wise but is within the reach of the lowly of heart. The doctrine of the immaculate conception, for example, is not an item of information passed on by an academic process. Rather, it is the fruit of popular Marian devotion, stubbornly asserting itself against the determined opposition of theologians and bishops. 'It is a victory for the affective over neat, rational systems.'[28]

The Glories of Mary is a book which presupposes a 'devout reader' who enters into a heart-to-heart relationship with an author who is sharing his own Marian life, and the extent to which he himself lives from her motherly mercy to sinners. The power of the book lies in the harmony between the truth Alphonsus writes and the life he lives. His aim is to bring the reader to love Mary, not just to accept his argument but to live it. Full truth is lived truth. The fact of being committed does not make Alphonsus unscientific:

As a theologian he was easier to read than any of his

predecessors. But when he was attacked for his doctrines, antagonists found that the simplicity was deceptive and that underneath the apparently unintellectual missioner was a scholar equipped at all points.[29]

It should not be said that Alphonsus was devout but not a theologian. As Kierkegaard claims: 'A theologian is one who not only talks of God but talks to him.' That is the depth and fullness of Alphonsus' science; he is more than an academic doctor, he is a doctor of the church. His whole human life resonates with God's life in him, which is truth between grace and life. To be in tune with him, it is necessary to live at his pitch of Marian devotion, otherwise the reader's personal lack of depth can be blamed on the writer.[30]

The last word on the book can be left to the author himself, even though he spoke it unwittingly. Towards the end of his life, crippled with arthritis, half blind, with failing memory, he was listening one day to some spiritual reading by the brother infirmarian. 'Brother, who is the author of that beautiful book?', he asked. The brother read the title to him: '*The Glories of Mary* by Alphonsus Liguori.'

15. *In Search of Christian Spirituality Today*

BY general agreement the word 'spirituality' is a vague and flexible term. It is often understood, for example, to refer to a person's or a community's prayer-life, religious practices or methods of prayer. In this paper, however, I understand christian spirituality as having to do with the whole life of a christian, with life orientation, with a person's or a community's 'life in the Spirit'. It refers to the full, human, lived faith-response to revelation and redemption through Jesus Christ.

The poles of christian spirituality are events now separated by some two thousand years. The first is the historical event of revelation and redemption given through Jesus of Nazareth. The second is the acceptance of this revelation and redemption by the christian through faith and baptism. Linking these two events is the history of the believing community which is the bearer of revelation and redemption, and which holds them available to people, especially through word and sacrament.

Since each individual throughout the ages is unique, and if spirituality is understood as a life-response in faith to the gifts of revelation and redemption, then it follows that there are as many spiritualities as there are active christians. Historically, certain distinctive approaches to spirituality have arisen, and have been named after individuals or communities who embodied them, eg Benedictine, Dominican, Franciscan. In modern times other spiritualities have appeared on the scene, such as holistic, liberation and creation spiritualities. All that can be claimed for any one of these, I suggest, is that it helps to highlight certain aspects of the christian way of life, or that it corrects or establishes certain emphases according to the needs of particular times, situations or groups. It can not be claimed that any named spirituality is the correct, ideal or universal christian spirituality.

I propose to indicate in the brief historical account which follows, that while some undesirable features have been introduced into christian spirituality at various times, there has been a wide range of authentic spiritualities from the beginning. Relying mostly on the scriptural tradition, I shall then propose certain important features which I believe should characterise any authentic christian spirituality, at the same time suggesting some characteristics particularly appropriate to our times.

The New Testament writings emerge from a community, or rather communities, struggling to understand, express and respond to their experience of the life, preaching, death and resurrection of Jesus. The texts already provide evidence of considerable variety in ways of understanding and responding to the content and meaning of the experience.

In the earliest New Testament texts, (1,2 Thess), there is the eager expectation of the Lord's Second Coming which is thought to be imminent. The practical response of some of the Thessalonians to this belief was to stop working. They saw no point, apparently, in the labour of spring planting if the end of the world was going to occur before the harvest. Much later, around the year AD 100, when the Johannine writings are taking shape, some sixty years or more have passed, and the Lord has not come. The Johannine writings reflect a community of believers settling in for the 'long haul', and adjusting their life accordingly. In the middle period, the writings of Luke reflect the growing belief that the Lord has in fact already returned, but in the Spirit. He is at once near and distant. Throughout, the early communities are struggling to find guidelines for an appropriate way of life for themselves as followers of Jesus. For example, whether or not to proclaim the gospel to the gentiles; whether circumcision was required; how to deal with sinners and apostates; the role of the law.

From the very beginning, then, there were many ways

of understanding the significance of the Jesus event, and many ways of responding in faith with an appropriate way of life. It is not possible to speak of a single theology of the New Testament, because there are many, nor to speak of a single spirituality.

There is now consensus among New Testament scholars that the central content of Jesus' message is not God, or morality or the immortality of the soul, but the kingdom of God: 'The most certain historical datum about Jesus' life is that the concept which dominated his preaching, the reality which gave meaningfulness to all his activity, was "the kingdom of God".'[1] It is also agreed that the kingdom preached by Jesus has to do with human existence in the present world. While it certainly has an eschatological dimension, it is not a purely personal, spiritual or otherworldly reality. It is thus in continuity with Old Testament ideas about salvation.

For the Hebrews, God was the God of their ancestors. He was the God of Abraham, the God of Isaac and the God of Jacob (Ex 3:6). In other words, he was the one who was present to them throughout their history in their daily, bodily, worldly existence. His saving acts on their behalf had to do with their personal, human and national welfare. They had no concept of an afterlife, and therefore no concept of salvation as having to do with the immortality of the soul. Only during the two centuries before Jesus do we find some vague and very uncertain ideas of some existence after death. Whatever God did for them was done here and now in the world.

Historically, however, despite these well-established facts from the Old Testament and the New, salvation and sanctification came to be widely understood as primarily personal and individual matters, and christianity came to be regarded as a religion of personal and even spiritual salvation.

Although the Old and New Testaments emanated from a Hebrew culture, they came to be interpreted according to the criteria of another, mainly Greek, culture. When Paul, for example, speaks of tension between flesh and spirit, he is referring to two dimensions of the human which in Hebrew terms are radically inseparable. In Greek thought, however, body and soul are separable. The soul is considered to be held in bondage by the body, and is prevented by the body from soaring to its own appropriate heights. The Greeks could speak of the 'immortality of the soul' only when it became free of the body. This, we may be sure, was why the Athenians 'burst out laughing' at Paul's proclamation of the resurrection of the body (cf Acts 17:16–32). For Paul, as a Hebrew, the resurrection of the body was non-negotiable. But for the Greeks, bodily resurrection could only mean continuing enslavement of the soul. In time, however, the bible came to be interpreted according to Greek thought-patterns. Sanctification came to be described as 'the ascent of the soul to God'. Salvation became a possibility when the soul simply shed the encumbrance of the flesh.

The dualism in this approach found extreme expression, in ways unacceptable to christianity, in such movements as gnosticism, manichaeism and docetism. All of these were condemned in turn by the church, but the underlying attitudes were never fully rooted out of christian consciousness. They recur again and again through history, most recently and obviously in puritanism and jansenism. Despite condemnation they left their mark on christian spirituality. Up to the present day it can be seen that a lot of spiritual writing has been dominated by the idea of the 'spiritual' person as the one who has become purified of all bodily and material concerns in order to attain to the pure realm of the soul.

During most of christian history the starting-point for a consideration of the story of salvation came to be the Fall, according to the Yahwist tradition, (Gen 2:4b–3:24), almost to the exclusion of the Creation tradition of the Priestly source, with its emphasis on the goodness of creation and of humanity (Gen 1:1–2:4a). The emphasis on the Fall encouraged a predominantly negative attitude towards humanity because of its sinfulness, and towards the material world which was understood to share in the fallenness of humanity. It encouraged a view of the world as a vale of tears in which people should not feel much at home. 'Flight from the world' came to be seen as a christian ideal, and salvation as an act whereby God transports the soul to another realm.

During the later middle ages spirituality became separated from the influence and discipline of sound theology. It widely became not only indifferent to theology but sometimes positively anti-theological and anti-intellectual, a situation that still obtains, as John Macquarrie points out:

> In the Western Church today there is some tension between theology and spirituality. The faithful say their prayers and aspire to holiness, but sometimes what they are doing seems threatened by the theologian, who may be reaching conclusions that seem hard to square with the faith that finds expression in prayer and worship. Though the separation of theology and spirituality is in part due to the pressure on theologians to defend the academic status of their subject in the universities, it is equally due to the indifference and even contempt shown for theology by some clergy and laypeople.[2]

It is indeed true that christianity is a religion of the heart rather than of the head. Nevertheless, history shows that when christian spirituality ignores the discipline of rigorous theological investigation and reflection, it leads to superstition, superficiality, emotionalism, naiveté and even materialism. During the past 500 years especially, much of spirituality has been tainted by such features.

While spirituality was inspired by and modelled on liturgy it retained its communal character, since liturgy of its nature emphasises this dimension of faith and christian life. But when spirituality became separated from liturgy, especially during the two or three centuries prior to the Reformation, it tended to become more and more privatised and individualistic. For the first time, treatises on methods of private prayer as a means of personal sanctification appear. Spiritual perfection becomes a goal for the very religious. A false distinction begins to be made between the evangelical precepts which were binding on everyone, and what came to be called the 'counsels of perfection', which were often thought of as optional extras for the chosen few, the elite, the 'athletes of God'. The existence of higher and lower states of life within the christian community begin to be taken for granted. Clergy and religious in particular are considered to belong to the higher states. Virtual universal acceptance of such an understanding is shown by the fact that nearly all those canonised as saints during the past 500 years have been clergy or religious.

The tendency towards individualism and the privatisation of spirituality received further impetus from the Reform movement in the sixteenth century. In the centuries that followed, the rise of the doctrine of separation of church and state carried it still farther. Living one's faith became a private option for the individual.

This brief survey of the history of spirituality shows that there has been a wide variety of christian spiritualities from the beginning. The spiritualities arose out of different experiences of life, different ways of interpreting scripture, and different ideas about humanity, about the world, and about God. It is also evident that the shape of spirituality was often affected by the personality, background and temperament of individuals and communities. It would seem very clear, for example, that the different interpretations of the Jesus event by St Paul and St Luke reflect the character, background and temperament of each of them. The same might be said in a comparison of the spiritualities of Francis of Assisi and Ignatius Loyola.

The search for an authentic spirituality must, it seems, be undertaken anew in every age according to the life-experience of each individual, community or even culture. Not that each generation has to make a completely new start. Every individual is born into a community. And every community has a tradition which, initially at least, shapes one's life, outlook, faith and spirituality:

> Belief on the deepest level means a personal participation in the life and the ethos of a commuity and its tradition and an assent to the fundamental symbolic forms of that tradition as true and normative, that is, as directing or guiding one's own thought, goals and

patterns of behaviour. Belief in ordinary life is thus not an act of subjective fancy; it represents *the* important spiritual link between ourselves and the objective social order in which we all live and act.[3]

It is evident that in the course of history certain understandings, attitudes and practices arose which can now be recognised as lacking in scriptural foundation, and sometimes actually at variance with the content of scripture. They can be recognised as theologically unsound, or socially or psychologically unhealthy. We are now in a position to review the situation, and hopefully to develop spiritualities suitable for our times and circumstances. The reason we are in such a position is that the past one hundred years have seen an unprecedented period of development in scriptural interpretation, theology, liturgical studies and the human sciences. Corresponding developments in the physical sciences provide an understanding and control of the workings of our material universe such as were never available to humanity before.

It will be the task of spiritual theology in the future to draw all these areas of study together, if it is to fulfil its purpose: to shed some light on that area of existence where faith and human living intersect. The most fruitful avenue of inquiry, initially at least, will be an exploration of the biblical tradition itself.

The biblical roots of spirituality

The biblical roots of christian spirituality show that the Old Testament contains a number of theological traditions which reflect different experiences of the Israelites through various stages of their history. There are two main strands of Old Testament theology which have been called 'saving theology' and 'blessing theology'. Both traditions are reflected, as we shall see, in the New Testament.

Saving theology emerges out of the experience of the Israelites as an oppressed people. They find themselves enslaved in Egypt, wandering homeless through the wilderness, attacked and invaded by foreigners, and struggling to establish themselves as a people in a land of

259

their own. Because of their situation they come to think of God as a saviour, a redeemer who will come from outside to set them free. They experience him as a great warrior who performs signs and wonders 'with mighty hand and outstretched arm' in order to bring them out of the bondage of Egypt and win their battles for them. Correspondingly, the Israelites experience themselves as helpless, weak and powerless. Their only hope is that someone from outside (God) will come and save them. God gave them a Covenant on Sinai. It contained a promise of his continuing assistance, and a code of law to guide their lives: they were to worship God alone. They were not to oppress one another, because they had all once been oppressed themselves. In the New Testament, this understanding is transferred to Jesus in those texts which refer to him as the new Moses, the one who gives a new covenant and a new covenant law. The name Jesus means 'Yahweh saves'.

Blessing theology is made up of three related strands: creation thought, wisdom, and royal (or Sion) theology. Blessing theology emerges out of an altogether different experience, the experience of the 'kingdom' under David and Solomon. It was during this period that the Israelites, for the first time, experienced themselves as a free, sovereign people. They had a fruitful land of their own. Their king was as glorious as any other. They were as strong as any surrounding nation. They were secure. For the first time they found themselves in full charge of their own destiny. They were able to do things, to achieve.

Although the kingdom lasted effectively no more than a hundred years of Israel's long history, the experience had a profound effect on their outlook for generations to come. Many of them looked back on the kingdom era as the glory days of Israel. They recalled it with pride and, even into New Testament times, longed for its restoration.

Life was good for the Israelites during the kingdom years, and the Old Testament shows that through the experience they begin to view God in a new light, to understand him differently. God is predominantly the Creator-God. He is the one who calls all of creation into existence, a creation that is 'good'. He is the guarantor of peace (*shalom*) and justice (*sedekah* = right relationships). Wisdom, is the gift of God, and mediates his presence to his people. 'Wisdom calls aloud in the streets' (Prov 1:20), ie in the midst of busy life. God continues to work signs and wonders on behalf of his people. But the signs and wonders are no longer such things as manna from heaven or water from the rock. In blessing theology they are the ordinary processes of nature, and the God-given capacity of men and women to manage and to achieve.

In contrast to saving theology which saw the human being as weak and powerless, blessing theology sees the human as the very image of God, as being given power to share responsibility for creation. Although raised in dignity in this way, humanity must still acknowledge God alone as the giver of creaturehood. Again, people are not to oppress one another, the motivation now being that all have the same Creator.

In the New Testament the same approach is used in attempting to explain the mystery of Jesus. It is found in those texts which refer to him as the Son of David, as the wisdom of God (eg 1 Cor 1:24), as a teacher of wisdom (Jn 1:17,18), as the creator (Col 1:15-16). Jesus is also seen as the source of life and blessing. In this tradition he is named, 'the Christ', ie the anointed king, the Messiah.

There is a significant statement in the book of Joshua which marks the transition from saving theology to blessing: 'The manna stopped the day after they had eaten the produce of the land. The Israelites from that day onwards ate the produce of Canaan and had no more manna' (5:12). The manna had been simply given from above by God, but to avail of the produce of the land required human labour and cooperation. While the transition from saving to blessing theology may be regarded as a step forward, it must be observed that the movement was not continuously forward. The time would come when Israel would be persecuted and enslaved again. They would then revert to saving theology and spirituality as being appropriate to their new situation.

In the bible, the human being is seen to exist in a network of relationships. To be a human person is to be immersed in community. The individual is never seen alone except as the result of sin or tragedy. When Cain kills Abel, and is sent out to be 'a restless wanderer on earth', it is the worst of all punishments. In the psalms, one of the greatest pains is to be alone. The human being is also seen to be in close relationship with the natural world. There are sympathetic vibrations, as it were, between person and planet. When Adam sins, for example, it results in the soil yielding him food only 'by the sweat of your face'. What is good for the person is good for the earth and vice versa.

Relationships with people and with the earth can be adequately understood only if all are seen as in relationship with God. It is part of the definition of the human being that he or she is in relationship with God who is in turn passionately involved with all creation.

The individual fits into this complex of relationships essentially by being the 'image' of God. Being the image of God means that one recognises and accepts the fact, and acknowledges one's creaturehood and dependence on him; one is to be fruitful and life-giving, a concept which includes, but is not limited to, procreation. Being in the image of God also means having 'dominion'.

Dominion is a concept in royal theology, and reflects the role of the king in Israel. It will be noted that the Genesis story of creation does not speak of God creating 'out of nothing'. Instead, the story begins with chaos, with earth as a formless void. God devotes the first period of creation to conquering and dividing the formlessness, changing chaos into orderliness, thus making the earth inhabitable for the living beings created during the second period. All this is the activity of the One who has dominion. When human beings are given dominion, they are raised up to share in God's dominion. Their task is therefore to subdue the earth and keep it inhabitable. The exercise of dominion is not, however, confined to keeping the earth inhabitable in the physical sense. It includes the task of promoting justice and peace, and thus bringing order into the possible chaos of human relationships.

The threefold relationship referred to here indicates that a comprehensive spirituality will include not only a relationship with God, but a close relationship with other people and with material creation. A more detailed examination of each relationship will help to bring out the full scope of an authentic christian spirituality.

The scope of christian spirituality:
a threefold relationship

With other people. In speaking of a person's threefold relationship with God, other people and the material world, these relationships are never experienced in isolation from the others. In the bible, they are so interwoven and interconnected that they can be properly understood only as different aspects of total human existence.

In scripture, to be human is to be in relationship with other people. It is not an option. While much of traditional spirituality, influenced by such movements as manichaeism, has emphasised the dangers to holiness involved in human relationships, the emphasis of scripture is on humanity as the locus of encounter with God, an approach which is highlighted in the mystery of the Incarnation. It is true that sin enters into human life through humanity, but it is equally true that it is through humanity, and only through humanity, that grace comes too.

In line with the scriptural emphasis, christian spirituality today, while not being naive about the dangers, will rather emphasise the possibilities for growth in human relationships. The christian does not have to choose between people and God; the choice is between people-with-God and people-without-God.

There are far deeper implications here for christian spirituality than the cultivation of charitable attitudes and behaviour advocated in traditional spirituality. Never in history have people been so aware, even from a purely secular point of view, of the interrelatedness of peoples and nations, and how economic, political and social structures affect the lives of ordinary people. All these realities must be seen today as the locus and the raw material for the christian response, and therefore for spirituality.

The Old Testament consistently demands a connection between holiness and justice, between caring for the poor and a true relationship with God. In the New Testament, the central theme of Jesus' preaching, and the central preoccupation of his life is the kingdom. While the kingdom is nowhere exactly defined, it is clear that it is not a purely personal, individual, interior reality. Neither is it an other-worldly hope. Rather the kingdom is a process whereby God intervenes in some way in human history and human affairs in order to overcome the evils that oppress people (cf Mt 11:2–5). Edward Schillebeeckx explains it like this:

> It does not denote some area of sovereignty above and beyond this world, where God is supposed to reside and to reign. What Jesus intends by it is a process, a course of events, whereby God begins to govern or to act as king or Lord, an action, therefore, by which God manifests his being-God in the world of men. Thus God's lordship or dominion is the divine power itself in its saving activity within our history, but at the same time the final, eschatological state of affairs that brings to an end the evil world, dominated by forces of calamity and woe, and initiates the new world in which God 'appears to full advantage'; 'your kingdom come'.
>
> God's lordship, therefore, is the exercise of his peculiar and divine function as sovereign Creator: as 'king' he is purveyor of salvation to that which he endowed with life. That this kingdom come means that God looks to us men and women to make his 'ruling' operational in our world.[4]

It is because God looks to men and women in this way that a true christian spirituality for today demands involvement in the world and its human processes, not flight from it. Tendencies throughout history to make christianity into a world-avoiding, interior religion, or a religion of personal and even spiritual salvation, have ignored this challenge of the gospel. Frequently, the eschatological dimension of the kingdom has been so emphasised that its present, here-and-now aspects have been ignored or greatly understated.

Because God is present and active in the events of

history, those events are the place of the christian's encounter with him. But when we say that God is present in history, there is a real sense in which we mean that he is present only if, and to the extent that, he is allowed to be present by free human beings. In other words, he is present only when people allow him into their lives to shape their attitudes and their activities.

In this context there is no inherent conflict between contemplation on the one hand, and action on behalf of the kingdom on the other. It is true that people commonly experience a certain tension between the two, but the tension arises from the feeling that it is difficult to find the time or energy for satisfactory attention to both, and not from any necessary exclusion of one by the other. Indeed, since there is no true sense in which we can contemplate God 'in himself', we can only contemplate him through what we believe are manifestations of his presence and activity in the world. What above all characterised the great mystics and prophets was not their intimate knowledge of God, but their extraordinary insight into their contemporary situations, and their capacity to discern there the presence—or often the absence—of God.

Christian spirituality today, Donal Dorr says, requires a dedicated effort on the part of christians to understand

> how our society works—and particularly how it is structured in ways that favour certain groups and give them an unfair advantage over others, even when the privileged ones do not intend to be unjust.
>
> We need a *commitment* to correcting injustices, not just on an ad hoc basis but by replacing the unjust structures with ones that are equitable.[5]

Jon Sobrino states it like this:

> To put it in straightforward but pointed terms, we can say that Jesus' intrinsic relationship to the kingdom means that our contact with him will come not primarily through cultic acclamation or adoration but through following Jesus in the service of God's kingdom.[6]

In view of our greater awareness today of how our

decisions and activities affect people thousands of miles away, the situation may be calling christians to seek new answers to the ancient question: 'Who is my neighbour?'

With the material world. Six times the first chapter of Genesis asserts the goodness of creation. Paul speaks of God's intention 'that the whole creation itself might be freed from its slavery to corruption and brought into the same glorious freedom as the children of God'. In Matthew's gospel the moment of Jesus' death 'the veil of the Sanctuary was torn in two from top to bottom', a sign that there was no more Holy of Holies, but that all places were sacred. The Book of Revelation represents God as saying, 'Look, I am making all things new.' Clearly, scripture sees material creation as good. And it sees the act of creation not as a once-for-all deed of God, but rather as an ongoing process closely connected with the destiny and salvation of humanity. In scripture too, there is never any suggestion that humanity is to be saved *from* the world; it is always a question of being saved *in* the world.

The gospels relate that Jesus used such material things as clay, water and even spittle as channels for communicating God's healing power and compassion to suffering people. The process continues in liturgy where material things, water, oil, bread, wine and salt are used as means of communication between God and humanity. It is probably true that christians are insufficiently aware of the sheer 'earthiness' of the sacraments.

The attitudes to the material both in scripture and liturgy more than suggest a need to reconsider the 'rejection of the material' theme in much of traditional spirituality. Created things are not to be seen as alternatives to God but rather as his gifts, sacraments of his bountifulness. As Teilhard de Chardin said: 'By virtue of the Creation and, still more, of the Incarnation, *nothing* here below is *profane* for those who know how to see.'[7]

The most convincing way a person can show gratitude and appreciation to the giver of a gift is by not only using the gift but enjoying it. The same must be true of our response to the gifts of God. They are to be not only used but to be enjoyed. Again, the choice for a christian is not between the material and God; it is a choice between the material-*with*-God and the material-*without*-God.

It is of course true that people can and do abuse created things in many ways, and that such abuse affects their relationships on other levels, that is, with God and with people. But the christian corrective to the abuse of creation is not non-use but proper use. The question is not whether or not to use and enjoy material things, but how to use and enjoy them according to what seems to be the intention of the Creator, and in a way that will not cause deprivation or suffering to others.

More than that. Since human beings are called to share in God's dominion over creation, they are called to share in his creative activity of making the earth continuously inhabitable. Nowadays, we are becoming more aware that the earth, and even perhaps the universe, has to be made inhabitable for an ever-increasing population. We need to be equally aware that the earth needs to be more than physically inhabitable. Its continuing inhabitability requires attention to its political, social and psychological dimensions as well.

Clearly, such a task cannot be carried out by flight from the world. Nor can it be achieved in passivity. The task can only be advanced through active involvement in developing the created potential of the material universe. It is to this that christians are called as part of their living response to the gifts of creation, revelation and redemption. It is, in other words, part of christian spirituality.

What has been said above about promoting the kingdom of God through human relationships is to be applied here in the context of subduing the earth and making it fruitful. This too is a contribution to the kingdom. To remain passive and long-suffering in this 'vale of tears' is no part of christian spirituality. Instead, christians are to make the world different and better by using the power that is in them. In the modern world, the abuse of power is so prevalent that power itself is often seen as an evil. In scripture, however, it is its opposite, powerlessness, that is regarded as evil. As with poverty, powerlessness is never idealised or even romanticised in the bible. Power is not an evil, it is a good. To have power is to share in God's dominion. It is a dimension of being his image. It is part of one's God-given capacity to do things, to achieve, to make a difference in the world.

With God. For the human being, in biblical terms, the relationship which holds all the other relationships together and in place is the relationship with God. It is precisely because of faith in God that one adopts certain attitudes and patterns of behaviour towards other people and the material world. If the faith-relationship with God is damaged or broken, the others are affected accordingly. Thus, when Genesis recounts the story of Adam's sin, it goes on to relate a litany of tragic consequences: Adam and Eve begin to argue, the earth yields its life-giving nourishment only with toil, Cain murders Abel, and the flood threatens the very existence of humanity.

The first and crucial response to human existence, then, is to rejoice in the dignity of being made in the image of God, and at the same time to acknowledge and accept creaturehood and dependence on him. It is significant that the first temptation in the Genesis story is the temptation to reject the primary relationship: 'you will be like gods'. When that temptation is yielded to, concern for life, peace and justice collapses. In the biblical conception of the unity of existence, all levels are affected by one act at one level.

What is important here for christian spirituality is that the Genesis account of creation and the fall is a mythical representation of the basic structures of human existence. In other words, the story of Adam and Eve is the story of every man and woman born into the world. Each one has the dignity of imagehood, with gifts of creation to use and enjoy—and the same temptation to cope with.

For the christian, Jesus of Nazareth is the 'image of the unseen God' in an altogether unique way. As 'the first-born of all creation', he is to be seen as the model par excellence of imagehood. What Jesus reveals is not God, Jon Sobrino says, but sonship or imagehood:

In Jesus we have the revelation of the Son of God and

all that means. The revelation of the Son in the history of Jesus shows us completely and definitively how human beings can correspond to the ultimate mystery of God in the midst of historical existence. Strictly speaking, Jesus is not the sacrament of the Father. He is not the epiphanic revelation of the ultimate mystery. Rather he is the revelation of the Son, of the proper way to approach and correspond with the Father.[8]

One of the clearest features in the life of Jesus was his relationship with his Father. Yet he consistently refused to usurp the role of his Father, and this in spite of the temptation do to so. The story of the temptations in the desert is to be seen as Jesus' confrontation and rejection of the temptation to do things in his own way instead of leaving himself open to the destiny laid out for him by the Father. Since the story is found towards the beginning of each of the synoptic gospels, it can easily be misread as meaning that at the beginning of his ministry Jesus confronted and rejected the temptation once and for all. The gospels relate, however, that he had to face the temptation again and again throughout his public life.

When Jesus acknowledges that there are certain things he does not know, but which the Father knows, he acknowledges the distinctness of the Father and refuses to take over the Father's role. In the garden of Gethsemane he prayed that his destiny might be altered, but concluded, 'let it be as you, not I, would have it'. He would be Son, and let the Father be Father.

Christian spirituality requires that the christian, following the example of Jesus, must always let God be God. In other words, the christian will not try to control God, not even by knowing him or pretending to know him. Strictly speaking, anything we say we know about God, we do not actually *know*; we *believe*. The essential feature of the christian's relationship with God is recognition and acceptance of the absolute otherness of God. Without it, the relationship is defective. In biblical terms, this means that relationships at other levels are correspondingly flawed.

Experience shows how easily, frequently and in how

many different ways christians succumb to the temptation to be like gods, to take over God's unique role in the universe, even to use him. They often lay claim to insights into the mind of God, a claim such as Jesus himself does not make. Such imagined insights become particularly obnoxious when they are used to control or harass other people. The relationship is equally flawed by those who presume to make decisions for God, to decide whom he is to love or hate.

As in the case of Jesus, the temptation to violate or ignore the primary relationship with God is not encountered and defeated once and for all. It has to be confronted and rejected again and again throughout the whole of life. I expect it would be generally agreed that for the most part people do not violate their primary relationship with God by a deliberate, fully thought-out decision or action. They do it mostly by simply forgetting. In the Jewish and christian traditions, the protection against forgetting is prayer.

I suggest that in christian spirituality the immediate and primary purpose of prayer is *remembering*. Adoration, praise, thanksgiving, contrition and petition all follow from remembering, from being aware of who we are in relation to God.

The Book of Deuteronomy describes how Moses prepared the Israelites for the imminent crossing into the Promised Land. He warns them of the dangers involved in settling in the land. The underlying problem is the danger of forgetting:

> Be careful not to forget Yahweh your God, by neglecting his commandments, customs and laws which I am laying down for you today. When you have eaten all you want, when you have built fine houses to live in, when you have seen your flocks and herds increase, your silver and gold abound and all your possessions grow great, do not become proud of heart. Do not forget Yahweh your God who brought you out of Egypt, out of the place of slave labour, who guided you through this vast and dreadful desert (8:11–15).

Afterwards, whenever the Israelites renewed and celebrated

the Covenant, they began by recalling the saving acts of God on their behalf. They remembered in prayer, both liturgical and private, as is evidenced in the psalms, and in the canticles and prayers throughout the Old Testament. In recalling the reasons for praise and thanksgiving, the psalms maintained the memory.

Jesus' story of the pharisee and the publican suggests the same need to remember. What is wrong with the pharisee's prayer is that he forgets or ignores the primary relationship. The focus of his prayer is not God, but himself. When he adverts to the publican he shows that his secondary relationships are correspondingly awry (Lk 18:1–14).

In liturgy too, the centrality of remembering is evident. In the reading of the word of God which is part of every sacramental celebration, the object is basically remembering, becoming aware of our relationship with God. This is clearest of all in the celebration of the Eucharist which is carried out, at the command of Jesus, 'in memory of me'. In every eucharistic celebration we call to mind the central events of our salvation in Jesus. And remembering, we give thanks. In the second eucharistic prayer, 'we thank you for counting us worthy to *stand* in your presence and *serve* you.'

Conclusion

The approaches to christian spirituality outlined above clearly suggest positive attitudes to God, to people, to material creation, and indeed to human powers. Apart from the fact that such approaches are supported by both scripture and liturgy, they would also appear to offer the most helpful and effective standpoint from which to cope with the negative aspects of human existence. It may be expected that a true christian spirituality will help christians to deal in some satisfactory way with the pain of human life, and for that reason I conclude by emphasising that a basically positive approach should not mislead into an attitude of naive optimism.

Some recent forms of spirituality seem to have been

characterised by such unwarranted optimism, and fail to measure up to the requirements of authentic christian spirituality, mainly for two reasons. First, they suggest an overemphasis on self-preoccupation, with a certain promise of some paradise of personal development to be achieved through a continuum of self-fulfilment. Secondly, they fail to take sufficiently into account the brokenness and pain of human existence.

Perhaps nobody has written more positively, optimistically and poetically about the glory of the universe and humanity's role in its evolution than Teilhard de Chardin. Yet he concludes one of his major works by saying: 'In one form or the other it still remains true that, even in the view of the mere biologist, the human epic resembles nothing so much as a way of the Cross.'[9]

It has been observed above that for a very long time christian spirituality has emphasised the fallenness of humanity, almost to the exclusion of the more positive attitudes reflected, for example, in Genesis. But the imbalance is hardly to be corrected by simply reversing the emphases, thus excluding or unduly minimising consideration of human weakness and sinfulness. Both traditions must be held in some tension or balance, since each tradition expresses something of the common experience of human existence.

It is doubtful if anyone experiences human life as a continuum of self-fulfilment or growth. Sooner or later everyone comes up against the limitations of life, even if they are only the limitations of time, energy and human powers. To a greater or less extent everybody experiences the pain of human life, and becomes aware of death as the only certainty. A true christian spirituality will acknowledge this reality, try to find some meaning in it, and search for ways of coping.

When the Israelites of old had progressed from slavery to freedom, the change affected their attitudes and behaviour before God. However, when later in their history they again experienced persecution and exile, they reverted to pleading with God to come 'from outside' to save them. Their story is the story of all ages and people, and for that

272

reason a spirituality is needed that will embrace the bad times as well as the good. In the bad times the human being, like the psalmist, will spontaneously cry out to God. For the christian, life and salvation are not humanly achievable, but are the pure gifts of God.

16. *The Parish Mission Apostolate of the Redemptorists in Ireland, 1851–1898*

THE first Redemptorists arrived in Ireland in 1851. A year earlier, the National Synod of Thurles had been held, which can be taken as the launching pad of Cardinal Paul Cullen's programme of ecclesiastical reform. Although the parish mission was one of the agencies of this reform, Cullen was not the first to advocate the parish mission, nor were the Redemptorists the first or only practitioners of it in the last century.[1]

The Redemptorists established their first foundation in Limerick in 1853. Their numbers were quite small. Until the founding of the second mission house in Dundalk in 1876, rarely could more than two mission teams be fielded at any given time. In the Limerick community the number of priests averaged eleven, and in Dundalk eight. To these must be added a smaller, unseen force involved in the ministry: the brothers. Their hidden life of religious observance, prayer and work provided spiritual fuel for the Redemptorist parish mission machine. This was also the contribution of the sister Order of Redemptoristines, contemplative nuns established in Dublin in 1859.

Besides their main work of parish missions, the priests were stretched by other activities such as service to their own mission churches, retreats to clergy and religious, as well as to confraternities, schools, magdalen homes and workhouses. As far as was possible, the winter months were closed to external works to further the home religious life of the communities.

The Redemptorists came to Ireland on the initiative of the Belgian province. From 1854 to 1865, the houses in

England and Ireland had depended on the Dutch province, but after 1865 Ireland formed part of the independent English province. Ireland finally became a separate province in 1898.

During this whole period, especially the earlier years, there was a cosmopolitan mixture of personnel: men from Belgium, Holland, Austria, Germany, France, Russia, Poland and Italy formed communities with the Irish, English and Scots. In the beginning, the Continentals were pioneers of the mission, and later they came to Ireland as refugees from anti-clerical regimes in their own countries, and teamed together on missions in Ireland and Britain. Their work from Limerick (1854–1890) and from Dundalk (1876–1890) is shown in the following figures.

	Missions	Renewals	Clergy Retreats	Other Retreats
Limerick	336	58	177	740
Dundalk	125	17	47	367

Although the influence of their parish missions may have been greater than the small work force engaged, nevertheless the overall impact on the Irish church can have been only patchy. However, the reports of Redemptorist parish missions and the observations of the missioners mirror a pastoral theology in its time: for instance, the decided dualism of salvation theology, the heavy reliance on sacrament and sacramental to underpin evangelisation, the primacy of confession in pastoral strategy, the defensive stance of ecclesiology, the weaning of the people from over-reliance on elements of folk religion to a chapel-centred practice of faith. The reports also give close-up glimpses of the country in a most distressful period of its history.

The parish mission can be described as an extraordinary, temporary and intensive apostolate designed to complement the ordinary parochial ministry. It is a type of revivalism which aims at providing a service to the existing forms of grace, and at bringing, possibly, a prophetic statement of the gospel way to the local church.

It is, ideally, a work of collaboration, where the missioners with their experience of mission ministry, and the parochial clergy with their knowledge of the local community, combine to structure the programme and give it its particular pastoral thrust.

The Redemptorists were heirs to the style of mission practised by their founder, St Alphonsus Liguori. It got its form and drive from its single-minded purpose of leading the faithful to save their souls. Its programme combined instruction in faith and morals, the preaching of repentance and conversion, the administration of the sacraments, and the ensuring of perseverance through fostering sacramental observance and the practice of 'the devout life'. Within this pastoral scheme, the programming of the mission was flexible.

The leader of the first Redemptorist missions in Ireland was the Austrian Joseph Prost,[2] a founding father of the Redemptorist mission in the United States. He had grown in experience of the parish missions in the Tyrol. Some features of the mission style he evolved and of the conditions under which a mission was accepted are outlined in his letter of May 1853 to Fr Roche, the parish priest of Wexford, on the eve of a mission there:

> . . . The superior of the mission must have full liberty to direct and to arrange all. . . . The missioners must have full liberty in prolonging the mission and to take as much time for it as they think proper in order to do their work well. Hence, no time can be appointed for the end of the mission. . . . No public collection for the expenses of the missioners is allowed. . . . We know very well the wants of the Catholic churches in Ireland and we would be very glad if we could procure money for them, but our rule teaches us, we know from our own experience that the least money speculation at a mission destroys all the fruits of a mission, and if one penny, or even a half-penny would be asked at the door, many sinners would remain away and be lost, for whose conversion the missioners come. . . .

Although all have free access to all our sermons and instructions etc, parishioners and strangers, to the confessionals, however, only those belonging to the parish are admitted, with the exclusion of all the strangers without exception. This is necessary to secure for the parishioners the benefit of confession during the mission. . . .

We recommend always that before the opening of the public mission prayers may be said for the good success of the mission. As your parish is large we will come in a large number, but do not be puzzled by it, because we find easily room even in a small house. The beds must be very simple as the fathers do not like to sleep in feather beds, but we like open beds the best. And as our journey and boarding is all at our own expense, nobody is burdened if we come in considerable number. It is beneficial for those who wish to make good confessions, as hurried confessions would be of little use. Please pray for us.

The pastoral values that Prost's letter sought to uphold were cherished in parish mission practice long after Prost departed. But his material arrangements were none too practical: the descent of a large number of missioners on a parish for an indefinite length of time would be acceptable to few parish priests, and reliance on Providence to foot the bills was hardly realistic.

After Prost, the celebrated Dutch missioner, Bernard Hafkenscheid[3] became leader of the missions in Britain and Ireland from 1853 to 1855. During his short stay in this country as 'coach', Fr Bernard established the strong, simple, spirited style of pulpit oratory that was the hallmark of the Redemptorist missioners in Ireland. In future the duration of the mission and the number of missioners to be employed would be fixed by agreement. And although the missioners continued to look for accommodation that was as reserved as possible—to enable them to follow their own routine of rest and religious observances—the idea of having an independent quasi-cloistered household to themselves was abandoned.

The daily timetable, however, still continued to look like a programme for an unending crisis. Typical was St Finbarr's parish in Cork in 1854, where the first Mass and instruction was at 4.45 am to accommodate workers. Those, both in industry and in domestic service, would not be released from their treadmill of work to attend the mission at a humane hour. The confessionals were manned from 6.30 am to 12.45 pm, and from 4.00 to 7.00 in the afternoon, and after the evening mission service, confession—for men and boys only—continued to near midnight.

This timetable was rationalised at the end of the first Redemptorist mission in Dundalk in 1859, the report of which states that it was 'the most important of our missions since the departure of Fr Bernard', referring not to any change in missiology but to a more workmanlike order of the day 'to be a model for towns of similar magnitude and importance'.

Robert Coffin, the Vice-Provincial from London, was in charge of the team, with three leading missioners of the Limerick community: Pecherin, the Russian, and Irishmen Harbison and Plunkett, as well as two Dutchmen. The parish priest, Dean Kiernan—later Archbishop of Armagh—'one of the most zealous and best informed ecclesiastics in Ireland' was brought into the deliberations, which led to the early morning rising being eased by more than an hour and the dropping of the later afternoon confessions. That same year, Coffin directed that missions should 'as a general rule' be of three weeks' duration.

The message in pulpit and confessional

The people responded to the missions with huge enthusiasm. They packed to overflow, not only the small thatched churches but the more commodious ones in the towns. Occasionally they responded vocally to pulpit rhetoric with cries of guilt and repentance. Central to the scenario was the dire poverty of the people. The country was prostrate after the Great Famine (1845–7) and haemorrhaging from mass emigration. After a mission in Bruree and Rockhill in 1863, the missioners returned for a renewal within twelve months to find that one third of the population had emigrated to America.

Apart from a thin stratum of well-to-do people in business, the professions and on large farms, the bulk of the Catholic population was miserably housed and clothed, largely deprived of education, especially at second and third level, and dependent on only menial employment, if any. In an agrarian economy where the great majority lived on and off the land, small farmers and labourers were often forced by oppressive landlordism into a barely subsistence standard of living. There are references to the throngs coming barefooted, to the use of one suit of clothing used successively by members of the same family, and to the lice-ridden plight of the poor. The grounds for hope for a good life were indeed slim. Emigration was an escape hatch to a better world on earth for many. Though a hard-headed resolve to right the wrongs on their home ground was not wanting, there was also a faith, too often uninstructed and flawed with superstition, in a better world to come. They conjured for themselves an 'aisling' out of their religion.[4] This the mission presaged. The mission, moreover, had features about it that made it an experience 'out of this world'. The missioners were strangers who came into their parish 'out of the blue'. The foreigners in particular, having acquired English only imperfectly, must have come across as positively exotic. In addition, they brought the splendours of the liturgy: Benediction, processions, communal praying, hymn singing and an array of sacramentals, into the drab lives of the people.

Preaching had a key place in the mission scheme of leading men to salvation. The preaching was catechetical and declamatory. These features were, in a measure, combined in all the preaching, but the forenoon instructions were essentially catechetical while the great evening sermons were declamatory or motivating to conversion and to perseverance. Typical of the subjects preached are those listed for the mission preached for the opening of the Redemptorist church in Limerick in 1862, a mission which lasted two and a half weeks and ended on Christmas day. (Page 280)

	Morning	**Evening**
Monday	–	End of man
Tuesday	Necessity of penance	Salvation
Wednesday	Sincerity	Mortal sin
Thursday	Examination of conscience	Sacrament of Confession
Friday	Sorrow	Death of sinner
Saturday	Purpose of amendment	Judgment
Sunday	General confession	Hell
Monday	Faith	Drunkenness
Tuesday	Superstition	Impurity
Wednesday	Cursing and swearing	Restitution
Thursday	Obscene words	Amende (Holy Hour of Reparation)
Friday	Eighth Commandment	Scandal
Saturday	Bad thoughts	Mercy of God
Sunday	Relapse	Proximate occasions of sin
Monday	Forgiveness of injuries	Duties of parents
Tuesday	Communion: preparation and thanksgiving	Prayer
Wednesday	Daily acts	(free for confession)
Thursday	States of grace	Perseverance

Instruction often included lectures on the different 'states': married — men and women separately — young unmarried, also men and women separately, or a lecture to 'the better classes so called'.[5]

During the first week, the motive of fear predominated in the evening sermons. Higher motives were emphasised as the mission progressed. The Redemptorists came to be dubbed hell-fire missioners. It is certain that motivating through fear had its place in their sermons, as indeed it always has had in conversion preaching. Did they overdo it? With hindsight, we may think so, but it should be remembered that until recent times, sermons on hell were the stock-in-trade of all preachers. The great Tom Burke, OP had it on his list of mission sermons.[6] The sermon on hell that James Joyce recalled has never been dismissed as something exceptional or untypical of the time. Fear is a highly memorable experience, especially if transmitted by means of a strong, simple and dramatic pulpit delivery. It can stand out in an individual's recall of the mission long after other telling motives put forward in sermons are either quietly forgotten or integrated in the complex guidance system that is a christian's.

Undoubtedly there were those missioners who passed the borderline that separates salutary fear from unwholesome terror. The extent to which the emotions in general should be stirred by the preacher is a matter of pastoral judgment. On this head the pioneer, Prost, faulted his successor as superior of missions, Bernard Hafkenscheid: 'He depended much on rousing the emotions of his hearers', whereas Prost 'sought above all to influence the understanding through instruction and dispassionate presentation so that good resolutions might grow out of a clearer perception of the truth'.[7] However, Bernard, a theologian who had won his doctorate in Rome, is unlikely to have been short on instruction.

The 'metanoia' or change of heart that was achieved with the help of the preaching was not considered to be the completion as yet of conversion. It was seen only as an intermediate step in the process. The change of heart needed to be sealed and delivered, as it were, by the sacraments, through which the grace of God was ultimately mediated. This, moreover was compromised by the fact that, in spite of the mission instructions, the *ex opere operato* effectiveness of the sacraments was not always understood by the people in the best christian sense. In this context, it should be stated that the sacrament of conversion, Penance, was effectively the central sacrament of the mission. It might be argued that this was an imbalance in the pastoral strategy of the mission, but the parish mission itself was, at this time, designed to have this thrust. It was central to the people, the culmination of 'doing the mission', and for the missioners the hearing of confessions was the most time-consuming and energy-sapping work of the mission. The confessional drew penitents from far and wide like a magnet. Many people found it difficult to confess to their own clergy—the sacrament had often been available only in houses at 'stations'; some were alienated by the involvement of their priests in politics, or embittered by some factor as alleged at Foxford in 1880, where the parish priest was thought to have neglected the people during a famine.

In addition, a theological obstacle was noted by Fr Van der Aa in a letter to Fr Mauron, the General, in 1860. He describes how many of the priests had studied only French moral theology and so had a taint of Jansenism. They were often afraid to hear the people, had them back several times without much cause, with the result that many thousands ignored or neglected the sacraments. 'There are thousands of adults aged thirty, forty, sixty years who have not made their first communion. The priests are in fear of them, ie the sacraments. Our missioners are like Redeemers for these poor people.' The Redemptorists would be mindful of the pastoral approach of their founder, St Alphonsus, who, in the face of the Jansenism that blighted his era, carried out a crusade that nurtured faith in the love of a merciful God. Van der Aa may have been generalising from some particular cases, because Alphonsus had already been introduced by this time to Maynooth.

Although the missioners were sometimes criticised, in the Irish situation, for letting the penitents off too lightly, their administration of the sacrament of penance was not without a strain of rigorism. In the 'box' the confession of sins came in for exceptional scrutiny, the favoured name 'confession' being a pointer to this. Not only were the norms for formal integrity prescribed by the Council of Trent sedulously applied, but the questioning of the penitent, carried out as part of the process, sought what was tantamount to material integrity. The shriving of one penitent could take the greater part of an hour as many were required to make a general confession. It was not unusual for the missioners to be in the confessional eight or nine hours a day and to hear no more than thirty or forty penitents during that time.

In this context, Vladimir Pecherin trailed like a comet

across the firmament of the Redemptorist mission to Ireland during the years 1851 to 1861, for he was the leading light among a few who questioned the accepted norms for confessions. He departed from, or notably reduced, the investigative practice of his confreres and did not push penitents to make general confessions. Pecherin (1807–1885) was born in the Ukraine. After studies in Petrograd (now Leningrad) he became a professor of Greek in Moscow University. He changed from the Russian Orthodox to the Roman Catholic faith and became a Redemptorist in 1840. He drew inspiration from St Francis of Assisi as a christian, St John Chrysostom as a preacher and St Alphonsus as a missioner. Gifted with a brilliant mind and a liberated spirit, he won fame in Ireland as an outstanding preacher and giver of retreats, especially to the clergy. He became something of a national hero on being acquitted of the charge of burning a Protestant bible at a mission in Kingstown (Dun Laoghaire) in 1855. He was the first Redemptorist to do an apostolic work in Ireland: a retreat to the Sisters of St Francis Xavier at Omagh in 1851.

The effects on his health of a crushing workload of missions, retreats and sermons may account for his decision to join the Trappists in Mount Melleray (on the title of passing to a more severe Order). However, after a brief stay there, he applied for readmission to the Redemptorists in 1861. He was refused by the authoritarian Superior General, Mauron, although his superior in Limerick, William Plunkett urged his readmission 'for his sake if not for ours', suggesting that Pecherin did not fit easily into the tightly uniform and regimented Redemptorist Congregation of the time. His wide range of intellectual interests could not get much play there; his passion for freedom and for the primacy of conscience was not then in favour, and his insights on religion and society were acceptable only to a few revolutionary spirits of his time.

For all that he had been rejected officially, Pecherin continued to hold a place in the respect and affections of his erstwhile companions. One of these, Harbison, gave him the last rites. He spent his later life as an exemplary chaplain to the Mater Hospital, Dublin. In his secluded lodgings he applied himself to mastering an astonishing range of languages and sciences. He also renewed contacts with kindred Russian spirits. He is buried in Glasnevin. Since that fine student of Pecherin, Dr Eoin MacWhite, died in a car accident in 1972, the drama of his life awaits a final scripting.[8]

Pecherin found it easier to justify his theology of penance because of his love of, and sympathy for, the oppressed Irish. He is of special interest in that his 'pastorale' of culpability, had it been accepted, might have countered the syndrome of guilt that got into the psyche of Irish Catholicism. He was deeply moved by their faith, poverty and deprivation of education. He argued that 'these people are so ignorant that one does not know the milieu of their sins and they do not see a great evil in being silent about them in confession' (Plunkett to Mauron, 1861). It may be significant that, in the same letter, the Vice-Provincial, Coffin, a convert, alone of Pecherin's superiors was not said to be concerned about his confessional practice. Roes, the Belgian superior in Limerick, complained to the Superior General in 1859 of Pecherin's speed, his giving a pat to, and readily absolving boys, 'even bad boys . . . and after all they are very bad boys who habitually relapse and frequent the occasion of their sins'—on the say-so of their mothers! 'They say he does not ask the number because the Irish people are not able to tell the number of their sins. Then they accuse him of not making general confessions where it ought to be.'

On the missions, the job of coping with confessions was made more difficult by the presence of large numbers from neighbouring parishes. In some of the early missions, many of the poor people remained overnight in the church if they could, or somewhere near it. It took little to bring the patience of both priests and people to near breaking-point. The missioner who had charge of arrangements in the church often had difficulty in containing the stampede for position. In 1859, the Provincial Superior actually found it necessary to forbid the use of a stick—it being the era when the use of the clerical blackthorn was not unknown—to maintain due order outside the confessionals.

The receiving of communion was virtually twinned with confession at the time. Mission statistics show that the number who confessed and who received was about the same. Indeed, there was then a sense of being at fault if communion were not received after confession. Often people wishing to complement their confession immediately with Holy Communion asked for Communion at or after sunset, having fasted from the previous midnight.

The tradition of doing their annual 'duty' at stations linked the two sacraments in the people's minds. In addition, there was a rigoristic fear that they might become sullied in the interval. St Pius X's Decree on frequent communion, of course, was to come later. The Eucharist got due recognition, however, in that the Mass was explained and daily attendance during the mission was urged. The evening Benediction and the solemn Holy Hour of Reparation brought splendour to eucharistic devotion in many parishes for the first time. In some of the parishes going back to the penal times there was no tabernacle. According to the report on a mission in a Derry parish in 1879, the poor and badly clothed who used to be ashamed to go out on Sundays may now be seen in multitudes bare-headed and bare-footed hurrying to hear early Mass.

Reports list large numbers of all ages for Confirmation in the early missions, although the numbers fell progressively as the years went by. The same pattern emerged in regard to marriages. Because of the failure to observe the *tametsi* decree and because of the expense of having a marriage blessed by a priest, many poor couples had their marriages regularised at the early missions. This was particularly notable in Dublin city missions.

No account of the Redemptorist missions would be complete without reference to their apostolate to children. The children of the poor in particular were uninstructed and undisciplined. Reports mention boys and girls as being in service without having received confession or communion. The most celebrated practitioner of the children's mission was the Englishman, John Furniss.[9] Though prematurely aged and unkempt in appearance, he captivated children with instructive stories and devices.

The high point of his mission was confession and a ceremonial first communion. He extended his reach to children by means of numerous booklets for his apostolate. Furniss preferred to run the children's mission by himself, and separately from the mission to adults. His unique style, which did not meet with universal approval, ended with himself.

There was special concern that the good effects of the mission would continue afterwards. Much would depend on the follow-up by the local clergy, but the mission itself also was structured for further perseverance. The full mission package provided for a renewal six to twelve months later. This was a summary repeat of the mission. Renewals were most frequent in the early years, but declined due to the increasing demand for confraternity or sodality retreats which the clergy regarded as renewal substitutes, and the pressing demands for missions on the small work force.

Perseverance was also promoted through the 'devout life': daily prayers—learnt by repetition during the mission—family rosary and fidelity to confraternity or sodality rules, which had been either founded or strengthened during the mission. Confraternities had the advantage of providing group identity and promoting regular frequenting of the sacraments. Devotion to the Mother of Perpetual Help was especially favoured, inspired by a meaningful image of Mary and the Child, originating in the Eastern church and entrusted to the Redemptorists by Pius IX in 1865. The works of St Alphonsus himself in this field had a wide circulation in popular editions even before the arrival of the Redemptorists in Ireland, when they had a zealous promoter in Dr Nicholas Callan of Maynooth.[10] Pious objects in the home were also encouraged, and vendors followed the missions with their stalls, not only giving a service but also a carnival atmosphere to the occasion.

Clearly, the revivalism of the parish mission was strongly underpinned with sacrament and sacramental. In addition the mission referred all the aids to christian living to the church, or chapel as it was then called. This was in keeping with the contemporary ecclesiastical reform. This sought to establish direct and central clerical control and wean the people from folk expressions of piety. In the not very distant past, the sacraments of baptism, confession, communion, marriage and the funeral rites had been centred in the homesteads. Favoured practices of piety were centred in holy places at holy times: pilgrimages, 'rounds' at holy wells, monastic remains, the patron ('pattern') day rituals. The centring of the whole panoply of grace-giving media in the local chapel was, moreover, a symbol of the ecclesiology of the time. This was a defensive ecclesiology which regarded the Catholic church alone as the almoner of grace, as the institution where salvation was secured.

The social world

A listing of the pastoral benefits of the Redemptorist parish mission team would begin by noting its way of countering defections to Protestantism. Earlier in the century, Protestants had begun a well-funded campaign, notably in poverty stricken areas, to win Catholics from 'popery and ignorance' — their 'second reformation'. They had some initial success. The Redemptorists did not conduct anti-proselytising missions as such. At the very beginning Prost had expressed his opposition to the polemical preaching popular with the Irish. When, on some occasions, Protestant polemicists challenged the missioners to a debate, they were ignored — much to the disappointment of the people. When the missioners were greeted with huge enthusiasm on arrival in Enniscorthy in 1857, a local explained that it was 'not only for the Fathers but for the Protestants here, for this kills them'! The whole mission, instructions in particular, upheld the church's teaching under attack by the Protestants. In the early missions especially, big numbers of converts were reported, although most of these were probably lost sheep returning to the fold.

The most frequently-mentioned benefit of the parish mission in reports of the time was the ending of local feuds. In small, closed rural communities, enmities could be deep, violent and ridden with litigation. After the mission in Killydysert in 1865, the *Limerick Reporter* and *Tipperary Vindicator* recorded the tribute of the Killydysert Petty Sessions to the mission: 'It has served to create new and fresh bonds of friendship between the voracious legal belligerents who had been systematic attendants at the temple of Justice for years previous to the arrival of these good and holy men.' The heyday of faction fighting was past. A famous survival of it, however, was the focal point of a mission and renewal at Emly in the troubled border lands of Limerick and Tipperary, 1862–3. As often in factions fights, if no serious cause for conflict could be found, any old bone of contention would do. In this case, it was a dispute about the age of a certain bull. The combatants squared off as three-year-olds and four-year-olds. For years battle was joined at fair days and other public occasions. Lives lost and blood spilt continued to fuel the fighting. Archbishop Leahy of Cashel arranged a mission which ended with a formal reconciliation of the two factions.

There were also some constantly recurring targets for denunciation. Excessive drinking, the bane of society, was the principal one. The denunciation of dances, wakes and 'American wakes' occur frequently. The special effort to restrain company-keeping derived from the incidence of illegitimate births.

Secret societies came in for severe denunciation. In this the missioners were following the standard discipline both of the church and the state. Special mention is made of Ribbonmen and Fenians. The Ribbonmen formed one of several societies organised to defend local interests or to right local wrongs. In the North such organisations were concerned chiefly with protecting Catholics from Protestants. They were a kind of counter to the Orange Order. Elsewhere they, or their kind, were an intimidating force that sought to right such abuses as unjust land structures, dues extracted from Catholics for the maintenance of the Church of Ireland (a State establishment until its disestablishment in 1869), or even from the excessive dues demanded from their flock by the Catholic clergy.

Fenianism, on the other hand, was, in its constitution at least, more national in its objectives and organisation. It was also wholly secular in its inspiration and impervious to church condemnation. This condemnation, in any case, was not always free of ambivalence. Such successes as the missioners reported after the retreat to the men's confraternity in Ennistymon in 1874 were rare: 'many who had joined the Fenian Brotherhood, and among the rest the local head, renounced Fenianism and were admitted to the sacraments'. On the other hand, at SS Peter and Paul church in Cork in the same year, young men in the Fenians swore an oath to one another not to attend the mission. In his reports to Rome on the canonical visitation, 1866 and 1867, Coffin, the Provincial, noted that there was a marked reduction in the number of men and boys for confession at the Redemptorist church in Limerick due to Fenianism.

A critical evaluation of the Redemptorist ministry from 1851 to 1898 would have to take account of the difference between the missions of the first decade or two and those of the latter part of the century. The earlier missions were characterised by unbounded expectancy and excitement on the part of the people, and by unregulated demands on the missioners. This changed as the novelty wore off and the missioners gained in experience. The 'primitive fervour' of the early missioners was tempered, of course, later by the increase in their number and by the stress arising out of the deepening conflict between Irish and English interests. More significant, however, was the change in the situation of the parish mission. The spread of ecclesiastical reform on several fronts enabled the parish mission to take its point of departure from higher ground. This change has been described as a transition from 'mission' in the early period to 'maintenance' in the latter. This ready-made distinction hardly fits the case: the parish mission of its nature is about both 'mission' and 'maintenance'. It is an itinerant apostolate whose thrust comes into play, equally though differently, in either a developed or undeveloped situation. A problem which did arise for the parish missions in the later period was due precisely to the more developed situation at the time. This was the clamour by parochial priests for retreats and confraternities, or for annual parish retreats. Leading

Redemptorist missioners deplored this trend in that it diverted some of the energies of the mission force from parish missions proper. But there were also limitations on the early missions due to the extremely neglected state of many parishes.

In the early years, the mission 'revivalism' had something of a Catholic *Blitzkrieg* about it. The people were given too much too fast, and the impact on a largely deprived congregation was not always positive. Side by side with the vast amount of good done, some consciences were unduly upset and some impressionable minds disturbed. Some incidents suggest that mass enthusiasm bordered on the hysterical. The mission programme of the pioneer, Prost, which required a long, gradual evangelisation in such a situation, had it proved viable, would have lessened this risk.

Communication between missioners and people was also a problem in the early years. Simplicity of diction and clear delivery—qualities required of the Redemptorist preacher—went some way to cope with the problem, but the missioners were up against great diversity in the communities: literate and illiterate, rich and poor, those competent in English and those not. The missioners, for their part, were largely limited to set piece uniformity in their sermons and instructions. The missioners from the Continent in particular laboured under this limitation. Irish-born missioners would be somewhat more adaptable. The need for Irish at many missions could not be supplied. The first competent Irish-speaking missioner, Michael Geoghegan, was not professed until 1863.

Over the whole period, the salvation theology of the missioners, obviously had the limitations that characterised the soteriology of the church at the time. 'Save your soul' was the clarion call that signalled the be-all and end-all of life on earth. Soul was understood in the dualist sense as opposed to body. The pitch was made to the individual in the singular. 'What does it profit a man if he should gain the whole world and suffer the loss of his soul?' (Mk 8:36) was the standard back-up scriptural text for the sermon on salvation. This translation (Douai), after the Vulgate, misleadingly lends itself to the dualist under-standing of 'soul'. This is not the sense of the gospel language, as may be seen from modern English versions. From this base, a strong other-wordly focus was given to preaching. The Last Things came first. The coming of Christ into the social order was not a primary concern. A christianity was proclaimed that was not really incarnate in the local situation. Because of this, a preacher felt free to preach everywhere on much the same terms.

To say all this is not to make an adverse criticism but to make an assessment. For the same theology had its merits in that all the guns of the missioner were trained single-mindedly on the moral conversion of the individual. And if the individuals in a community did become more temperate, just, chaste, charitable and neighbourly, it followed that the social and communitary dimension of christian life was enhanced, and at the same time gave the people a new sense of belonging to, and identity with, their parish.

Related to their 'save your soul' soteriology was the relative aloofness of their apostolate from the sin of the world of nineteenth century Ireland: the radically unjust political, social and economic order that poisoned the whole of life, urban and rural, and caused secret societies to sprout out of the ground. Many individual Redemptor-ists did privately deplore this sin, but their personal *saeva indignatio* was not translated into any prophetic denuncia-tion of the evil. They did, however, show their sympathy for the oppressed. It would, of course, be too facile to judge them in the light of the theology and apostolate of liberation in favour in our time. Besides, one of their greatest assets from the pastoral point of view was their blanket detachment from political involvements of any kind.

Tensions: the foundation of the Irish Province

In any case, a public campaign of denunciation by itinerant missioners would give rise to more problems than it would solve. It should be recalled that until 1898, Irish Redemptorists formed part of the English Province, and they teamed with their English and Scots confreres on missions both in Ireland and across the Irish Sea. The Catholic faith, their common religious vocation and their commitment to the same apostolate helped them to cope with their national differences until late in the century. Ultimately, however, these differences led to the setting up of an independent Province for Ireland.

The mix of cultures, Continental, British and Irish, brought a considerable enrichment to the Redemptorists in Britain and Ireland in the last century. The Continentals merged reasonably well with both the Irish and the English, but the Irish and the English themselves in the period were, chemically speaking, not for mixing.

One factor in the differences between them, usually overlooked, was the difference between the Irish Catholic and the English Catholic as such. This explains why their common faith, far from softening their political differences, often only gave these an added dimension. The Irish, deprived and under siege on several fronts, affirmed themselves by claiming a certain superiority in terms of their Catholic faith. Prost recalls in his diary how a professor in the ecclesiastical college in Wexford tried to get him to admit that the Irish were the best Catholics in the world! The Irish identity emerged as a Catholic identity. In 1872, at a retreat to the men's confraternity in Mullingar, the men attended sporting green scarves, and Irish saints had been chosen as patrons of the different sections. This identity of nation and church became both a badge of defiance and a triumphalist banner unfurled over a vaunted 'spiritual empire' of the Irish at home and in the diaspora.

This was paralleled by a contrasting affirmation on the part of English Catholics. Socially and politically they had more affinity with the English Protestant than with the Irish Catholic. They had their roots in an élitist tradition that they saw as giving them 'class', and were distanced from the populist tradition of Irish Catholicism. This was given expression in no uncertain terms in 1860 by a Mrs Charlton who, when introduced by the Marquis of Westminster as a Roman Catholic, retorted: 'Yes, but an

English Catholic, not an Irish one, which is all the difference in the world. English Catholics are responsible beings who are taught right from wrong, whereas Irish Catholics, belonging to a yet savage nation, know no better and are excusable on that account.'[11]

The converts of the 'second spring', many of whom became Redemptorists, only emphasised this different identity. Edward Norman muses quizzically that 'the Anglican converts had not quite believed that the church of the Fathers could have a Kerry accent'.[12] The implication is that they believed it to have had, ideally, an Oxford accent. The differences underlying the two identities were real enough, but in themselves, might well have issued in a creative tension. But, as often happens, the differences were overlaid with distortions of the realities, distortions that gave rise to antipathy and bitterness. For example, Provincial Swinkels' letter to Mauron in 1860, refers to accusations made by Dutch, German and Belgians who unfairly accuse English converts like Coffin and others of being a group apart in the church, wanting to govern, proud and unreliable: 'One cannot rely on them, because just as they changed over once, they may change again. . . .' Likewise, it was tendentious and an irritant to the Irish to find their grumblings against the injustices in their land deplored by their superiors in Rome and London as 'excessive nationalism'. For nationalism in any form was a brand name in disfavour in ecclesiastical circles for the questionable reason, among others, of the threat to the Papal States by the Italian Risorgimento.

In such a situation, the Irish and English inevitably had different perspectives in regard to the Redemptorist apostolate: the conversion of England on the one side, the missionising of Ireland on the other. In the early years, when there was a large Continental presence and only a few Irish members, the Continentals urged a larger investment in Ireland. The English confreres, however, in the glow of the second spring, saw themselves as ushering in the summer for the church in England.

Soon an Irish voice was raised in protest at the failure to expand the Congregation in Ireland. William Plunkett

(1824–1900), professed in 1851, was the first Irish Redemptorist and the first to be given a post of authority—he was superior of Limerick, 1860–65. Plunkett was a cadet of the Anglo-Irish aristocratic house of Fingal. Educated in England, he served in the Welsh Guards. He was a man of devout and gentle disposition and a zealous, though weak, parish missioner. His name appeared in the list of possible candidates for the see of Meath. Late in life he volunteered for the mission to Australia, became superior there and died in Sydney.

In 1861, he wrote to Douglas, asking him to present to the Superior General the case for a novitiate in Ireland:

> Your Reverence knows very well that the English and Irish do not agree very well together. I'm not speaking for myself as I was educated in England and lived among Englishmen and I can get on very well with them, in fact I like them in some things better than my own compatriots. But I am afraid that as long as we have our novitiate in England that we shall have few postulants and fewer professed subjects, because it requires more than ordinary virtue to hear one's country abused—and it is done even unintentionally in England by the English Fathers—and to have to listen to disparagement of everything that is done in Ireland, particularly as regards to ecclesiastical affairs.

In 1863, he warned Mauron that 'in time we may have a schism, as in America',[13] but got poor comfort from Mauron who replied in his lofty manner that he should leave the problem in the hands of God, for any measures that Mauron himself would take 'would be for the good of your Province and your house (Limerick)'. Added to Mauron's authoritarian style of government was that of the area superior, Coffin, whose policies, moreover, Rome supported absolutely. The result was that during the long rule of these two superiors, there was no effective hearing for the grievances of the subjects.

Robert Coffin was a man of splendid talents.[14] A gifted missioner, he translated many of St Alphonsus' works for the English public. But as a superior he was imperious and did not brook opposition to his policies. Plunkett said that Coffin always had the effect on him of a novice master. His policy for the Province was hampered severely by the shortage of English vocations. Irish vocations were an asset but only if they did not increase to such an extent that they would create a case for an independent Irish Province. His virtual one-man rule was facilitated by Mauron's suspension of the provision in the Rule for dealing with local grievances, namely, an extraordinary canonical visitation from the Superior General or his delegate. During his long reign (1855–93) there was not a single such visitation of the houses in England and Ireland, though the rule envisaged this 'from time to time'. Likewise, no general chapter of the Congregation was held over that forty-year period. Had these legal rights been protected, the differences between the two sides might not have fermented into bitterness and the process of separation might have matured amicably.

Not all of Coffin's restraints on growth in Ireland were without merit. He screened aspirants rigorously on grounds of health and education. Many of the eager Irish recruits proved unequal to the demands made on their health by studies first and by apostolic work later: tuberculosis was the great scourge. A juniorate was established in Limerick in 1884 for fostering vocations, by Coffin's successor as Provincial, Hugh McDonald, a Scot. In the meantime, in spite of the increase in the number of Irish, Coffin proceeded with foundations in Scotland and England before being pressured from Rome to set up a second house in Ireland at Dundalk in 1876.

The Dundalk foundation was intended as a base for missions in the northern part of the country. It was the creation of Henry Harbison (1820–88), a native of Moneymore, Co. Derry. In 1854 he became the first and most brilliant of the many talented Irish diocesan clergy to join the Redemptorists in the last century. An outstanding preacher and indefatigable confessor, he was a great favourite with bishops and clergy and was instrumental in popularising the Redemptorist parish mission and clergy retreat.

Robert Coffin's last major work for the Province before his elevation to the see of Southwark was the opening of a mission to Australasia by the Province in 1882. The Irish Redemptorists participated in this mission from the beginning and took it over completely in 1898.

Nicholas Mauron died in 1893. By the time the General Chapter met in 1894, the Anglo-Irish rivalry had come to the boil. After the mandatory third foundation was made, in Belfast, in 1896, the Irish Province was established in 1898. Of the many arguments for and against separation put forward, the truly apostolic ones were the loss to the Irish emigrant communities in Britain resulting from the separation, and the gain to the mission ministry in Ireland, especially in the West where a foundation was already projected.

Andrew Boylan (1842–1910) was the first Provincial of the Irish Province. More than that, he was really the founding Father of the new Province. He had been the bursar in Maynooth before joining the Redemptorists — a college wag said he was leaving Maynooth to follow Christ! He earned immense respect and affection from both sides of the Redemptorist divide, and from the ecclesiastical establishment in Ireland and did much to heal the wounds left by the battle for separation. He established a house for missions at Esker in Co. Galway in 1901 and founded the mission of the Irish Province in the Philippines in 1906. When Boylan was elevated to the episcopal see of his native Kilmore in 1907, he had effected the transition from the cosmopolitan Redemptorist mission of the nineteenth century in Ireland to the native Irish Province of the twentieth century.

Notes

Chapter 1. The Role of the Moral Theologian in the Life of the Church
(pp. 8–23)

1. The term 'hierarchical magisterium' is used throughout this paper in preference to the commonly used term 'the magisterium'. Unhappily, both terms can be misleading with regard to teaching and learning in the church's life and mission. To speak of 'the magisterium' can too easily give the impression that the church is divided into two groups, 'teachers' and 'taught'. On the other hand, the expression 'the hierarchical magisterium' suggests a too-juridical approach to teaching and learning. The balance would not be set right even by introducing the pre-nineteenth century practice of speaking of theology as 'the theological magisterium'. All three terms tend to obscure the fact that as christians, we have only one teacher, the Holy Spirit, whom the Lord has given us to lead us into all truth. Consequently, prior to any teaching activity we are fundamentally a listening and learning community. Compliance with juridical requirements for a legitimate exercise of teaching authority in the church is not a substitute for following the normal human process of listening, learning and discerning (cf Kelly 1986 (1), 3–9).

2. Since the word 'critical' carries very negative overtones in current everyday usage, I have deliberately refrained from speaking of the 'critical' role of moral theology, lest that should portray moral theology as confrontational and destructive. Instead, I have used the expression 'scientific discernment' as a blanket term to cover all the tools of the science of theology, eg a careful examination of the sources (scripture, tradition and experience as seen dynamically in dialectical interpenetration), a study of the history of theology itself and an application of the best philosophical analyses that are available. In fact, the original meaning of 'critical' carried the same flavour as such expressions as 'opportunity for growth' or 'healing diagnosis'. If 'critical' still had this positive flavour in everyday language, there

would be no problem about speaking of the 'critical' role of moral theology.

3. I made a similar point with reference to the exchange of correspondence between Cardinal Ratzinger and Charles Curran. I felt it was unfortunate that both parties were making dissent the main issue: 'Dissent is a negative word. It belongs to the same stable as terms like deny, oppose, contradict. There is nothing positive or affirmative about it. Focusing on the issue of dissent, therefore, has two unfortunate consequences. It creates a climate of confrontation and it makes true dialogue virtually impossible' (Kelly 1986 (2),647). In response, Curran wrote: 'As a Catholic theologian, I should always explain the official church teaching and then show how I relate to it. Clarity, honesty and truth require that positions be labeled as dissent when they are such .... The primary function of the theologian is to interpret, explain and understand. The vast majority of times, this does not involve any dissent. However, on occasions the interpretive function of the theologian will result in a dissenting position. A responsible theologian should never try to hide or dissimulate dissent. Dissent is dissent and not just dialogue' (Curran 1986, 100).

4. 'We have to be ready to accept the discipline of ecumenism, not acting unilaterally, but seeking to explore together the mind of Christ' (Hume 1987, 2).

Key to References
Curran 1986
Charles E. Curran, *Faithful Dissent*, Sheed and Ward, Kansas City: London 1986. The second half of this book contains the full documentation of the exchange of correspondence between the Congregation for the Doctrine of the Faith and Curran.
Dulles 1983
Avery Dulles, 'The Two Magisteria: An Interim Reflection', ch. 8 of his book, *A Church to Believe in*, New York: Crossroad 1983.
Fuchs 1984
Josef Fuchs, 'Teaching Morality: The Tension between Bishops and Theologians within the Church', ch. 9 of his book, *Christian Ethics in a Secular Arena*, Dublin: Gill and Macmillan 1984.
Hume 1987
Cardinal Basil Hume, 'Address to the meeting of the Presidents

of the European Episcopal Conferences, (6–8 March 1987); full
text in *Briefing*, vol 17, no 6, Supplement.

ITC Theses 1976

Twelve Theses (6/6/76) summarising the conclusions of a plen-
ary session of the International Theological Commission held
on 25 September–1 October 1975. They were drawn up by
Otto Semmelroth and Karl Lehmann and were approved by
the 'great majority' of the Commission. A translation of these
theses is found in ch. 8 of Sullivan 1983 under the title, 'The
Magisterium and the Role of Theologians in the Church', 174–
218. It is this translation with the page numbers of the book
which is being referred to when the reference code ITC Theses
1976 is used. Another translation with a commentary by
Semmelroth and Lehmann is published by the US Catholic
Conference (1977).

Kelly 1986(1)

Kevin T Kelly, 'Formation for Collaboration', *The Way*, Supplement 56, (Summer 1986), 3–15.

Kelly 1986(2)

Kevin T Kelly, 'Serving the Truth', *The Tablet*, (6 June 1986),
647–9.

McCormick 1986

Richard McCormick, 'The Search for Truth in the Catholic
Context', *America* (8 November 1986), 276–81.

McCormick 1987(1)

Richard McCormick, 'The Vatican Documents on Bioethics',
America (17 January 1987), 24–8, 39.

McCormick 1987(2)

Richard McCormick, 'Notes on Moral Theology: 1986', *Theological Studies*, (March 1987), 87–105.

Malone 1986

Bishop James Malone, 'How Bishops and Theologians Relate',
June 1986, Address at Marquette University. Full text in
Origins (31 July, 1986), 169–74.

Orsy 1986

Ladislas Orsy, 'Reflections on the Text of a Canon', *America* (17
May 1986), 396–9.

Chapter 2. Historicity and Moral Norm (pp. 24–44)

1. Cf A Auer, 'Die Erfahrung der Geschichtlichkeit und die
Krise der Moral', *Theol. Quartalschrift* 149 (1961), 4–22. Idem,
'Die normative Kraft des Faktischen. Die Begegnung von

Ethik und Sozialempirie', in A Seckler, ed, *Begegnung* (Festschrift H Fries), Graz:Vienna:Cologne 1972, 615–32. W Kerber, ed, *Sittliche Normen. Zum Problem ihrer allgemeinen und unwandelbaren Geltung*, Düsseldorf 1982. K Demmer, *Deuten und Handeln. Grundlagen und Grundfragen der Fundamental-moral*, Freiburg i Ue/Freiburg i Br 1985; idem, 'Christi vestigia sequentes, eiusque imagini conformes', *Lumen Gentium* 40. Appunti di teologia morale (ad uso privato degli studenti), Rome 1986. S Bastianel, *Autonomia morale del credente*, Brescia 1980. GB Sala, 'L'imperativo morale e la storicità dell'uomo', *La Civiltà Cattolica* 2957 (1 September 1973), 361–77. RM McInerny, 'Truth in Ethics, Historicity and Natural Law', *Proceedings of the American Philosophical Association*, Washington, DC, 43 (1969), 71–82.

2. K Demmer (see note 1).

3. Discourse of 29.10.1951: *Acta Apostolica Sedis* 43 (1951), 835–54.

4. Cf Josef Fuchs, 'Moral Truth—between objectivism and subjectivism' in *Christian Ethics in a Secular Arena*, Washington, DC: Georgetown University Press/Dublin: Gill and Macmillan 1983.

5. On this problematic, see also Josef Fuchs, '"The Sin of the World" and Normative Morality' in *Personal Responsibility and Christian Morality*, Washington, DC: Georgetown University Press/Dublin: Gill and Macmillan 1983, 153–75.

6. G Martelet, *Amour conjugal et renouveau conciliaire*, Paris 1967 (cf discourse of Paul VI on 31.7.1968). D Capone, La Humanae Vitae nel ministero sacerdotale, *Lateranum* 44 (1978), 195–227; references there to the article on homosexuality. P Chirico, 'Morality in General and Birth Control in Particular' *Chicago Studies* 48 (1969), 125–43; idem, 'Tension, Morality and Birth Control', *Theological Studies* 28 (1967), 258–85.

Chapter 3. Thomistic and Analytic Philosophers on the First Principles of Morality: A Conflict of Interpretations
(pp. 45–59)

1. See K Kluxen, *Philosophische Ethik bei Thomas von Aquin*, Mainz 1964, 61–71. See also Oscar J Brown, *Natural Rectitude and Divine Law in Aquinas*, Toronto 1981, both for a treatment and bibliography on St Thomas on natural law.

2. J Finnis, 'The Claim of Absolutes', *The Tablet*, vol 241, no 7656 (4 April 1987), 364–6.
3. V MacNamara, *Faith and Ethics: Recent Roman Catholicism*, Dublin: Gill and Macmillan 1985, 2.
4. E D'Arcy, '"Worthy of Worship" A Catholic Contribution' in *Religion and Morality*, edited by G Outka and JP Reeder Jr, New York 1973, 173–203, at 173.
5. MJ Charlesworth 'Analytic Philosophy', New Catholic Encyclopedia, vol 1, New York: McGraw-Hill 1967, 470–73.
6. E D'Arcy, 'Worthy of Worship', 181.
7. Elizabeth Anscombe has studied this problem in depth in her book, *Intention*, Oxford 1957.
8. E D'Arcy, *Conscience and its Right to Freedom*, New York 1961.
9. Ibid, 49.
10. Ibid, 52.
11. Ibid, 56–7.
12. DJ O'Connor, *Aquinas and Natural Law*, London 1967, 66.
13. D'Arcy, *Conscience*, 69.
14. O'Connor, *Aquinas*, 76.
15. Herbert McCabe, OP, 'Aquinas on Good Sense', *New Black-friars* (October 1986), vol 67, no 798, 419–31.
16. Alan Donagan, 'The Scholastic Theory of Moral Law in the Modern World' in *Aquinas: A Collection of Critical Essays*, ed A Kenny, New York 1969, 330.
17. Ibid, 336.
18. E Kant, *The Moral Law, or Kant's Groundwork of the Metaphysic of Morals*, tr HJ Paton, London 1948, 95.
19. Alan Donagan, *The Theory of Morality*, Chicago 1977.
20. E D'Arcy, 'The Withering-Away of Disbelief' *Consultation of the Secretariat for Non-Believers*, The Vatican, Rome 1985, 164–5.
21. G Grisez, 'The First Principles of Practical Reason: A Commentary on the Summa Theologiae, 1–2, Question 94, article 2' *The Natural Law Forum*, 10 (1965), 168–201.
22. Ibid, 175.
23. See D Mindling, OFM Cap, *Germain Grisez: Commitment and Choice*, Rome 1987, for a developed analysis of Grisez's theory in its various parts.
24. G Grisez, 'The First Principle', 180.
25. See E D'Arcy 'The Withering-Away', 166–7.
26. G Grisez, 'A Contemporary Natural Law Ethics': Conference given at the Dept of Philosophy, Marquette University, 5 October 1985, 4. Grisez gives an enlightening account of the evolution of his own thought in this talk.
27. See D Flippen, 'Natural Law and Natural Inclinations', *The*

New Scholasticism 50 (1986), 284–316; B Johnstone, 'The Structures of Practical Reason', *The Thomist* 50 (1986), 417–47; P Simpson, 'St Thomas on the Naturalistic Fallacy', *The Thomist* 51 (1987), 51–70. For the incipient theological debate see G Abba, 'I *Christian Moral Principles* di G Grisez e la *Seconda Pars* della *Summa Theologiae*', *Salesianum* 48 (1986), 637–80.

Chapter 4. Reciprocity of Consciences: A Key Concept in Moral Theology (pp. 60–72)

1. Cf M Nédoncelle, *La réciprocité des consciences: Essai sur la nature de la personne*, Paris 1942. Idem, *De la Fidelité*, Paris 1953.
2. Cf R Girard, *Des choses cachées depuis la fondation du monde*, Paris 1978.
3. Cf BF Skinner, *Beyond Freedom and Dignity*, New York 1974. My position against Skinner's behaviour manipulation is developed in full in B Häring, *Manipulation: Ethical Boundaries of Medical, Behavioural and Genetic Manipulation*, Slough 1975.
4. *Gaudium et Spes* no 16.
5. *Lumen Gentium* no 37.
6. *Gaudium et Spes* no 62.
7. A striking example of those calling for sanctions against any dissent is given by the lawyer JP Hale in his article 'Where he started and where he stands. A case against Charles Curran', *Commonweal* (30 January 1987) 47–51. He writes: 'For theologians like Curran, once you give sexual intercourse an independent life of its own, it would follow that it was not only within marriage that one had occasion or need to express affection. If sexual intercourse were essentially an expression of affection like a powerful handshake, it would be beyond argument that one could have affection for someone other than one's spouse. . . . And so Fr Curran moved down what he perceived as the logical line to arrive at the legitimacy of masturbation, fornication and sodomy' (49–50). Here we have not only a striking lack of fairness but also, perhaps, an attempt to disturb the peace by suggesting that many Catholic moral theologians do, in fact, approve of 'masturbation, fornication and sodomy'. For those who take such assertions at their face value, this may lead to a breakdown of sexual morality. Where are 'reciprocity of consciences' and 'earnest dialogue'?

8. St Alphonsus warns: 'Imposing on others uncertain obligations is not a sign of holiness, but of arrogance and stubbornness' (*Risposta Apologetica* 1764). Text is to be found in *Cinque Apologie del Beato Alfonso Maria di Liguori*, Turin 1829, 23.

Chapter 5. Moral Theology and Transformative Justice
(pp. 73–84)

1. Cf Josef Fuchs, *Christian Morality: The Word Becomes Flesh*, Washington, DC: Georgetown University Press/Dublin: Gill and Macmillan 1987. J Mahony, *The Making of Moral Theology*, Oxford: Clarendon Press 1987.

Chapter 6. Official Catholic Social Teaching and Conscience
(pp. 85–104)

1. Pastoral Constitution on the Church in the Modern World, par 42, in David O'Brien and Thomas A Shannon, eds *Renewing the Earth: Catholic Documents on Peace, Justice, and Liberation*, Garden City, NY: Doubleday Image Books 1977, 216.
2. Pope Pius XI, *Quadragesimo Anno*, par 11, in Terence P McLaughlin, ed, *The Church and the Reconstruction of the Modern World: The Social Encyclicals of Pius XI*, Garden City, NY: Doubleday Image Books, 1957, 222.
3. Pope Pius XI, *Divini Redemptoris*, par 34, in McLaughlin, 379.
4. Pope John XXIII, *Mater et Magistra*, par 226–42, in O'Brien and Shannon, 105–8.
5. Pope Paul VI, *Octogesima Adveniens*, par 4, in O'Brien and Shannon, 353, 354.
6. Jean-Yves Calvez and Jacques Perrin, *The Church and Social Justice: The Social Teachings of the Popes from Leo XIII to Pius XII*, Chicago: Henry Regnery 1961, 58–62.
7. Marie-Dominique Chenu, *La 'Doctrine Sociale' de L'Église Comme Idéologie*, Paris: Editions du Cerf 1979, especially 79–96; Donal Dorr, *Option for the Poor*, Maryknoll, NY: Orbis Books/Dublin: Gill and Macmillan 1983, 157 ff.
8. Benjamin L Masse, *Justice for All: An Introduction to the Social Teaching of the Catholic Church*, Milwaukee Bruce 1964, 70–88.
9. These different approaches are developed in my *American*

Catholic Social Ethics: Twentieth Century Approaches, Notre Dame, Indiana: University of Notre Dame Press 1982.

10. For a further development of this change, see my *Directions in Catholic Social Ethics*, Notre Dame, Indiana: University of Notre Dame Press 1985, 5–42.

11. Pope John XXIII, *Mater et Magistra*, par 236, in O'Brien and Shannon, 107.

12. Pope John XXIII, *Mater et Magistra*, par 217 ff, in O'Brien and Shannon 102 ff.

13. Pope John XXIII, *Pacem in Terris*, par 35–6, 80 ff, in O'Brien and Shannon, 132, 142 ff.

14. National Conference of Catholic Bishops, 'The Challenge of Peace: God's Promise and Our Response', *Origins* 13 (1983), 1–32; National Conference of Catholic Bishops, 'Economic Justice for All: Catholic Social Teaching and the US Economy', *Origins* 16 (1986), 409–55.

15. *Origins* 13 (1983), 3, 15.

16. J Brian Benestad and Francis J Butler, eds, *Quest for Justice: A Compendium of Statements of the United States Catholic Bishops on the Political and Social Order 1966–1980*, Washington, DC:National Conference of Catholic Bishops 1981.

17. For a negative criticism of the bishops' approach, see J Brian Benestad, *The Pursuit of a Just Social Order: Policy Statements of the US Catholic Bishops, 1966–1980*, Washington, DC: Ethics and Public Policy Center 1982.

18. Archbishop Joseph Bernardin, 'NCCB Committee Report: Studying War and Peace', *Origins* 11 (1981), 403, 404.

19. All this documentation is found in *Origins* 12 (1983), 690–96.

20. Ibid, 691.

21. Ibid, 693.

22. *Origins* 13 (1983), 2, 3.

23. *Origins* 16 (1986), nos 134, 135, 426.

24. Ibid.

25. The first draft of the pastoral letter was not published in its entirety, but parts of it appeared in *National Catholic Reporter* 18 (2 July, 1982), 11 ff. I am citing the document 'First Draft: Pastoral letter on Peace and War: God's Hope in a Time of Fear' which was sent to the bishops and others. The section on deterrence is found on pp 25–38.

26. 'Second Draft: Pastoral Letter on Peace and War', *Origins* 12 (1982), 315–18.

27. 'Third Draft of Pastoral Letter: The Challenge of Peace: God's Promise and Our Response', *Origins* 12 (1983), 713–16. The teaching on deterrence in the final document is found in *Origins* 13 (1983), 16–19.

28. Jim Castelli, *The Bishops and the Bomb: Waging Peace in a Nuclear Age*, Garden City, NY: Doubleday Image Books 1983, 169, 170.
29. *Origins* 16 (1986), no 134, 426.
30. 'Pastoral Letter on Catholic Social Teaching and the US Economy: First Draft', *Origins* 14 (1984), 337–83.
31. Rembert G Weakland, 'The Economic Pastoral: Draft Two', *America* (21 September, 1985), 129, 130.

Chapter 7. Sterilisation: The Dilemma of Catholic Hospitals
(pp. 105–122)

1. *Washington Post*, 22 May 1977, A3.
2. Charles F Westoff and Elise F Jones, 'The Secularization of US Birth Control Practices', *Family Planning Perspectives* 9, no 5 (1977), 203–7.
3. Personal communication.
4. The letter was provided to me by several bishops. It has not, to the best of my knowledge, been published.
5. *Origins* 15 (1986), 733–44. *America* 154 (1986), 372.
6. *Origins* 15 (1986), 737. *Crux of the News*, 28 April 1986.
7. John M O'Lane, MD, 'Sterilization and Contraceptive Services in Catholic Hospitals', *American Journal of Obstetrics and Gynecology* 133, no 4 (1979), 355–7.
8. 'Statement on Tubal Ligation', National Conference of Catholic Bishops, *Origins* 10 (1980), 175.
9. *Documentum circa sterilizationem in nosocomiis catholicis*, Translated in *Origins* 6 (1976), 33 and 35.
10. Cf *Policy Manual* of St Joseph's Hospital, London, Ontario 1973, Foreword.
11. *Acta Apostolica Sedis*, 22 (1930), 560.
12. *Acta Apostolica Sedis*, 32 (1940), 73.
13. *Acta Apostolica Sedis*, 45 (1953), 674–5.
14. For the English version cf *The Birth Control Debate*, Robert G Hoyt, ed, Kansas City: *National Catholic Reporter*, 1968, 115–40 at 124.
15. John C Ford, SJ and Gerald Kelly, SJ, *Contemporary Moral Theology II: Marriage Questions*, Westminster: Newman 1963, 319.
16. Ibid, 288.
17. Cf note 14, 123.
18. Gerald Kelly, SJ, *Medico-Moral Problems*, St Louis: Catholic Hospital Association, 1958, 158.

19. Cf note 14, 93.
20. Walter J Burghardt, SJ, 'Rome and Rebellion', *New York Times*, (8 April 1980).
21. Bernard Häring, CSsR, *Medical Ethics*, Notre Dame: Fides 1973, 90.
22. *Washington Star* (22 June 1980), 1.
23. *30 Giorni*, May 1986.
24. 'Edges of Life' I, *Commonweal* 107 (1 August 1980), 421.
25. *National Catholic Reporter*, 4 July 1986, 14: 'Because it was planned as a celebration of moral theology loyal to the church's teaching authority, Curran, McCormick and their friends were not invited to the party.'
26. In what follows, the data and citations are taken from the notes compiled by the late Sister Emily George and are used with the permission of the authorities of the Sisters of Mercy of the Union.
27. Johannes Gründel, 'Zur Problematik der operativen Sterilisation in Katholischen Krankenhausern', *Stimmen der Zeit* 199 (1981), 671–7.
28. BC Butler, 'Authority and the Christian Conscience', *Clergy Review* 60 (1975), 3–17.

Chapter 8. Basic Ecclesial Communities and Moral Theology
(pp. 123–143)

1. FB Avila, *A Situação Socio Econômica e Política do Brasil*, Itaici 1984.
2. Instituto Brasileiro de Geografia e Estatística, *Relatório Anual* (1987).
3. *Evangelii Nuntiandi*, no 58. Documents of the Conference of Puebla, no 641.
4. *Evangelii Nuntiandi*, no 14.
5. Conference of Medellín, *Introduction and Documents on Peace and Justice*, 1968. G Baum, 'Class Struggle and the Magisterium' in *Theological Studies*, 45 (1984), 690–92.
6. Baum, Art cit, 692–7. Dorr, Donal, *Option for the Poor*, Maryknoll, NY: Orbis Books/Dublin: Gill and Macmillan 1983, ch 8–11.
7. Puebla, nos 1134–65.
8. RF Moreno, *Teologia Moral Desde Los Pobres*, Madrid 1968, 108–10. G Gutiérrez, *The Theology of Liberation*, New York 1973, passim.
9. RF Moreno, op cit, 47–65.

10. E Dussel, *Ética Comunitária*, Petropolis 1986.
11. Sacred Congregation for the Doctrine of the Faith, *Libertatis Conscientia*, 1986, nos 69–70.
12. Jan Sobrino, *Christology at the Crossroads*, London 1978.
13. Donal Dorr, *Spirituality and Justice*, Maryknoll, NY: Orbis Books/Dublin: Gill and Macmillan, 1985, 100.
14. John Paul II, *Dives in Misericordia*, no 14.
15. JM Bonino, *Towards a Christian Political Ethics*, London 1983, 47.
16. For a brief evaluation of Latin American hermeneutics, see A Tambasco, 'First and Third World Ethics', in R Daly, ed, *Christian Biblical Ethics*, New York 1984, 139–51.
17. Bernard Häring, *The Law of Christ*, vol 1, Cork 1963, 73–80.
18. G Baum, 'The Magisterium in a Changing Church', *Concilium* 3 (1967), 34–42, and see 'The Teaching Authority of Believers', *Concilium* 180 (1985).
19. Segundo Galilea, *The Beatitudes*, Maryknoll, NY: Orbis Books/Dublin: Gill and Macmillan 1984.
20. *Evangelii Nuntiandi*, nos 30–33. Letter of John Paul II to Brazilian Bishops, April 1986.
21. E Dussel, for example in *Para una Ética da Libertação latino-americana*, Sao Paulo: Piracicaba 1982.

Chapter 9. Learning through Suffering
(pp. 144–160)

1. Many of these themes are explored in the Apostolic Letter of John Paul II, *On the Christian Meaning of Human Suffering*, Washington: United States Catholic Conference 1984, no 23.
2. 'Affliction' [*malheur*], she writes, includes physical, psychological and social elements. But it involves a sorrow at least akin to physical pain, an 'almost bodily disorder: together with psychological trauma and social degradation'. Simone Weil, *Waiting for God*, trans Emma Craufurd, with an introduction by Leslie A Fiedler, New York: GP Putnam's Sons 1951, 117.
3. On the role of narrative in theology see: Michael Goldberg, *Theology and Narrative: A Critical Introduction*, Nashville Abingdon 1982.
4. Fyodor Dostoyevsky, *The Brothers Karamazov*, trans with an introduction by David Magarshack, New York: Penguin Books 1981, 595–6. This story is cited by Stephen E Toulmin in *An Examination of the Place of Reason in Ethics*, Cambridge: Cambridge University Press 1971, 210.

5. Manlio Arueta, *One Day of Life*, trans Bill Brow, New York: Vintage Books 1983.

6. Toulmin, op cit, 212–13

7. H Richard Niebuhr, *The Responsible Self*, New York: Harper & Row 1963, 60.

8. Ibid, 143.

9. Cf Edward Schillebeeckx, *Christ: The Experience of Jesus as Lord*, trans John Bowden, New York: Crossroad 1983, 699.

10. Arthur C McGill, *Suffering: A Test of Theological Method*, Philadelphia: Westminster Press 1982, 47.

11. For a fundamental, theological discussion of the moral use of force, see Karl Rahner, 'The Theology of Power', in *Theological Investigations*, vol IV, trans Kevin Smyth, New York: Crossroad 1982, 391–409.

12. See the illuminating analysis by Herbert Fingarette, 'The Meaning of Law in the Book of Job', *Hastings Law Journal* 29 (1978), 1581–1617, reprinted in *Revisions: Changing Perspectives in Moral Philosophy*, eds Stanley Hauerwas and Alasdair MacIntyre, Notre Dame, Indiana: University of Notre Dame Press 1983, 249–86.

13. Schillebeeckx, *Christ*, 727. '. . . we cannot look for the ground of suffering in God, although suffering brings the believer directly up against God.'

14. Paul Ricoeur, 'Interpretation of the Myth of Punishment', in *The Conflict of Interpretations*, trans Robert Sweeney, Evanston: Northwestern University Press 1974, 354–77.

15. Ibid, 355. This would seem close to the basic analysis of the experience of suffering which was proposed at the beginning of this essay.

16. *The Christ*, 699. '"Suffering" in itself, no longer suffering through and for others, took on a mystical and positive significance.' It lost its critical power and acquired a reactionary significance. I suggest that the mistake here was to transfer the interpretation of the suffering itself from its proper historical sphere of interpretation into the realm of the contemplative 'visions'. Thus can be seen the importance of a clear grasp of the structures of experience and its interpretation for the detection and correction of distorted interpretations.

17. Fingarette, art cit 265.

18. In what may well be the classic statement of this kind of suffering (or *misère*) Pascal wrote: 'When I consider the short duration of my life absorbed in the eternity which precedes and follows it . . . the small space I fill or even see, swallowed up in the immensity of spaces which I do not

know and which do not know me, I am afraid and astounded to see myself here rather than there, why now rather than then. Who has put me here? By whose order and arrangement have this place and time been destined for me?' Blaise Pascal, *Pensées sur la Réligion et sur quelques autres sujets*, Textes, intro by Louis Lafuma, Paris: Éditions du Luxembourg 1951, 55. The point which I wish to make is that not all the structures which give rise to suffering are of the internal necessity of things. Some of these structures do not reflect the original nature of things (or of the human will) but are of sin and contrary to the will of God. Cf Josef Fuchs, '"The Sin of the World" and Normative Morality' in *Personal Responsibility and Christian Morality*, Washington, DC: Georgetown University Press/ Dublin: Gill and Macmillan 1983, 153–75.

19. The contrast experience has been a significant theme in Schillebeeckx writing: see 'Questions on Christian Salvation of and for Man' in *Towards Vatican III: The Work That Needs to Be Done*, ed David Tracy *et al*, New York: Seabury, *Concilium*, 1978, 27–42; *The Schillebeeckx Reader*, ed Robert J Schreiter, New York: Crossroad 1984, 54.

20. Cf Schillebeeckx, 'Questions', 42. He develops the notion of the critical knowledge emerging from the contrast experience as critical of 'the dominating knowledge of the sciences and technology'.

21. On the narrative as mediation of memory, specifically the memory of suffering, see Johann Baptist Metz, *Faith in History and Society: Towards a Practical Fundamental Theology*, trans David Smith, New York: Crossroad Book, Seabury Press 1980, 110. Metz writes: 'It is in this solidarity that memory and narrative of salvation acquire their specific mystical and political praxis.' 229.

Chapter 10. Alcoholism: A Course in Theology? (pp. 161–180)

1. Sean O'Riordan, CSsR, 'Round the Reviews', *The Furrow*, vol 3, no 1 (1952), 31–40.

2. a) John C Ford, SJ, 'Alcoholism' in *New Catholic Encyclopedia*, vol 1, New York: McGraw-Hill 1967, 273–9; b)*Living and choosing: an approach to alcohol education*, Dublin: Health Education Bureau 1984; c) Max Glatt, *Alcoholism*, Teach Yourself Book 1976, Hodder 1982; d) Royal College of Psychiatrists, London, *Alcohol and Alcoholism*, Tavistock 1979; e) Royce,

James S, SJ, *Alcohol Problem and Alcoholism*, Collier Macmillan 1981.
3. *Dying for a Drink*, video cassette, Dublin: Radharc.
4. Mark Keller, 'Alcohol, Use of' in *The Encyclopedia of Bioethics*, vol 1, WT Reich, ed, New York: Free Press/London: Collier Macmillan 69–74.
5. John C Ford, SJ 'The sickness of alcoholism: still more clergy education?' in *Homiletic and Pastoral Review*, vol 87, no 2 (November 1986), 10–18.
6. Mary Purcell, *The Making of Matt Talbot, 1856–1925*, Irish Messenger Office 1972.
7. James Healy, SJ, 'The Priest and Alcohol', *The Furrow*, 33 (October 1982), 610–16.
8. Social Welfare, Committee, 'The Catholic Approach to Alcohol Misuse', *Briefing*, 17/4 (20 February 1987), Catholic Media Office, 49–64.
9. The Pastoral Constitution on the Church in the Modern World, *GS* 32.

Chapter 11. Structural Sin
(pp. 181–198)

1. As well as considering psychological, pastoral and historical aspects of moral theology (notably in relation to St Alphonsus), Father Sean O'Riordan has devoted considerable attention to the social dimension of moral behaviour. See particularly the following articles: 'The nature and function of pastoral psychology', *Studia Moralis* 1 (1963), 345–87; 'The sociology of moral theology', *Studia Moralis* 9 (1971), 149–77; 'The human psychology of repentance', *Studia Moralis* 21 (1983), 79–102.
2. Cf Bernard Häring, *Sin in the Secular Age*, Slough: St Paul Publications 1974, 61–4.
3. Karl Rahner, *El Pecado de la Iglesia: La Iglesia del Vaticano II*, Barcelona 1966 (2nd ed), 433–48. Also A Peteiro, *Pecado y hambre actual*, Estella 1972, 20.
4. Häring, op cit, 102.
5. P Schoonenberg, *Man and Sin*, London: Sheed and Ward 1965, 104–18. A similar interpretation can be found in Karl Rahner, *Foundations of Christian Faith*, London: Darton, Longman & Todd 1978, 106–15. For the implications of such interpretations for moral theology see Josef Fuchs, 'The

310

"sin of the world" and normative morality' in *Gregorianum* 61 (1980), 51–76.

6. D Soelle, *Teologia Politica*, Salamanca 1972, 93–119.
7. Ibid, 99.
8. F Moreno, *Teologia Moral desde los Pobres*, Madrid 1986, 127–8. See his exposition on the development of moral theology in Latin-American theology, 126–38; also bibliography, note 2, 210–11.
9. EF Pironio, 'Teologia de la Liberacion', *Criterio* 1608 (1970), 822–3.
10. G Gutiérrez, *A Theology of Liberation*, London: SCM 1974, 175–6.
11. Moreno, op cit, 133.
12. *Reconciliation and Penance in the Life of the Church*, no 13, 28.
13. *Ecclesia*, no 149 (12 November 1983), 2.
14. Cf C Boff, 'O Pecado social', *Rev Ecc Bras* 37 (1077), 675–701; A Bertuletti '"Peccato Sociale", una categoria controversa', *Teologia* 1 (1985), 40–58; M Sievernich, 'Social sin and its acknowledgment', *Concilium* 190 (1987), 52–63.
15. Pironio, art cit, 822.
16. G Santamaria, 'El pecado collectivo', *Orbis Catholicus*, 2, 11 (1959), 364.
17. *Christian Freedom and Liberation*, no 74.
18. See for example the observations made by K Popper, *The Open Society and its Enemies*, London: Routledge and Kegan Paul 1945.
19. Pironio, art cit, 822.
20. Soelle, op cit, 102–3.

Chapter 12. The Functions and Disfunctions of the Idea of Sin (pp. 199–211)

Works consulted
(a) Narcissus the seeker
Apuleius, Lucius, 'Cupid and Psyche' in *The Transformations of Lucius*, (otherwise known as *The Golden Ass*), translated, R Graves, Penguin 1950.
Gay, V, 'Kohut on Narcissism: psychoanalytic revolution from within', *Religious Studies Review* 7 (1981), 199–203.
Grimm, The Brothers, 'Snow Drop' in *Household Tales*, 1953.
Homans, P, 'Introducing the psychology of the self and Narcissism in the study of religion', *Religious Studies Review* 7 (1981), 193–9.

Leclaire, S, *On tue un enfant, un essai sur le narcissisme primaire et la pulsion de mort*, Paris 1975.

Moore, TW, 'Narcissus', *Parabola* I (1976).

Pohier, J, 'Cette année, j'ai tué deux enfants', *Connexions* 25 (1978), 115–34. 'Wozu ou Warum? Refléxions inspirées de la psychanalyse sur le sense de la question, "pourquoi sommes-nous sur terre?", *Concilium* 128 (1977), 37–46. 'Le pêché, à quoi ça sert?', *Vie Spirituelle Supplément*, 19–39.

Steindl-Rast, D, 'Paths of Obedience, fairy tales and the monk's way', *Parabola* 5 (1980), 33 ff.

(b)Adam the Paradise Seeker

Barthelemy, D, *Dieu et son image, ébauche d'une théologie biblique*, Paris 1963.

Philibert, P, 'Duty or pleasure?, *Spirituality Today* 32 (1980), 347–57.

Plé, A, *Par devoir ou par plaisir?* Paris 1980.

Pohier, J, *Au nom du Père, rechèrches théologiques et psychoanalytiques*, Paris 1972.

(c) What is sin?

Dwyer, G, 'Original sin: theological abstraction or dark reality?, *Catholic Mind* (May 1979), 11–23.

Fagan, S, 'No more sin?', *Doctrine and Life* (June 1976).

Farrelly, J, review of G Vandervelde, 'Original sin: two major trends in contemporary roman catholic reinterpretation, *Thomist* 32 (1979), 482–8.

Fuchs, J, 'The "sin of the world" and normative morality', *Gregorianum* 61 (1981), 51–76.

Jossua, JP, 'Original sin and theological displacements, *Theology Digest* 28 (1980), 133–6.

McDermott, B, 'The theology of original sin, recent developments', *Theological Studies* (1977), 478–512.

MacIsaac, S, *Freud and Original Sin*, New York 1974.

Maly, E, *Sin, biblical perspectives*, Dayton 1971.

Peter, C, 'Original sin: a test case in theology', *Concilium* 10 (1971), 106–12.

Philibert, P, 'A spiritual portrait of the christian as seen in recent church teaching', *Spirituality Today* 32 (1980), 257–68.

Power, D, 'Confession as ongoing conversion', *Heythrop Journal* 18 (1976), 180–90.

Sabourin, L, 'Original sin reappraised', *Biblical Theology Bulletin* 3 (1973), 51–81.

Schottroff, L, 'Sin's reign of terror in Romans', *Theology Digest* 28 (1980), 129–32.

Sugerman, S, 'Sin and madness' *Cross Currents* 21 (1971), 129–54.

Taylor, M, *The Mystery of Sin and forgiveness*, New York 1971.

Zalotay, J, 'Original sin', *Concilium* 10 (1971), 98–105.

Chapter 13. The Fate of the Moral Manual since St Alphonsus
(pp. 212–239)

1. A list of the editions is found in: M De Meulemeester, *Bibliographie générale des écrivains Rédemptoristes*, première partie, Louvain 1933, 62–8.
2. Alphonsus de Liguori, *Theologia Moralis*, ed L Gaudé, Rome 1905. Referred to henceforth as Gaudé.
3. P Antoine, *Theologia Moralis Universa*, revised edition, 1818; the references here are to tom. 5, 28–301.
4. P Dens, *Theologia Moralis et Dogmatica*, Dublin ex typ Richardi Coyne 1829, 150–213.
5. Brief notes on Dens are to be found in *New Catholic Encyclopedia* vol 4, London 1908, and *Dictionnaire de Théologie Catholique*, tom 4, Paris 1911.
6. A notable difference would be the emphasis of Alphonsus on grace and the sovereign goodness of God throughout the whole treatment of the question. It is not that Dens would deny these, but the categories of thought with which he works, being legally casuistic, do not easily highlight them.
7. C Roncaglia, *Universa Moralis Theologia*, editio absolutissima a P Optato Bellotti, Luca 1834. There is a short note on Roncaglia's life in *Dictionnaire de Théologie Catholique*, tom 13, Paris 1937.
8. FP Kendrick, *Theologia Moralis*, vol 3, Philadelphia 1843, 208–21. Short biographical material in *Catholic Encyclopedia*, vol 8, and in J Healy, *The Just Wage, 1750–1890*, The Hague 1966.
9. TM Gousset, *Théologie morale à l'usage des curés et des confesseurs*, tom 2, Brussels 1849, 251–68. Also, his earlier work, *Justification de la théologie morale du Bienheureux Alphonse Marie de Ligorio*, 1832. Biographical details in J Healy, op cit, and in *Dictionnaire de Théologie Catholique*, tom 6, Paris 1920.
10. He distances himself, somewhat, from Alphonsus' views on the sexual conduct of fiancés: if young people are to prepare for marriage how are they to avoid seeing each other?
11. Ibid, 267.
12. These dates refer to (a) the Decree of the Sacred Congregation

of Rites of 18 May 1803, 'super revisione et approbatione operum Ven Alphonsi in ordine ad eius beatificationem' and (b) Responsum S Poenitentiariae super Doctrina Morali B Alphonsi, 5 July 1831. These statements (particularly the much-quoted 'nihil in his censura dignum repertum fuerit') were, in time, used in a fairly literalist way, ignoring the theological subtleties needed in the interpretation of such Roman documents.

13. The standard account is J Guerber, *Le ralliement du clergé à la morale française Liguorienne*, Analecta Gregoriana 193, Rome, Gregorian University 1973.
14. Besides the theological arguments of Lanteri, Gousset and Pallavicini, all mentioned by Guerber and which were most definitely crucial in this regard, one should not underestimate the impact of the popular missions preached by congregations like the Redemptorists at this time. The great appeal of these missions was, in part, due to the sensible pastoral practice of confession which they incorporated.
15. P Scavini, *Theologia Moralis Universa*, vol 4, Paris 1859, 118–125.
16. Healy, op cit 313.
17. Further biographical details can be found in *Dictionnaire de Théologie Catholique*, vol 6, Paris 1920.
18. In his list of the extraordinary signs he does not start, as most others did, with the sign of weeping/sighs. In fact, he places this sign last, as if to suggest slight French distrust of the exuberance of the Italian moralists.
19. E Müller, *Theologia Moralis*, vol 3, Vienna 1879, 355–65.
20. A Konings, *Theologia Moralis*, vol 2, London 1880, 179–84. Short biographical data, *Catholic Encyclopedia*, vol 8, London 1910.
21. AJ Haine, *Theologia Moralis Universa*, vol 3, Rome: Louvain 1899, 363–73.
22. Balanced assessments of Alphonsus' status can be found in 'Theologie Morale', *Dictionnaire de Théologie Catholique*, tom 10, Paris 1928, and in T Bouquillon, *Theologia Moralis Fundamentalis*, vol 1, New York 1890, 43–128.
23. A Harnack, *Dogmengeschichte*, 4th ed, 3, 755; quoted in J Mausbach, *Catholic moral teaching and its antagonists*, New York 1914, 57–8.
24. One can note JH Newman's opposition to Alphonsus' views on reservation (*Apologia*, 1902 ed, 279) and the careful assessment of Alphonsus in Mausbach, op cit, 57–65.
25. RP Blakeney, *St Alphonsus Liguori*, London: Reformation Society Office 1852.

26. Blakeney, op cit, iii, xiii, 31, 89.
27. P Gardella, *Innocent Ecstasy*, Oxford University Press 1985, 102.
28. A list of articles in the *Vindiciae Alphonsianae*, xii–xiv and lxi–lxvii, is an indication of this.
29. T Slater, *A Manual of Moral Theology*, vol 2, New York: Benziger Brothers 1908, 216–25.
30. H Noldin, *Summa Theologiae Moralis*, vol 3, Rome 1912, 469–90.
31. Art 5 (*De absolvendis consuetudinariis*, 476–7) and Art 6 (*De absolvendis recidivis*, 477–81) follow as applications of Art 4 (*De obligatione absolvendi poenitentes in genere*, 468–76).
32. J Aertnys and C Damen, *Theologia Moralis secundum doctrinam S Alfonsi de Ligorio*, tom 2, Turin 1920, 346–90.
33. L Wouters, *Manuale Theologiae Moralis*, Bruges 1933.
34. Roman documents are often quoted, without their theological weight being assessed. His theological sources are, in the main, Redemptorist ones, especially Ter Haar on the question of the *recidivi et habituati*.
35. E Genicot, *Institutiones Theologiae Moralis*, vol 2, quam recognovit I Salsmans, Brussels 1940, 321–35.
36. H Jone and U Adelman, *Moral Theology*, Cork: Mercier Press 1955, 422–33.
37. 'Thus, if the invalidity of a marriage is commonly known the penitent must be told even though he has been till now in good faith, and even if it is foreseen that he will not pay any attention to the information.' Jone-Adelman, 424.
38. 'One necessary proximate occasion of sin is company-keeping with the prospect of an early marriage', ibid, 428.
39. Bernard Häring *The Law of Christ*, vol 1, Cork: Mercier Press 1961. Chapters 8–12 discuss many of these questions. While he does not deal with the *habituati et recidivi* in the limited sense that the manuals of the time dealt with them, it is the same human and theological problems that he grapples with. His language of dealing with the problem is so new that many manualists simply did not understand what Häring was trying to say.

Chapter 14. Sign of Contradiction or Sign of Hope? (pp. 240–252)

The following abbreviations are used in the notes:
PA: *Pietas Alfonsiana erga matrem gloriosam Mariam*, Louvain 1951.
NDM: *Nuovo Dizionario di Mariologia*, Milan 1986.

1. Rum-Marcuzzi, 'Stampa Mariana', *NDM*, 1381. Capone, 'II libro delle Glorie di Maria', *PA*, 67.
2. St Alphonsus, *The Glories of Mary*, Brooklyn 1931, 337–9.
3. J Koehler, 'Storia della Mariologia', *NDM*, 1398.
4. J Delumeau, *Catholicism between Luther and Voltaire*, London 1977, 228–9.
5. GR Cragg, *The Church and the State of Reason*, Penguin 1966, 282.
6. *The Glories of Mary*, 702.
7. L Gambero, 'Culto', *NDM*, 426–7.
8. K Barth, *Church Dogmatics*, IV, 3, Edinburgh 1958, 603.
9. Paul VI, *Marialis Cultus*, 3.
10. *Constitution on the Sacred Liturgy*, no 103.
11. EA Johnson, 'The Symbolic Character of Theological Statements about Mary', *Journal of Ecumenical Studies* (1985), 324–8.
12. Karl Rahner, *Mary Mother of the Lord*, New York 1964, 30.
13. S Meo, 'Mediatrice', *NDM*, 933.
14. JH Newman, *Difficulties felt by Anglicans*, London 1850, 445.
15. JJ Preston, *Mother Worship*, North Carolina Press 1982, 339.
16. K Leech, *True God*, London 1985, 366.
17. LJ Biallas, *Myths, gods, heros and saviors*, Connecticut 1986, 15–36.
18. JJ Preston, ibid, 340.
19. P Hebblethwaite, 'The Mariology of Three Popes', *The Way Supplement* 51 (Autumn 1984), 61.
20. J Moltmann, Editorial, *Concilium* 168 (October 1983), 14.
21. *Marialis Cultus*, 37.
22. B Pascal, *The Provincial Letters*, 9, Penguin 1967, 134.
23. JM Antier, 'Pilgrimages in France,' *Lumen Vitae*, 39 (November 1984) 372.
24. *The Glories of Mary*, 29.
25. JH Newman, ibid, 429.
26. J Westerhoff, 'On knowing the bi-cameral mind', *Concilium* 174 (1984), 63–7.
27. N Lash, 'Performing the Scriptures' in *New Testament as Personal Reading*, Illinois 1983, 7–18.
28. H McCabe, *God Matters*, London 1987, 212.
29. O Chadwick, *The Popes and European Revolution*, Oxford 1981, 231.
30. Capone, art cit, 20–33.

Chapter 15. In Search of Christian Spirituality Today
(pp. 253–273)

1. Jon Sobrino, SJ, *Christology at the Crossroads*, New York 1978, 41.
2. John Macquarrie, 'Prayer and Theological Reflection' in Jones, Wainwright and Yarnold, eds, *The Study of Spirituality*, New York 1986, 584–5.
3. Langdon Gilkey, *Message and Existence*, Minneapolis 1979, 27–8.
4. Edward Schillebeeckx, *Jesus*, New York 1979, 141–2.
5. Donal Dorr, *Spirituality and Justice*, Maryknoll, NY: Orbis Books/Dublin: Gill and Macmillian 1984, 16.
6. Sobrino, *Christology*, 50.
7. Pierre Teilhard de Chardin, *Le Milieu Divin*, London 1960, 38.
8. Sobrino, *Christology*, Preface to English edition, xxiv.
9. Pierre Teilhard de Chardin, *The Phenomenon of Man*, London 1959, 313.

Chapter 16. The Parish Mission Apostolate of the Redemptorists in Ireland, 1851–1898
(pp. 274–296)

1. The unpublished doctoral thesis of John Sharp, 'Reapers of the Harvest: the Redemptorists in the United Kingdom 1843–1898', London University 1968, includes a survey of the Redemptorists' work in Ireland. I thank Dr Sharp for giving me access to his work. The present article, researched before I saw 'Reapers', focuses on a pastoral assessment of the Redemptorist apostolate in Ireland. For the early period, see Samuel J Boland, 'Early Redemptorist missions in England and Ireland (1848–1865)' in *Spicilegium Historicum CSsR*, Rome 1985, 283–320. The domestic periodical of the Irish Redemptorists, *Search*, has several brief well-researched 'spots' by Patrick O'Donnell CSsR. The General Archives (Rome) and the Provincial Archives (Dublin) have relevant material. The main sources for this study have been the local Archives in Limerick (1853–98) and Dundalk (1876–98). On the pioneers of parish missions in Ireland, cf James H Murphy, 'The role of Vincentian parish missions in the Irish counter-reformation of the mid-nineteenth century' in *Irish Historical Studies* 94 (November 1984), 152–71. See also P O'Donnell 'Before the Redemptorists: missions and missioners', in *Search* 12 (1981), 28–38.

2. Prost's diaries in the Austrian Provincial Archives leave a record of his work as a missioner. An abstract from the diaries on his work in Ireland is published by E Hosp, 'First Redemptorist Missions in Ireland, according to Father Joseph Prost's diaries' in *Spic CSsR* 1960, 453–85.

3. Gerard Scheper, *P Bernard Hafkenscheid*, Regensburg 1884; A Redemptorist (unnamed), *A Son of St Alphonsus, Father Bernard Hafkenshied*, Dublin 1903.

4. 'Aisling' is the Gaelic for a secular 'vision splendid'. This was a conceit of Gaelic poets of the eighteenth century envisaging deliverance from oppression.

5. For other plans of instructions and sermons see Sharp, *Reapers*, Appendix, 307–10.

6. Cf William J Fitzpatrick, *Life of Thomas Burke*, London 1894, 146. The first three sermons were Death, Judgement, Hell.

7. Hosp, loc cit, 480.

8. There has been a revival of interest in Pecherin in recent decades in Ireland, his native Russia, Western Europe and the United States. Cf Victor S Frank, 'A Displaced Person: the strange life of Vladimir Pecherin (1807–1885)' in *Dublin Review* 449 (1949), 139–53; E MacWhite, 'Vladimir Pecherin (1807–1885)' in *Studies* (1971), 295–310 and (1972), 23–40; E MacWhite, 'Towards a biography of Father Vladimir Pecherin (1807–1885)': a progress report and bibliography edited and prepared for publication by PJ O'Meara in *Proceedings of the Royal Irish Academy*, Dublin, vol 80, section c, no 7 (1980), 109–58. See also the documentation edited by A Sampers in *Spic CSsR*, 1973, 1974 and 1980. For the court case on the charge of bible-burning, see James Doyle, *Report of the Trial of the Rev Vladimir Pecherin*, Duffy, Dublin 1856. A century later, Victor Frank (op cit, 139), heard a fragment of a street ballad celebrating the court victory: 'The waving of hats and handkerchiefs, the like was never seen, at Dublin and Kingstown, for Father Pecheerine.'

9. T Livius, *Father Furniss and his Work for Children*, London 1896; Charles Shepherd, CSsR, 'A Forgotten Apostle: John Furniss, CSsR' in *The Clergy Review* (March 1978), 99–104; J Sharp, 'Juvenile Holiness: Catholic Revivalism among Children in Victorian Britain' in *Journal of Ecclesiastical History* (1984), 220–38.

10. P O'Donnell, 'St Alphonsus' writings in nineteenth-century Ireland before the arrival of the Redemptorists', *Search* 12 (1981), 23–38; J Sharp, 'The influence of St Alphonsus Liguori in nineteenth-century Britain', *Downside Review* (January 1983), 60–76.

11. Cf JH Jackson, *The Irish in Britain*, London 1963, 144.
12. E Norman, *Roman Catholicism in England from the Elizabethan Settlement to the Second Vatican Council*, Oxford 1983, 73.
13. An allusion to the American, Fr Isaac Hecker, who left the Redemptorists and founded the Paulists in 1858.
14. On Coffin's talents and deficiencies see Sharp, *Reapers*, 51–9 and 69–75.